INTRODUCTION

This volume has been written with the intention of providing the most accurate guide to the organisation and strengths of the Waffen SS armoured units that fought in Normandy in the summer of 1944.

It comprises minutely detailed Divisional strength tables; ready for action states and Panzer allocations and deliveries for divisional sub-units – most of which have never been reproduced in book form before. These tables clearly show that with few exceptions, all units were virtually at full strength. Due to the poor quality of some of the original documents, the clarity of some charts is poor. Rather than trying to enhance them with the possibility of losing some information, we have chosen to show them as originally found.

Also provided are weapon, vehicle and unit symbol guides to help understand the rather complex Order of Battle charts.

We have avoided describing unit actions as these have already been covered in numerous other World War II publications.

Hopefully this will be the first of several volumes covering both SS and Wehrmacht (Army) Panzer units in the latter half of World War II.

We sincerely hope that these volumes will become the standard reference for wargamers, military enthusiasts and historians.

ACKNOWLEDGMENTS

The authors would like to thank the following people without whom this volume would not have been possible.

Herr Meyer, Frau Traudl, Herr Moritz and other members of staff at the Bundesarchiv-Militärarchiv, Freiburg, Germany.

Our patient families for their continued support and encouragement.

Herr Werner Volkner who gave friendly advice and helped with certain translations.

Finally a special thanks to Kris Machala who gave us the opportunity to produce this book.

CONTENTS

ORGANISATION

Organisation of an SS Panzer Division in June 1944

On 1st June 1944, the Waffen SS Panzer Divisions stationed in the west had organisations based on the 'Type 43' model Panzer Division. All would begin transforming into 'Type 44' units during the Normandy Campaign, although under the severe combat conditions many Divisions found the rather complex structural changes almost impossible to achieve.

The differences between a 'Type 43' and a 'Type 44' Panzer Division were manifold. One of the main changes involved a centralisation of supply units within the combat Battalions, leading to a reduction in supply personnel, thus releasing more troops for combat duties.

A list of Panzer Divisional units below clearly outlines all major organisational changes:

- Stab der Division (Divisional HQ)
  Administration section
  Mapping unit
  Divisional security company, later to include military police company

- SS Panzer Regiment (Tank Regiment)
- Regiments Stab (Regimental HQ)
  With signal, reconnaissance, engineer and flak units

- I. Abteilung (1st Battalion) – Panzer V's
  Abteilung Stab (Battalion HQ)
  With signal, reconnaissance, engineer and flak units
  4 Companies each of 17 tanks
  1 Workshop platoon*

** In the Type 44 organisation both Battalion workshop units were amalgamated to form one large regimental company*

- II. Abteilung (2nd Battalion) – Panzer IV's
- Abteilung Stab (Battalion HQ)
  With signal, reconnaissance, engineer and flak units
  4 Companies each of 22 tanks
  1 Workshop company

OR

- II. Abteilung (2nd Battalion) – Mixed Panzer IV's and StuG's
- Abteilung Stab (Battalion HQ)
  With signal, reconnaissance, engineer and flak units
  2 Companies each of 22 Panzer IV's
  2 Companies each of 22 StuG's
  1 Workshop company

On 1st June 2.SS, 9.SS and 10.SS Panzer Divisions had mixed 2nd Battalions. SS Panzer Regiments 1 and 12 both had full companies of armoured engineers mounted in halftracks.

- SS Panzer Grenadier Regiment (Armoured Infantry Regiment)
  Each SS Panzer Division possessed two such regiments

- Regiments Stab (Regimental HQ)
  HQ company and regimental band – later all bands were amalagamated to form a divisional band
  I to III Panzer-Grenadier Battalions (truck mounted)
  Each comprising an HQ, 3 rifle companies and a heavy support company.

In the 'Type 44' Division, each Battalion also had a supply company. Generally one of the two Panzer-Grenadier regiments had one of its battalions mounted in armoured halftracks (SdKfz 251), although 1.SS and 12.SS Panzer Divisions had one armoured battalion in each of their Panzer-Grenadier regiments. Each Panzer-Grenadier regiment also possessed several support units:

- Infanteriegeschutz Kompanie (Infantry Gun Company) with 6 x 15cm infantry guns, either towed or self-propelled
- Flak Kompanie (Anti-Aircraft Company) with 12 x 2cm flak guns
- Pionier Kompanie (Engineer Company) mounted in trucks or medium armoured halftracks
- Aufklärungs Kompanie (Reconnaissance Company)
  Some regiments formed reconnaissance companies. They were mounted in Volkswagens and were often attached to the Regimental HQ.

- SS Panzer Aufklärungs Abteilung (Panzer Reconnaissance Battalion)

  Usually a 'Type 43' unit with an HQ Company mounted in armoured half-tracks, one wheeled armoured car company, one tracked armoured car company, two light armoured reconnaissance companies, one heavy support company (in medium half-tracks) and one supply company. On changing to the 'Type 44' unit, the wheeled armoured car company was reassigned to the Battalion HQ company.

- SS Panzerjäger Abteilung (Anti-Tank Battalion)

  The 'Type 43' unit had an HQ of 3 self-propelled guns (SPs) and three companies each of 14 SPs. (By June 1944 Jagdpanzer IV's had replaced Marders).

  A 'Type 44' Battalion had an HQ of 3 SPs, two companies each of 14 SPs, one company of 12 towed anti-tank guns and a supply/support unit. Later this organisation was reduced to an HQ of 1 SP, two companies of 10 SPs and a towed company of 12 pieces.

SS Panzerjäger units as of June 1944:

9.SS Still forming. It would not be ready for combat operations until August 1944.

10.SS Still forming. It would be ready for action by August 1944.

12.SS Partially equipped as a 'Type 43' unit. It converted to a 'Type 44' in July/August.

1.SS and 2.SS Panzer Divisions had Sturmgeschütz in place of Panzerjäger units. Each battalion was organised with an HQ section, 3 assault gun companies and a workshop company.

- SS Panzer Artillerie Regiment (Armoured Artillery Regiment)
- Regiments Stab (Regimental HQ)

- I Abteilung (1st Battalion) was armoured and included 6 x 150 mm SP guns *(Hummel)*, and 12 x 105mm SP guns *(Wespe)*.

- II Abteilung (2nd Battalion) had 3 batteries of towed 105mm guns

- III Abteilung (3rd Battalion) had 3 batteries of towed 150mm guns, and 1 battery of 105mm guns (kanone) Under the 'Type 44' model a further (105mm) battalion was formed utilising existing weapon stocks.

- SS Werfer Abteilung (Rocket Projector Battalion)

  Only two Divisions (1.SS and 12.SS) possessed a nebelwerfer abteilung. 1.SS had 3 batteries of 15cm and one battery of 21cm werfers. 12.SS had 4 batteries of 15cm werfers.

  Each battery should have included a 5cm anti-tank gun, but these were never issued.

  A nebelwerfer abteilung had been planned for 2.SS Panzer Division, but it was redeployed and became a 2.SS Panzer Korps level unit.

- SS Flak Abteilung (Anti-Aircraft Battalion)

  With an HQ section, 3 heavy batteries of towed 88mm flak guns, 1 battery of towed 3.7cm flak guns and a 60cm searchlight section.

  1.SS Panzer Division had one extra battery of 3.7cm flak guns.

- SS Panzer Pionier Bataillon (Armoured Engineer Battalion)

  Stabs Kompanie (HQ Company)

  (With signal and armoured reconnaissance units.)

  2 motorised companies, 1 armoured company (in medium armoured halftracks) and up to 2 bridging columns.

- Panzer Nachrichten Abteilung (Armoured Signals Battalion)

  Had an HQ section and radio and telephone communication companies, each equipped with a mixture of softskin vehicles and armoured halftracks. The battalion organisation also included a light supply column.

- SS Feldersatz Bataillon (Replacement and Training Battalion)

  From 2-5 companies in strength, with a substantial complement of light and heavy weapons.

- SS Division Nachschubtruppen (Divisional Supply Battalion)

  The logistical heart of the Division comprising:

  HQ Section.

  6-8 trucked transport companies (each of 60-120 tonne capacity)

  1 Workshop company. Later integrated into the Panzer instandsetzungs abteilung.

- Panzer Instandsetzungs Abteilung (Workshop Battalion) with an HQ section, 3 or 4 motorised repair companies and a replacement parts company.

- SS Wirtschafts Bataillon (Administration Battalion)
  With an HQ section, bakery company, butchers company, field post office and an administrative supply section.

- SS Sanitäts Abteilung (Medical Battalion)
  Initially comprised an HQ, 2 medical companies, 1 field hospital and 3 ambulance platoons. Later the ambulance platoons were consolidated into a single company.

- SS Feldgendarmerie Kompanie (Military Police Company)
  Usually 5 platoons in strength. Initially part of the Divisional supply troops (Versorgungstruppe), it later moved to the Divisional HQ section during the 'Type 44' reorganisation.

Organisational Chart for a 'Type 43' SS Panzer Division

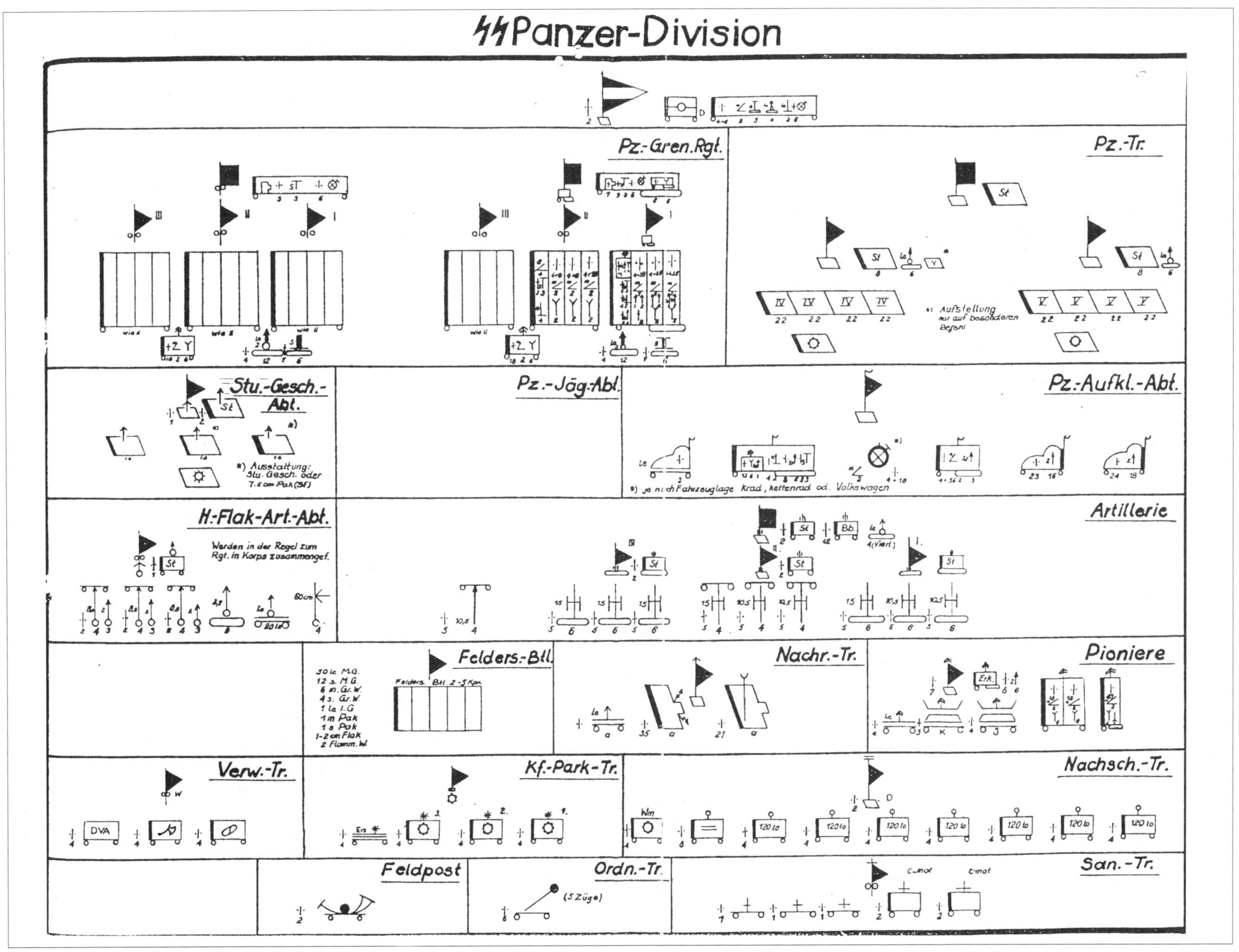

Organisational Chart for a 'Type 44' SS Panzer Division

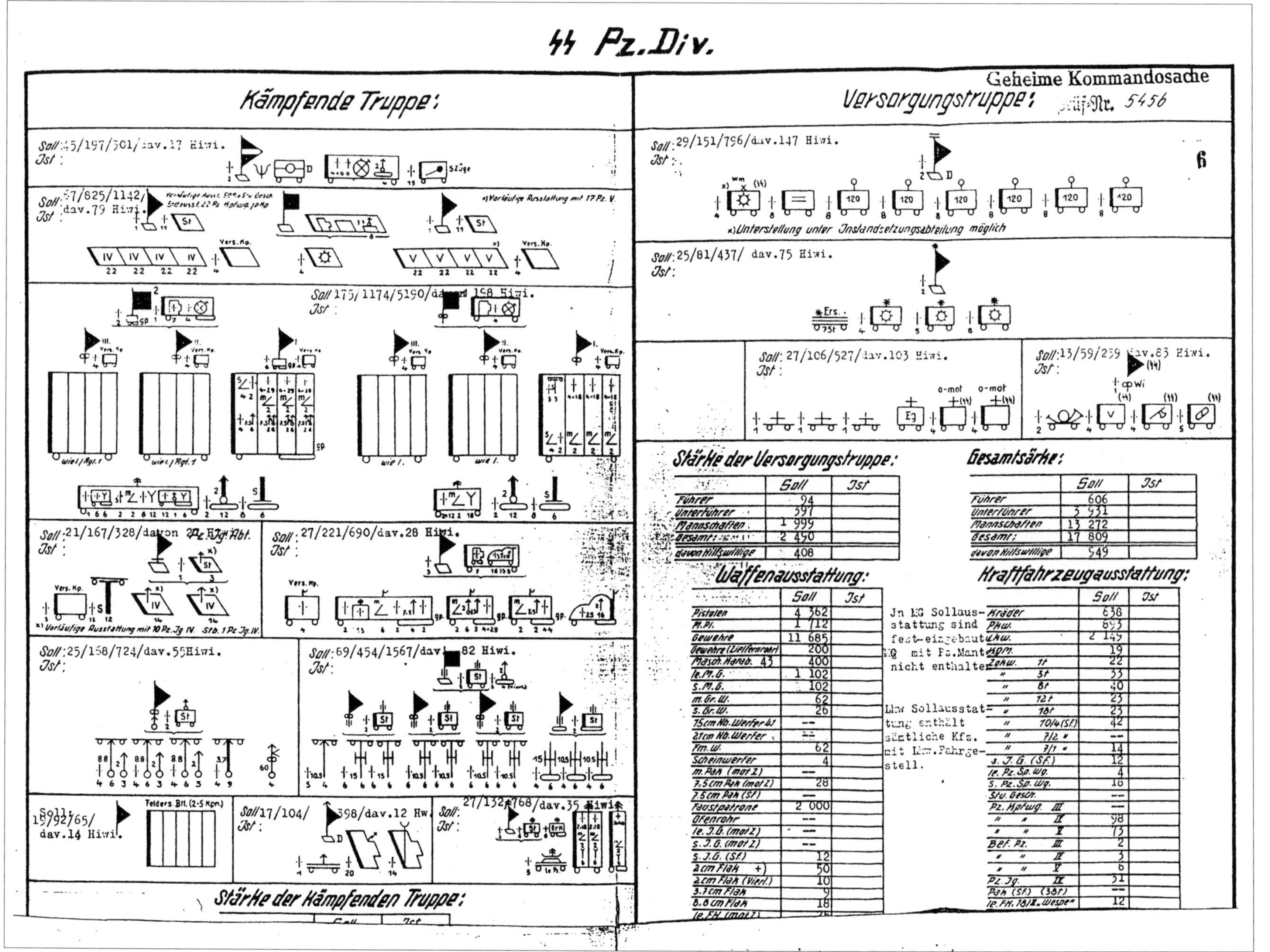

Stärke der Versorgungstruppe:

	Soll	Ist
Führer	94	
Unterführer	397	
Mannschaften	1 999	
Gesamt:	2 490	
davon Hilfswillige	408	

Gesamtstärke:

	Soll	Ist
Führer	606	
Unterführer	3 931	
Mannschaften	13 272	
Gesamt:	17 809	
davon Hilfswillige	549	

Waffenausstattung:

	Soll	Ist
Pistolen	4 362	
M.Pi.	1 712	
Gewehre	11 685	
Gewehre (Zielfernrohr)	200	
Masch.Karab. 43	400	
le.M.G.	1 102	
s.M.G.	102	
m.Gr.W.	62	
s.Gr.W.	26	
15cm Nb.Werfer 41	--	
21cm Nb.Werfer	--	
Fm.W.	62	
Scheinwerfer	4	
m.Pak (mot Z)	--	
7,5cm Pak (mot Z)	28	
7.5cm Pak (Sf)	--	
Faustpatrone	2 000	
Ofenrohr	--	
le.J.G. (mot Z)	--	
s.J.G. (mot Z)	--	
s.J.G. (Sf.)	12	
2cm Flak +)	50	
2cm Flak (Vierl.)	10	
3.7cm Flak	9	
8.8cm Flak	18	
le.FH (mot Z)	[illegible]	

Jn MG Sollausstattung sind fest-eingebaute MG mit Pz.Mantel nicht enthalten

Lkw Sollausstattung enthält sämtliche Kfz. mit Lkw.Fahrgestell.

Kraftfahrzeugausstattung:

	Soll	Ist
Kräder	636	
Pkw.	893	
Lkw.	2 149	
Kom.	19	
Zgkw. 1t	22	
" 3t	33	
" 8t	40	
" 12t	23	
" 18t	23	
" 10/4 (Sf.)	42	
" 7/2 "	--	
" 7/1 "	14	
s.J.G. (Sf.)	12	
le.Pz.Sp.Wg.	4	
s.Pz.Sp.Wg.	16	
Stu.Gesch.	--	
Pz.Kpfwg. III	--	
" " IV	98	
" " V	73	
Bef.Pz. III	2	
" " IV	3	
" " V	6	
Pz.Jg. IV	31	
Pak (Sf.) (38t)	--	
le.FH.18/II „Wespe"	12	

Panther Battalion

Organisational differences between 'Type 43' (alter Art) and 'Type 44' (Freie) Units

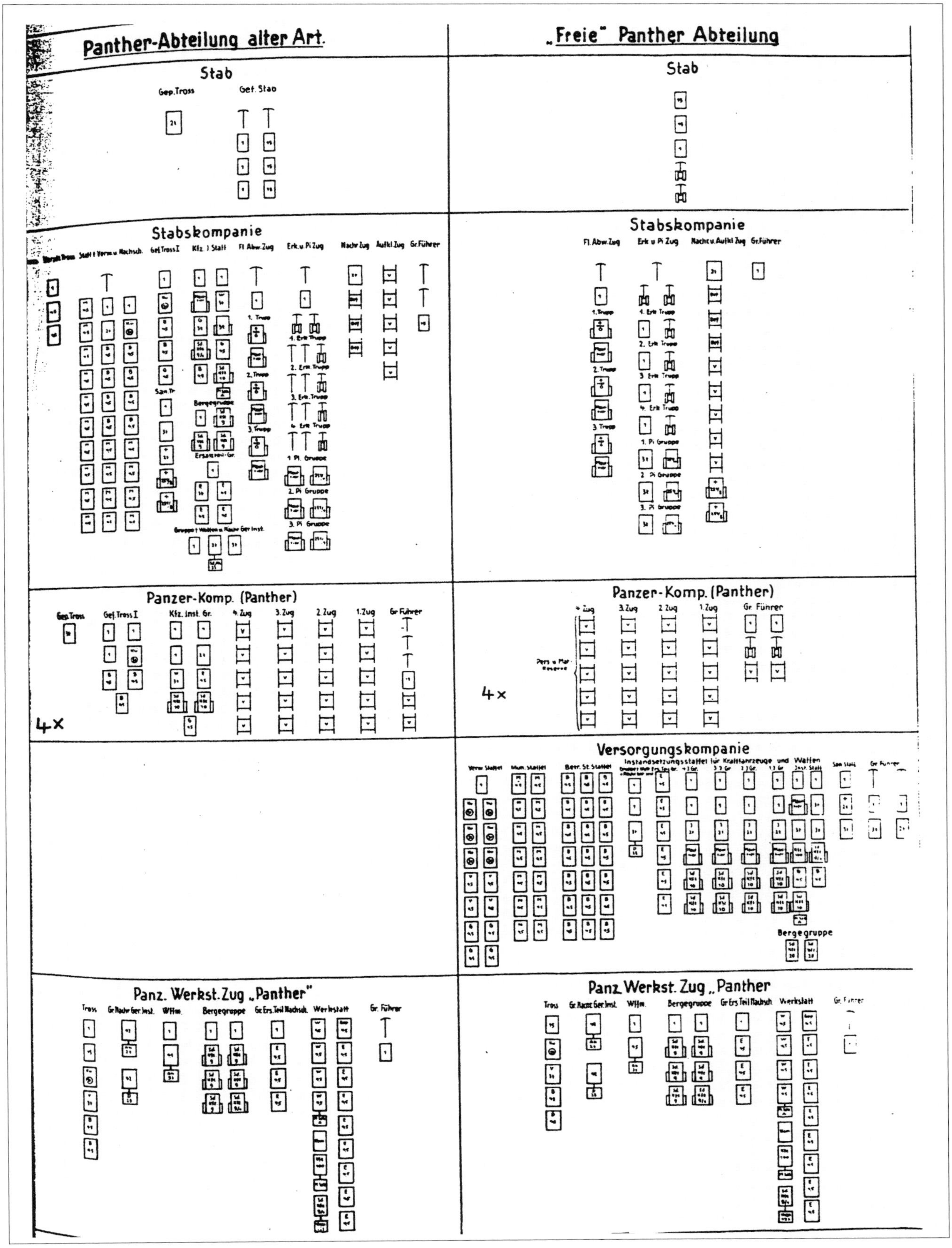

Panzer IV Battalion
Organisational differences between 'Type 43' (alter Art) and 'Type 44' (Freie Gliederung) Units

Panzer IV Abt. alter Art.	Panz. IV Abt. „Freie Gliederung"
Stab	Stab
Stabskompanie	Stabskompanie
m. Panz. Kp. a. (4x)	m. Panz. Kp. a. (4x)
	Versorgungskompanie
Werkstatt Kp. (ohne 2. Zug)	Werkstatt Kp. (ohne 2. Zug)

Armoured Panzer-Grenadier Battalion
Organisational differences between 'Type 43' (alter Art) and 'Type 44' (Freie Gliederung) Units

Panz. Gren. Btl. (gp.) alter Art	Panz. Gren. Btl. (gp.) „Freie Gliederung"
Stab u. Stabskomp.	Stab
Stabskompanie: Gep.Tr., Gef. Tross II (Btls.V-Tross, Nachsch.St., Inst.Staffel), Gef. Tross I (J.Trupp, Gef.Tross I, Nachr.St., Sr.Führer); Stab	Stab
Panz. Gren. Kp. c (gp.) — Gep.Tr., Gef.Tr.I, Inst.Trupp, schw.Zug, 3.Zug, 2.Zug, 1.Zug, Pz.Zerst.Tr., Gr.Führer — 3x	Panz. Gren. Kp. c (gp.) — schw.Zug, 3.Zug, 2.Zug, 1.Zug, Pz.Zerst.Tr., Gr.Führer — 3x
4. schw. Panz. Gren. Kp. (gp.) — schw.Pz.Jg.Zug, schw.Kan.Zug, le.J.G.Zug, Gep.Tr., Gef.Tr., J.Gruppe, Gr.Führer	4. schw. Panz. Gren. Kp. (gp.) — schw.Pz.Jg.Zug, schw.Kan.Zug, le.J.G.Zug, Gr.Führer
	Versorgungskompanie — Inst.Trupp (1. J.Trupp, 2. J.-Trupp, 3. J.-Trupp, 4. J.-Trupp, 5. J.-Trupp), I.Staffel (Waffen u. Ger.), Kfz. J.Staffel, Mun.Staff., Betr.St.Staff., Vers.Staffel, San.Staff., Gr.Führer

Theoretical Distribution (and type) of MSPWs in a Panzer Division
with one Panzer-Grenadier Battalion mounted in armoured halftracks
i.e.
2.SS Panzer Division
9.SS Panzer Division
10.SS Panzer Division

Soll an m.SPW einer Panz.Div. mit 1 Gren.Btl.

Einheit	K. St. N. Nr.	Datum	1	2	3	4	5	6	7	8	9	10	11	16	s.IG Sf
			m. Schtz. Pz. Wg. Sd. Kfz. 251/												
Stbs.Kp.Pz.Abt.Panther	1150a	1.11.43							3	2					
" " " " IV	1150b	1.11.43							3	2					
1 Stb.Pz.Gr.Rgt.a/b(gp)	1104a gp	1.11.43			2										
1 Stbs.Kp.a Pz.Gr.Rgt.(gp)	1153a gp	1.11.43	1		5							4	3	6	
1 Stb.u.St.Kp.Pz.Gren.Btl.(gp)	1108a gp	1.11.43			3					1			2		
3 Pz.Gren.Kp.c(gp)	1114c gp	1.11.43	27	6	6						6	21			
Fh. schw.Kp. (gp)	1121a gp	1.11.43			1								1		
2 schw.Gesch.Kp. (6 s.IG)	1120a	1.11.43	6		2								2		12
Gesch.Zug a (gp)	1123a gp	1.11.43	4												
schw.Kan.Zug (7,5)	1125a gp	1.11.43	1		1						6				
schw.Pz.Jg.Zug (gp)	1145 gp	1.11.43	1									4			
Pz.Gren.Pi-Kp.	1118	1.11.43			1				7						
Pz.Aufkl.Abt.Stab	1109 gp	1.11.43			7					1			2		
schw.Kp. wie ob.+PiZg.			6		2				7		6	4			
Stb.Kp. Pz.Jg.Abt.	1155d	1.11.43								1					
Pz. Art.							4								
Pz.Pi.Btl.Stab	703a	1.11.43			4				3						
Pz. Pi. Kp.	714	1.11.43	1	2	1				21			3			
Pz.Nachr.Abt.															
Pz. Fu. Kp.	971 n	1.10.43			2+8x										
Pz. Fe. Kp.	976 n	1.10.43	2xx										6Fe		
Summe Soll:			49	8	45	-	4	-	44	7	18	36	16	6	12 =233+

x = 2 Kdo.Fg.+
8 Fu. Fg.

xx = anstelle 251/19

Theoretical Distribution (and type) of MSPWs in a Panzer Division
with two Panzer-Grenadier Battalion mounted in armoured halftracks
i.e.
1.SS Panzer Division
12.SS Panzer Division

Soll einer Pz. Div. an m. SPW mit 2 Gren.-Batl.

Einheit	K. St. N. Nr.	Datum	m. Schtz. Pz. Wg. Sd.Kfz.251/ 1	2	3	4	5	6	7	8	9	10	11	16	s.IG Sf	
Stabs Kp.Pz.Abt.Panther	1150a	1.11.43							3	2						
" " " " IV	1150b	1.11.43							3	2						
2 Stab Pz.Gr.Rgt.a(gp)	1104a gp	1.11.43			4											
2 Stbs.Kp.a Pz.Gr.Rgt(gp)	1153a gp	1.11.43	2		10							8	6	12		
2x Stb.u.Stbs.Kp. Pz.Gren.Btl.(gp)	1108a gp	1.11.43			6					2			4			
6x Pz.Gr.Komp.c(gp)	1114c gp	1.11.43	54	12	12						12	42				
2x Führ.schw.Kp. (gp)	1121a gp	1.11.43			2								2			
2x schw.Gesch.Kp. (6 s.I.G. Sf)	1120a	1.11.43	6		2								2		12	
2x Gesch.Zug a(gp)	1123a gp	1.11.43	8													
2x schw.Kan.Zug (7,5)	1125a gp	1.11.43	2		2						12					
2x schw.Pz.Jg.Zug(gp)	1145 gp	1.11.43	2									8				
2 Pz.Gren.Pi-Komp.	1118	1.11.43			2				14							
Pz.Aufkl.Abt.Stab	1109 gp	1.11.43			7				~~7~~	1			2			
schw.Kp. (wie oben)u.Pi-Zug			6		2				7		6	4				
St.Kp. Pz.Jg.Abt.	1155d	1.11.43								1						
Pz. Artl.							4	~~4~~								
Pz.Pi.Btl.Stab	703a	1.11.43			4				3							
Pz. Pi-Komp.	714	1.11.43	1	2	1				21			3				
Pz. Nachr. Abt.																
Pz. Fu. Komp.	971n	1.10.43			2+8[x]											x 2 Kdo.Pz + 8 Fu.Pz
Pz. Fe. Komp.	976n	1.10.43	2[x]										6Fe			x anstell 251/19
Summe Soll:			83	14	64	-	4	-	51	8	30	65	22	12	12	= 353+12

Distribution of Panzers for a Type '43' Panzer Division

Übersicht über das Soll an Pz. Kpfw. und gep. Kfz.
einer Pz. Div. nach Gliederung 43

E i n h e i t	Nr.d. KStN	Datum	Pz.Kpfw. IV	Pz.Kpfw. V	Pz. Bef. Wg.	Schtz.Pz. Wagen le.	Schtz.Pz. Wagen m.	Pz. Sp. Wg. le.	Pz. Sp. Wg. s.	Art. B.Wg. III	s. I.G. Sf.	7,5 Pak Sf	
Stab Pz.Rgt. 1)	1103	1.11.41	5		3								
Stbs.Kp.Pz.Abt.b	1150b	25.1.43	5		3		1+						+ 251/8
" " " " Panther 2)	1150a	1. 6.43		5	3		5+						+2 251/8
4 m. Pz. Kp.a	1175a	25.1.43	88										
4 " " " Panther 2)	1177	10.1.43		88									
Summe Pz. Rgt.			98	93	9		6						
Stb.Pz.Gr.Rgt.(gp)	1104a(gp)	1. 6.43					2						
Stbs.Kp.aPz.Gr.R.(gp) 3)	1153a(gp)	1. 4.43					20						
Stb.Pz.Gr.Btl.(gp)	1108a(gp)	1. 4.43					6+						+1 251/8
3 Pz.Gr.Kp.c	1114c(gp)	1. 4.43					63						
Fhr.schw.Kp.a (gp)	1121a(gp)	1. 3.43					2						} schw. Kp.
Gesch.Zg. a (gp)	1123a(gp)	1. 3.43					4						} 27 SPW
Pi. Zg. a (gp)	1124a(gp)	1. 3.43					7						}
Schw.Kan.Zg.(7,5)	1125 (gp)	1. 5.43					8						}
Schw.Pz.Jg.Zg.(gp)	1145 (gp)	1. 3.43					6						}
2 s.I.G. Kp. (Sf) 4)	1120a	1. 5.43					8				12		
Summe Pz. Gren. Rgt.							126				12		
Stab Pz.Aufkl.Abt.	1109 (gp)	1. 4.43				15	1+						+ 251/8
1. Pz.Sp.Kp. 5)	1162	1.11.41						18	12+				+. 6-233 = Kan.Zg.
2. " " " c	1162c	5. 2.43				25							
3. Pz. A.Kp.(gp) 6)	1113 (gp)	1. 3.42				37							
s.Kp.wie s.Kp.Pz.Gr.Btl.							27						
Summe Pz. Aufkl. Abt.						77	28	18	12				

Stbs.Kp.Pz.Jg.Abt.Sf 7)	1155d	1. 6.43					1+					3	+ 251/8
3 schn.Pz.Jg.Kp(Sf) 7)	1148d	1. 6.43										42	
Summe Pz. Jäg. Abt.							1					45	
St.Batr.Art.Rgt.(mot) 8)	577	1.11.41				1							
3 Batr.le.FH ein.P.D. 8)	435	1.11.41				3							
2 St.Btr.Art.Abt(mot) 8)	585	1.11.41				2							
2 Btr.s.FH ein.P.D. 8)	463	1.11.41				2							
1 "10cm Kan." " 8)	457	1.11.41				1							
Stab Art.Abt.(Sf)	407	16.1.43								2			
Stbs.Btr.Art.Abt.(Sf) 8)	583	16.1.43				1							
2 Btr.le FH (Sf) 8)	431b	16.1.43				2				4			
1 " s. " (Sf) 8)	461b	16.1.43								3			
Summe Pz. Art. Rgt.						12				9			
Stab Pz.Pi. Btl. 9)	703a	1. 3.43				2							
le. Pi. Kp. (mot)	712	neu											
Pi. Komp. (gp)	714 (gp)	1. 4.43					v25						
Summe Pz. Pi. Batl.						2	25						
Pz.Div. Fsp.Kp.a 10)	976a	1. 3.43					16						
Pz.Div. Fu. Kp. 10)	971	1. 6.42			3		1+	2	27				+ 251/6
Summe Nachr. Abt.					3		17	2	27				
Zusammenstellung													
Pz. Rgt.			98	93	9		6						
Pz. Gren. Rgt.							126				12		
Pz. Aufkl. Abt.						77	28	18	12				
Pz. Jäg. Abt.							1					45	
Pz. Artl. Rgt.						12				9			
Pz. Pi. Batl.						2	25						
Pz. Nachr. Abt.					3		17	2	27				
Summe Pz. Division			98	93	12	91	203	20	39	9	12	45	

Distribution of light/medium armoured halftracks and armoured cars in a 'Type 43' Reconnaissance Battalion

Gliederung Pz. A. A. Pz. Div.

Einheit	K.St.N. Nr.	K.St.N. Datum	le. Schtz. Pz.Wg. 1	3	5	7	8	9	m. Schtz.Pz.Wg.251/ 1	3	7	8	9	10	11	Pz. Sp. Wg. 234	Gesamt 250	251
Stab Pz. A.A.	1109 gp	1.11.43		2						7		1			2		2	10
Pz.Späh-Kp.a	1162a	1.10.43														25		
Pz. " " c	1162c	1.11.43			9			16									25	
Pz.Aufkl.Kp.	1113 gp	1.11.43	22	2		4	3										31	
" " "	1113 gp	1.11.43	22	2		4	3										31	
Führ.schw.Kp.gp	1121 a	1.11.43								1								}
Gesch.Zug/a(2 le IG)	1123 a gp	1.11.43							4									}
Pi Zug a gp	1124a gp	1.11.43									7							} 25
schw.Kan.Zug(7,5)gp	1125 gp	1.11.43							1	1			6					}
" Pz.Jg.Zug(3 Gesch) gp	1145 gp	1.11.43							1					4				
Gesamtsumme:			44	6	9	8	6	16	6	9	7	1	6	4	2	25	89	35

Distribution of light/medium armoured halftracks and armoured cars
in a 'Type 44' Reconnaissance Battalion

Gliederung Pz. A. A. Pz. Div.

Einheit	K. St. N.		le. Schtz. Pz. Wg.						m. Schtz. Pz. Wg. 251/								Pz.Sp.Wg. 234	Gesamt	
	Nr.	Datum:	1	3	5	7	8	9	1	2	3	7	8	9	11	17		250	251
Stab Pz. A. A.	1109gp	1.4.44									7		1		2		16.oder 19.le.Sp.Wg.		10
Pz.Sp.Komp.c	1162c	1.4.44			9			16										25	
Pz.Aufkl.Komp.	1113gp	1.4.44	22	2		4	2											30	
" " "	1114cgp	1.7.44							10	2	2			2		7			23
Führ.schw.Kp.gp.	1121agp	1.4.44									1				1				
8 cm Gran.W.Zg. (6 Gran.W.)gp	1126agp	1.4.44							1	7									
Pi. Zug a gp.	1124agp	1.4.44										7							25
schw.Kan.Zug(7,5)gp	1125 gp	1.4.44							1		1			6					
Gesamtsumme:			22	2	9	4	2	16	12	9	11	7	1	8	3	7	16 oder 19 le.Sp.Wg.	55	53

Theoretical Strengths of Medium (MSPW) and Light (LeSPW) halftracks for 1.SS, 2.SS and 12.SS Panzer Divisions

MSPW	1.SS	2.SS	12.SS
Panzer Regiment	10	10	10
Panzer Grenadier Regiment			
Regiment Stab	18	9	18
Pionier Kompanie	28	14	28
Infanteriegeschuetz Kompanie	10	5	10
Panzer Grenadier Bn. Stab	12	6	12
Panzer Grenadier Kompanie	126	63	126
Schwere Kompanie	34	17	34
Panzer Aufklärungs Abteilung			
Abteilung Stab	10	10	-
3. Kompanie	21	21	-
4. (SchwereKompanie)	24	24	24
Panzerjäger Abteilung Stab	1	1	1
Panzer Pionier Bataillon Stab	5	5	5
Panzer Pionier Kompanie	25	25	25
Panzer Funk Kompanie	8	8	8
Panzer Artillerie Regiment	4	4	4
TOTAL	336 MSPW	222 MSPW	305 MSPW

LeSPW			
Panzer Aufklärungs Abteilung			
Panzer Aufklärungs Stab	-	-	15
1.(Panzerspähwagen) Kompanie	25	25	25
2. Kompanie	30	30	30
3. Kompanie	-	30	30
TOTAL	55 LeSPW	85 LeSPW	100 LeSPW

'TYPE 44' PANZER DIVISION ORGANISATION

Theoretical Strength differences between Waffen SS and Army 'Type 44' Panzer Divisions

	WAFFEN SS	ARMY
Personnel	17809	14727
Pistols	4362	3276
Machine Pistols	1712	1607
Rifles	12285	9094
Heavy MGs	102	72
Light MGs	1102	1239
Medium Mortars	62	52
Heavy Mortars	26	18
7.5cm Anti-tank Guns (Towed)	28	13
8.8cm Flak	18	12
Light Field Guns (Towed)	25	13
Light Field Guns (SP)	12	12
Heavy Field Guns (Towed)	12	8
Heavy Field Guns (SP)	6	6
10cm Cannon	4	4
Heavy Infantry Guns	12	12
2cm Flak	50	52
2cm Quad Flak	14	9
3.7cm Flak	17	17
Main Battle Tanks	180/200*	180/200*
Jagdpanzer IVs	31	31
Armoured Cars	22	16
Light Halftracks	63	55
Medium Halftracks	241	232
Motorcycles	638	468
Field Cars	893	641
Trucks	2168	1661
Prime Movers (including Flak Mounts)	197	125

**Theoretical strengths allowed for either 17 or 22 tanks per company. Divisional personnel strengths varied slightly depending on which option was used*

Unit Symbols
Organisational Chart 1

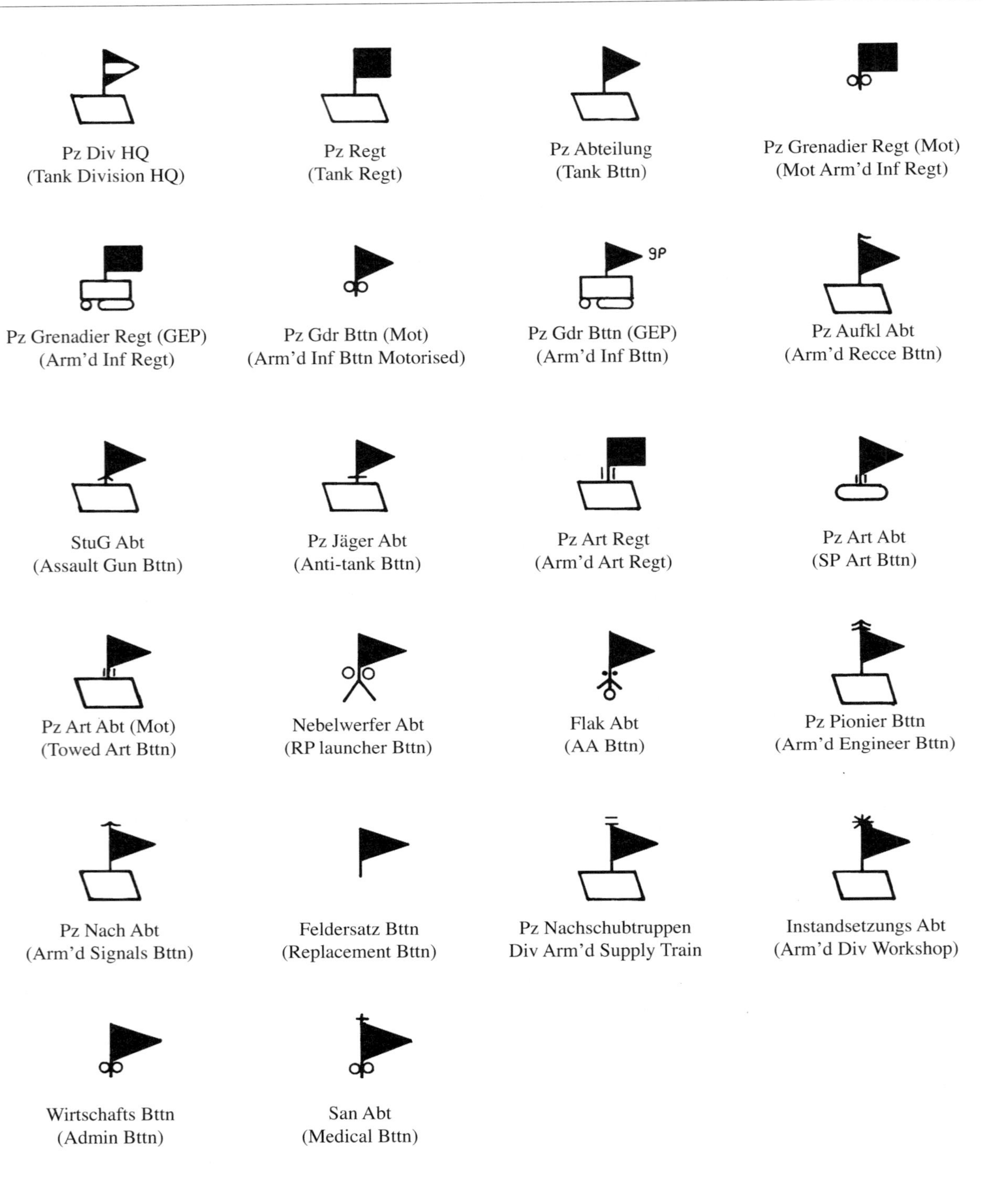

Unit Symbols
Organisational Chart 2

Pz Div HQ
Mapping Office

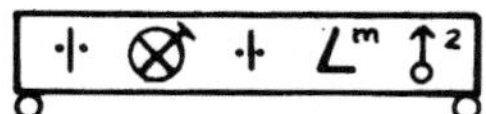

Div Escort/Security Company
(Equipped with MGs; mortars; AA guns)

Military Police Co
(5zg means 5 Zug – Platoons)

Div Music Corps

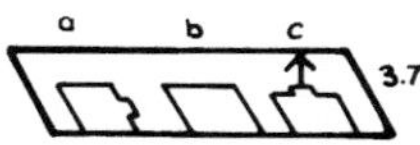

Pz Regt HQ
(a Signals/ b Recce /c Flak platoons
with 8 x 3.7cm SP flak guns)

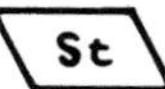

Pz Abt Stabs Kompanie
(Pz Bttn HQ Company)

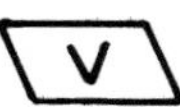

Pz Kompanie
(V = type of tank, here
Panther)

Pz Maintenance & Repair Co

Pz Pionier Kompanie
(Arm'd Engineer Co of Pz Regt. Usually 9 Co.
Equipped with flamethrowers; mortars; Mgs)

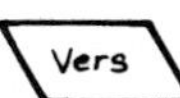

Supply Co within Pz Regt
or Bttn

9P

Arm'd HQ Co of Pz Gdr Regt
(LAH had two)

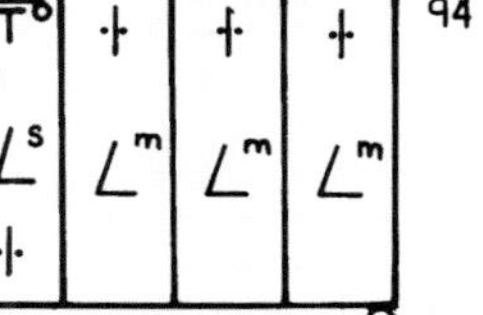

Pz Gdr Bttn
(Motorised with 3 rifle Co, 1 Heavy Co.
94 = % Strength of Bttn)

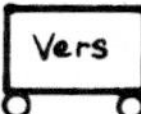

Motorised Supply Co
(Every Bttn in 44 Pz Div
had one such)

Heavy (150mm) SP Inf Gun Co
(Usually 13 Co of Pz Gdr Regt.
6 Guns per Co)

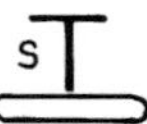

7.5cm SP A/T Gun (Marder)

Unit Symbols
Organisational Chart 3

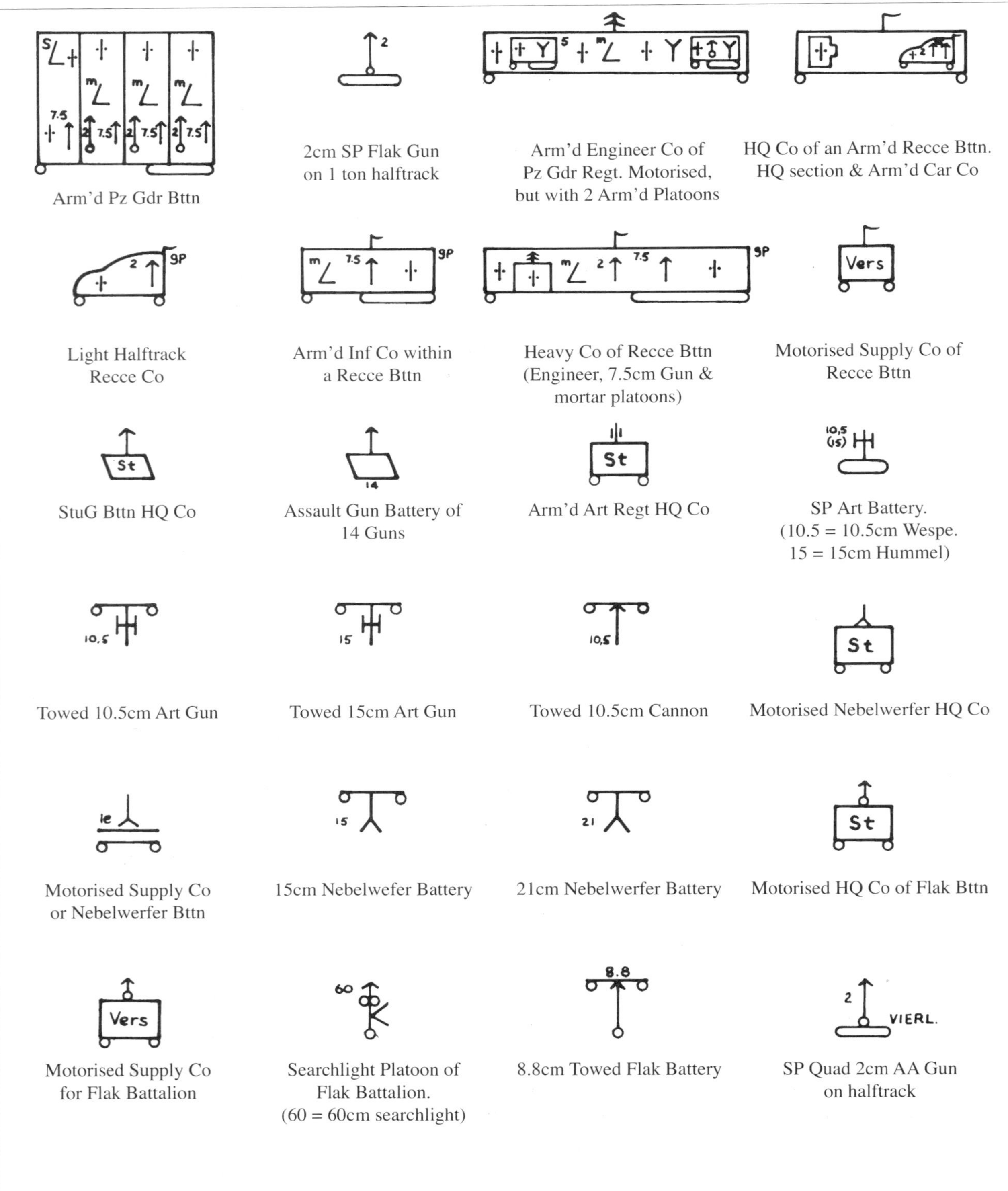

Arm'd Pz Gdr Bttn

2cm SP Flak Gun on 1 ton halftrack

Arm'd Engineer Co of Pz Gdr Regt. Motorised, but with 2 Arm'd Platoons

HQ Co of an Arm'd Recce Bttn. HQ section & Arm'd Car Co

Light Halftrack Recce Co

Arm'd Inf Co within a Recce Bttn

Heavy Co of Recce Bttn (Engineer, 7.5cm Gun & mortar platoons)

Motorised Supply Co of Recce Bttn

StuG Bttn HQ Co

Assault Gun Battery of 14 Guns

Arm'd Art Regt HQ Co

SP Art Battery. (10.5 = 10.5cm Wespe. 15 = 15cm Hummel)

Towed 10.5cm Art Gun

Towed 15cm Art Gun

Towed 10.5cm Cannon

Motorised Nebelwerfer HQ Co

Motorised Supply Co or Nebelwerfer Bttn

15cm Nebelwefer Battery

21cm Nebelwerfer Battery

Motorised HQ Co of Flak Bttn

Motorised Supply Co for Flak Battalion

Searchlight Platoon of Flak Battalion. (60 = 60cm searchlight)

8.8cm Towed Flak Battery

SP Quad 2cm AA Gun on halftrack

Unit Symbols
Organisational Chart 4

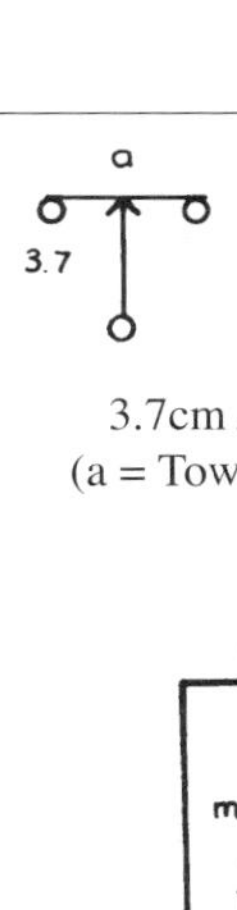

3.7cm AA Guns
(a = Towed/ b = SP)

Pz Pionier Battn HQ
(Motorised)

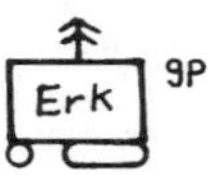

Arm'd Scout Platoon of Pz Pionier Battn
(Arm'd halftracks)

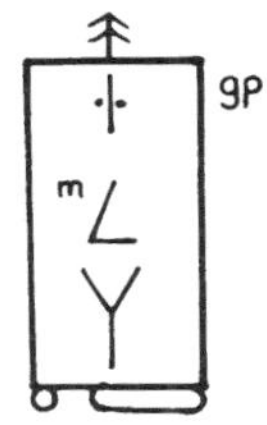

Arm'd Engineer Co of Pz
Pionier Battn

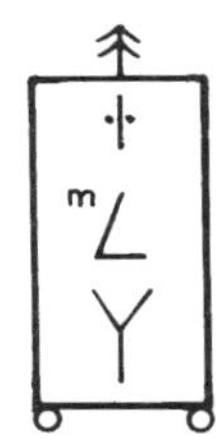

Arm'd Engineer Co
(Motorised) Pioneer Battn

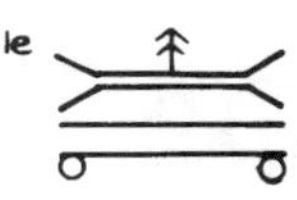

Bridging Column, Pioneer Battn
le = Light

Pz Nach Kompanie
(Arm'd Field Tel Co
of Signals Battn)

Pz Nach Kompanie
(Arm'd Radio Co
of signals Battn)

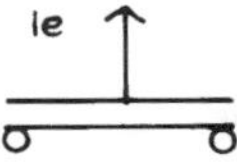

Light Supply Co fo Arm'd Signals Battn

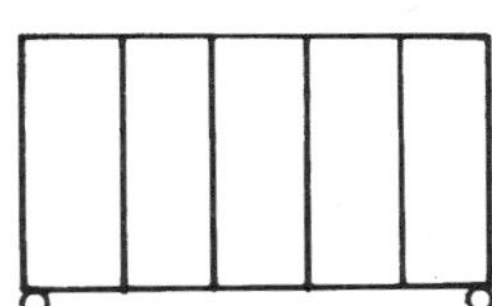

Felders Battn
(Field Replacement Battn.
Recruits & replacements to
Div in the field)

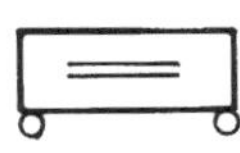

Supply Co supporting a
Supply Battn

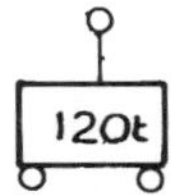

Motorised Supply Column
(120t = Tonnage carried by the unit)

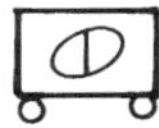

Bakery Co (Mot)
Part of Div Admin Battn

Butchery Co (Mot)
Part of Div Admin Battn

Supply Office (Mot)
Part of Div Admin Battn

Unit Symbols
Organisational Chart 5

Maintenance/Repair Co (Mot)
Div Workshop Battn

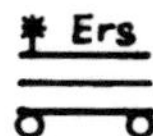

Replacement Co (Mot)
Div Workshop Battn

Weapons Repair Co
Div Workshop Battn

Field Post Office (Mot)
of Div Admin Battn

Medical Co (Mot)
of Medical Battn

Div Field Hospital

Ambulance Co (Mot)

Div
Correspondence
Platoon

M/C Platoon
Recce/Despatch

LMG

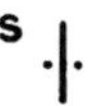

HMG

Medium Mortar (8cm)

Heavy Mortar
(120cm)

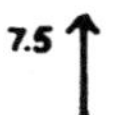

7.5cm Gun

2cm AA Gun
on halftrack
(7.5cm)

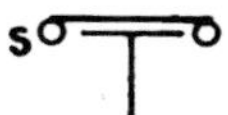

Towed Heavy
Anti-tank Gun

2cm Cannon
on halftrack

2/3.7cm SP AA Gun
on Pz IV chassis

Flamethrower
(Sometimes on
halftrack)

Towed Medium
Anti-tank Gun (5cm)

Quad 2cm AA Gun

THE MELDUNG

The Meldung was a one page monthly Divisional report detailing exact manpower, vehicle and heavy weapon stocks. A weekly report was also prepared, but this gave only a very brief account of Divisional readiness, stating manpower and tank strengths only.

The Meldung Described:

1. PERSONELLE LAGE
Detailed manpower strengths giving authorised strengths, shortages, casualty and replacement figures and numbers of staff absent from the Division

2. MATERIELLE LAGE
Comprised 4 sections:
- Gepazerte Fahrzeuge – Armoured vehicles
- Kraftfahrzeuge – Motorcycles and field cars
- noch Kraftfahrzeuge – Trucks and tracked prime movers
- Waffen – Anti-tank, artillery and machine guns

Each section gave authorised and actual strengths and included 'ready for action' and 'in short term repair' figures. Percentage figures were also included.

Below is an example of how the strength tables worked (1.SS Panzer Division, 1st June 1944).

Example:

		Stu. Gesch
Soll (Zahlen)		45
einsatzbeit	zahlenm.	44
	in % des Solls	97.7
in kurfristiger instandsetzung	zahlenm.	1
(bis 3 Wochen)	in % des Solls	22

Translation:

		Assault Guns
Authorised number		45
Ready for action	number	44
	% of authorised number	97.7
in short term repair	number	1
(under 3 weeks)	% of authorised number	22

What the tables do not show are vehicles/weapons in for long term repair.

The Meldung Translated:

MELDUNG	Report
Verband	Formation
Unterstellungsverhältnis	Placed under the command of:
PERSONELLE LAGE	Personnel situation
Soll	Authorised strength
Fehl	Shortfall
Offizier	Officer
Uffz.	Non-commissioned officer
Mannsch.	Other ranks
Hiwi	Russian volunteer
Verluste	Losses
Tot	Dead
Verw.	Wounded
Verm.	Missing
Krank	Sick
Sonst	Others
Ersatz	Replacement
Genesene	Recovered
Über 1 Jahr nicht beurlaubt	Absent from the Division over 1 year (non-leave)

MATERIELLE LAGE	Material/Stock situation
Soll (Zahlen)	Authorised number
Einsatzbereit	Ready for action
In kurzfristiger Instandsetzung (bis 3 Wochen)	In short term repair (For less than 3 weeks)

GEPANZERTE FAHRZEUGE Armoured vehicle

Stu Gesch	Assault Gun
III	Panzer III
IV	Panzer IV
V	Panzer V *(Panther)*
VI	Panzer VI *(Tiger)*

Schtz Pz.	Armoured halftrack
Pz. Sp.	Armoured car
Art. Pz. B.	Artillery observation tank
(O. Pz. Fu Wg)	Armoured radio vehicle
Pak Sl.	Anti-tank gun (Self-propelled)

KRAFTFAHRZEUGE	Motor vehicle
Kräder	Motorcycle
Ketten	Tracked motorcycle
M.angetr. Bwg.	Motorcycle with sidecar
Sonst	Other (type)
Pkw	Field car
gel.	Cross country type
O	Ordinary type

NOCH KRAFTFAHRZEUGE	Additional motor vehicles
Lkw	Truck
Maultiere	Tracked truck
Tonnage	Tonnage
Zgkw } RSO }	Tracked prime movers

WAFFEN	Weapons
s Pak	Heavy anti-tank gun
Art.-Gesch	Artillery
MG	Machine gun
Sonstige Waffen	Other weapons
Pferdefehlstellen	Horse stocks on strength

Blank Meldung
(Original German Monthly Divisional Strength Return)

Verband:

Meldung vom .... 194 .... Unterstellungsverhältnis:

1. Personelle Lage am Stichtag der Meldung:

a) Personal:

	Soll	Fehl
Offiziere		
Uffz......		
Mannsch.		
Hiwi....		
Insgesamt		

c) in der Berichtszeit eingetroffener Ersatz:

	Ersatz	Genesene
Offiziere		
Uffz. und Mannsch.		

b) Verluste und sonstige Abgänge in der Berichtszeit vom .... bis ....

	tot	verw.	verm.	krank	sonst.
Offiziere					
Uffz. und Mannsch.					
Insgesamt					

d) über 1 Jahr nicht beurlaubt:

	Köpfe		% d. Iststärke
insgesamt:			
davon:	12 - 18 Monate	19 - 24 Monate	über 24 Monate

Platzkarten im Berichtsmonat zugewiesen. ....

2. Materielle Lage:

	Gepanzerte Fahrzeuge							Kraftfahrzeuge				
								Kräder			Pkw	
	Stu. Gesch.	III	IV	V	VI	Schtz. Pz. Pz. Sp. Art. Pz. B. (o Pz. Fu. Wg.)	Pak Sf.	Ketten	m. angetr. Bwg.	sonst.	gel.	O
Soll (Zahlen)												
einsatzbereit zahlenm.												
einsatzbereit in % des Solls												
in kurzfristiger Instandsetzung (bis 3 Wochen) zahlenm.												
in kurzfristiger Instandsetzung (bis 3 Wochen) in % des Solls												

	noch Kraftfahrzeuge						Waffen			
	Lkw				Ketten-Fahrzeuge					
	Maultiere	gel.	O	Tonnage	Zgkw.	RSO	s Pak	Art.-Gesch.	MG. ( )	sonstige Waffen
Soll (Zahlen)										
einsatzbereit zahlenm.										
einsatzbereit in % des Solls										
in kurzfristiger Instandsetzung (bis 3 Wochen) zahlenm.										
in kurzfristiger Instandsetzung (bis 3 Wochen) in % des Solls										

SS K.K.St. 1 (Nr 19c)

*) Zgkw. mit 1-5t, **) Zgkw. mit 8-18t
( ) davon MG. 42

3. Pferdefehlstellen:

1.SS PANZER DIVISION

'Leibstandarte Adolf Hitler'

The 1.SS Panzer Division had been withdrawn from the Eastern Front in April 1944 and was transported to Belgium for rest and refitting.

In mid-June it began its move to the Normandy Front where it was placed under the command of 1.SS Panzer Korps. It was not until early July that all divisional units were consolidated, thus enabling it to fight as a complete unit.

On 1st June 1944, 1.SS Panzer Division had the following units on strength:

Stab der Division
SS Panzer Regiment 1
SS Panzer Grenadier Regiment 1
SS Panzer Grenadier Regiment 2
SS Panzer Aufklärungs Abteilung 1
SS Sturmgeschütz Abteilung 1
SS Panzer Atillerie Regiment 1
SS Werfer Abteilung 1
SS Flak Abteilung 1
SS Panzer Pionier Bataillon 1
SS Panzer Nachrichten Abteilung 1
SS Divisionsnachschubtruppen 1
SS Panzer Instandsetzungs Abteilung 1
SS Wirtschafts Bataillon 1
SS Sanitäts Abteilung 1
SS Feldgendarmerie Kompanie 1
SS Kriegsberichter Zug 1

- SS Panzer Regiment 1

In early May 1944, 1. *(Panther)* Abteilung began equipping with new tanks. The refit was expected to be completed by 20/6/44.

Tanks received by I. Abteilung

From II Abteilung Panzer Regiment 33	24 Pz V
From II Abteilung Panzer Regiment 35	21 Pz V
Delivered on 14/6/44	8 Pz V
Delivered on 16-17/6/44	26 Pz V
TOTAL	79 Pz V

(Including 6 Command Panthers)

Tanks received by II. Abteilung

From 116 Panzer Division	10 Pz IV
Delivered on 7/5/44	35 Pz IV
Delivered on 8/6/44	33 Pz IV
Delivered on 16/6/44	20 Pz IV
Delivered in May 1944	5 BEF Pz IV*
TOTAL	103 Pz IV

**Command Tanks*

Also received in the same period

2cm Flak Panzer 38(t)	12
SdKfz 7/1 Quad 2cm Flakwagen	6
Bergepanthers (Recovery tanks)	2
Medium armoured halftracks	10 (SdKfz 251)

SS Sturmgeschütze Abteilung I

Delivered on 4/5/44	20 StuG
Delivered on 7/5/44	25 StuG
TOTAL	45 StuG

SS Panzer Regiment 1
Tank Strengths December 1942 – April 1943

31/12/42	Pz II	Pz III	Pz IV	Pz VI	BEF Pz	TOTAL
a: Ready for action	12	4	30	-	-	46
b: Under repair	-	-	-	-	-	-
c: In the process of delivery	-	-	47	9	10	66

15/1/43	Pz II	Pz III	Pz IV	Pz VI	BEF Pz	TOTAL
a: Ready for action	12	4	30	-	10	56
b: Under repair	-	-	-	-	-	-
c: In the process of delivery	-	5	47	9	-	61

20/1/43 - 1/2/43	Pz II	Pz III	Pz IV	Pz VI	BEF Pz	TOTAL
a: Ready for action (on strength)	12	9	77	9	10	117

25/2/43	Pz II	Pz III	Pz IV	Pz VI	BEF Pz	TOTAL
a: Ready for action	9	4	46	7	8	74
b: Under repair	2	-	6	2	2	12

5/3/43	Pz II	Pz III	Pz IV	Pz VI	BEF Pz	TOTAL
a: Ready for action	10	1	35	8	8	62
b: Under repair	1	3	11	1	-	16

31/3/43	Pz II	Pz III	Pz IV	Pz VI	BEF Pz	TOTAL
a: Ready for action	11	10	28	5	10	64
b: Under repair	-	2	13	3	-	18

10/4/43	Pz II	Pz III	Pz IV	Pz VI	BEF Pz	TOTAL
a: Ready for action	11	11	37	6	9	74
b: Under repair	-	1	4	2	-	7

20/4/43	Pz II	Pz III	Pz IV	Pz VI	BEF Pz	TOTAL
a: Ready for action	11	9	36	6	9	71
b: Under repair	-	3	5	2	-	10
c: In the process of delivery	-	-	-	10	-	10

30/4/43	Pz II	Pz III	Pz IV	Pz VI	BEF Pz	TOTAL
a: Ready for action	11	12	42	8	9	82
b: Under repair	-	-	-	-	-	-
c: In the process of delivery	-	-	-	5	-	5

30/4/43	Pz II	Pz III	Pz IV	Pz VI	Bef Pz	TOTAL
a: Ready for action	11	12	42	8	9	82
b: Under repair	-	-	-	-	-	-
c: In the process of delivery	-	-	-	5	-	5

Bef Pz: Command tank   Pz Beo III: Artillery observation vehicle

SS Panzer Regiment 1
Tank Strengths May 1943 – July 1943

10/5/43	Pz II	Pz III	Pz IV	Pz VI	Bef Pz	PzBeo II	TOTAL
a: Ready for action	11	12	42	8	9	-	82
b: Under repair	-	-	-	-	-	-	-
c: In the process of delivery	-	-	25	5	-	9	39

31/5/43	Pz II	Pz III	Pz IV	Pz VI	Bef Pz	PzBeo III	TOTAL
a: Ready for action	11	11	53	7	9	9	100
b: Under repair	-	-	4	6	-	-	10
c: In the process of delivery	-	-	10	-	-	-	10

20/6/43	Pz II	Pz III	Pz IV	Pz VI	Bef Pz	PzBeo III	TOTAL
a: Ready for action	11	11	53	7	9	9	100
b: Under repair	-	2	4	6	-	-	12
c: In the process of delivery	-	-	26	-	-	-	26

30/6/43	Pz II	Pz III	Pz IV	Pz VI	Bef Pz	PzBeo III	TOTAL
a: Ready for action	4	12	63	11	9	8	107
b: Under repair	-	1	4	2	-	1	9
c: In the process of delivery	-	-	16	-	-	-	16

10/7/43	Pz II	Pz III	Pz IV	Pz VI	Bef Pz	PzBeo III	TOTAL
a: Ready for action	4	5	41	5	6	8	69
b: Under repair	-	7	37	8	3	1	56
c: In the process of delivery	-	-	-	5	-	-	5

20/7/43	Pz II	Pz III	Pz IV	Pz V	Pz VI	Bef Pz	PzBeo III	TOTAL
a: Ready for action	4	10	55	-	14	6	8	97
b: Under repair	-	2	19	-	3	3	1	28
c: In the process of delivery	-	-	53	98*	-	-	-	151

** Includes 2 Berge Pz V*

In early August 1943 the Division was transferred to Italy after handing over the majority of its tanks to the 2.SS and 3.SS Panzer Grenadier Divisions.

Bef Pz: Command tank   Pz Beo III: Artillery observation vehicle assigned to Pz. Art. Rgt.

SS Panzer Regiment 1
Tank Strengths August 1943 – December 1943

Tanks taken to Italy	Pz II	Pz III	Pz IV	Pz V	Pz VI	Bef Pz	PzBeo III	TOTAL
a: Ready for action	4	-	-	-	-	6	8	18
b: Under repair	-	-	-	-	-	3	1	4
c: In the process of delivery	-	-	53	98*	-	-	-	151

** 71 Pz V issued to 11 SS Pz. Rgt. 1*

Whilst in Italy the Division was re-equipped with new tanks including a Panther Abteilung (Battalion)

31/8/43	Pz II	Pz III	Pz IV	Pz V	Pz VI	Bef Pz	PzBeo III	TOTAL
a: Ready for action	4	1	54	62	20	7	5	153
b: Under repair	-	-	4	9	7	2	4	26

20/9/43	Pz II	Pz III	Pz IV	Pz V	Pz VI	Bef Pz	PzBeo III	TOTAL
a: Ready for action	4	1	46	71	26	9	2	159
b: Under repair	-	-	12	-	1	-	7	20

10/10/43	Pz II	Pz III	Pz IV	Pz V	Pz VI	Bef Pz	PzBeo III	TOTAL
a: Ready for action	3	1	53	58	25	9	9	158
b: Under repair	1	-	5	12	2	-	-	19

20/10/43	Pz II	Pz III	Pz IV	Pz V	Pz VI	Bef Pz	PzBeo III	TOTAL
a: Ready for action	3	1	53	58	25	9	9	158
b: Under repair	-	-	5	12	2	-	-	19
c: In the process of delivery	-	-	40	-	10	-	-	50

In November/December 1943 the Division returned to the Eastern Front receiving some new tanks on arrival. Fresh tanks were also collected at Magdeburg.

6/11/43	Pz II	Pz III	Pz IV	Pz V	Pz VI	Bef Pz	PzBeo III	TOTAL
a: on strength 4	1	93	96	27	9	9		244
b: In the process of delivery	-	-	-	-	10*	-	-	-

(42 StuGs, 9 StuHs, 31 Marders were also on strength)

20/11/43	Pz II	Pz III	Pz IV	Pz V	Pz VI	Bef Pz	PzBeo III	TOTAL
a: Ready for action	2	1	18	10	12	9	8	60
b: Under repair	2	-	69	75	13	-	1	160
c: In the process of delivery	-	-	3	-	10*	-	-	13

10/12/43	Pz II	Pz III	Pz IV	Pz V	Pz VI	Bef Pz	PzBeo III	TOTAL
a: Ready for action	1	-	12	5	4	3	4	29
b: Under repair	3	1	57	71	20	6	5	163
c: In the process of delivery	-	-	-	30	10*	-	-	40

** The 10 Pz VI were transferred to SS Pz. Abt. 101*

20/12/43	Pz II	Pz III	Pz IV	Pz V	Pz VI	Bef Pz	PzBeo III	TOTAL
a: Ready for action	1	-	9	7	3	2	3	25
b: Under repair	2	1	57	67	20	6	6	159
c: In the process of delivery	-	-	-	30	-	-	-	30

SS Panzer Regiment 1
Tank Strengths December 1943 – January 1944

31/12/43	Pz II	Pz III	Pz IV	Pz V	Pz VI	Bef Pz	PzBeo III	TOTAL
a: Ready for action	-	-	14	7	2	2	5	30
b: Under repair	4	1	44	46	19	6	3	123
c: In the process of delivery	-	-	-	30	-	-	-	30

31/1/44	Pz III	Pz IV	Pz V	Pz VI	TOTAL
a: Ready for action	-	15	22	2	39
b: Under repair	1	19	27	4	141

(In January/February 10-12 more Panthers were received from the batch of 30 Panthers assigned in early January 1944)

1/3/44	Pz III	Pz IV	Pz V	Pz VI	TOTAL
a: Ready for action	1	-	12	1	14
b: Under repair	3	30	46	17	96

SS Panzer Regiment 1/SS Sturmgeschütz Abteilung

Between 4/7/44 and 5/8/44, 1.SS Panzer Division had the following Panzers and StuGs ready for action

Date	Pz V	Pz IV	StuG	BefPz
4/7/44	29	60	44	
7/7/44	31	59	39	
8/7/44	29	60	42	
9/7/44	30	60	41	
11/7/44	29	63	42	
13/7/44	29	58	36	
15/7/44	29	61	34	
16/7/44	41	61	36	
17/7/44	48	59	35	
18/7/44	46	59	35	
20/7/44	17	46	19	8
25/7/44	31	41	32	7
28/7/44	33	30	22	6
30/7/44	35	68	25	6
31/7/44	33	60	29	6
5/8/44	43	55	29	5

Theoretical Organisation* of 1.SS Panzer Division
1st June 1944

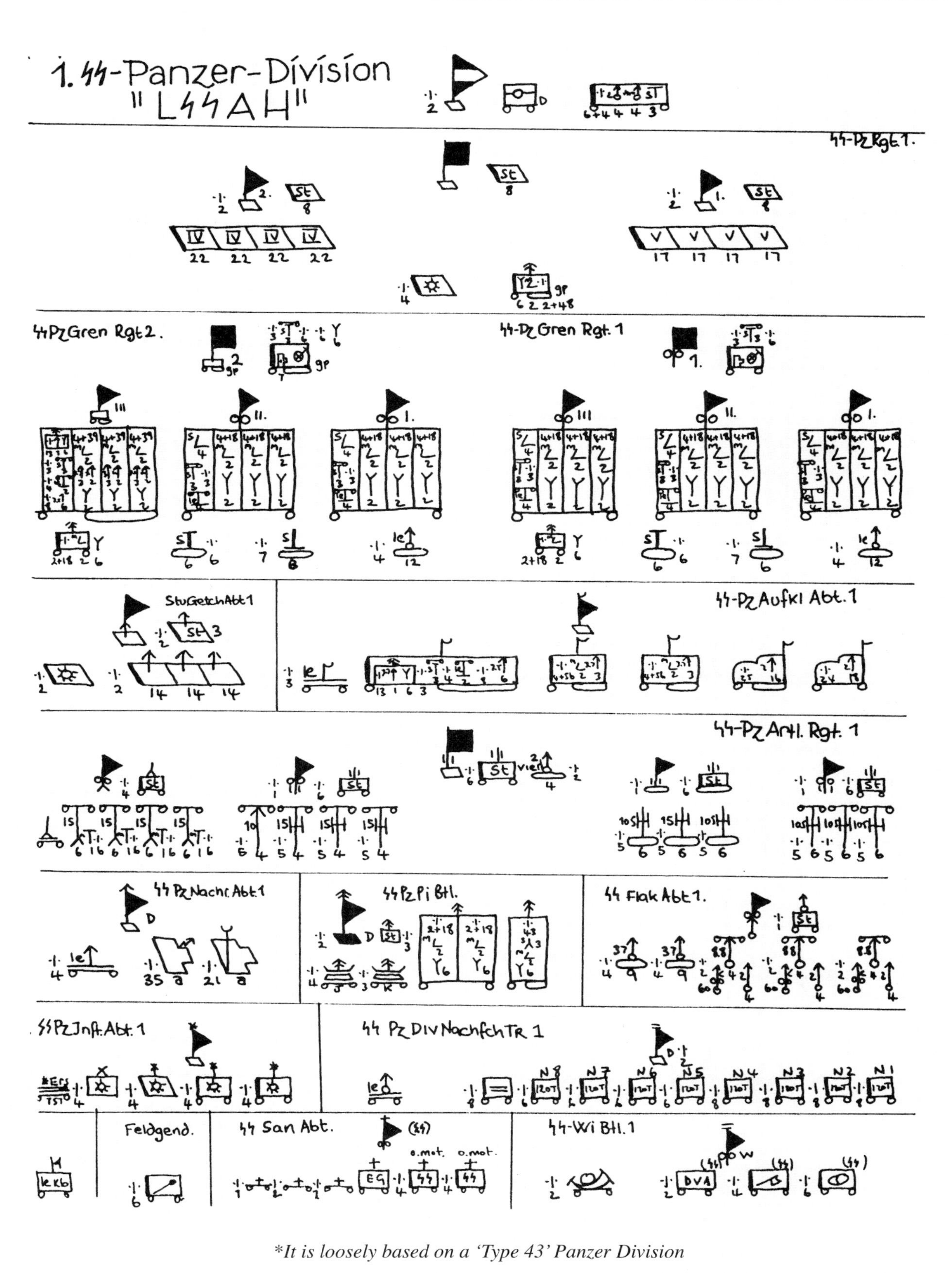

It is loosely based on a 'Type 43' Panzer Division

Theoretical Vehicle Strengths of 1.SS Panzer Division (Type 43 Organisation) 1st June 1944

PERSONNEL	
Officers	683
NCOs	4781
Other ranks	14761
Hiwis	1251
TOTAL	21,476
ARMOURED VEHICLES	
Sturmgeschütz (Assault Guns)	45
Panzer III	21
Panzer IV	101
Panzer V Panther	81
SdKfz 7/2 (SP 3.7cm Flak)	18
Armoured Personnel Carriers Armoured Cars Artillery Observation Vehicles	364
SIG 150mm Infantry Howitzers	12
SP Anti-tank Guns	26
MOTORCYCLES	
Motorcycle Combinations	756
Solo Motorcycles	1039
FIELD CARS	
4 Wheel Drive/Cross-country	1206
2 Wheel Drive/Normal Road	402
TRUCKS	
Maultiers (Semi-track Trucks)	15
Cross-country Type	1727
Normal Road Type	2145
HALFTRACKED VEHICLES	
SdKfz 10 (1 Ton) SdKfz 11 (3 Ton) SdKfz 6 (5 Ton)	283
SdKfz 7 (8 Ton) SdKfz 9 (12 Ton)	97
RSO (Fully Tracked Tractor)	3

Theoretical Weapon Strengths of 1.SS Panzer Division (Type 43 Organisation) 1st June 1944

7.5cm Anti-tank Guns (Towed)	31
5cm Anti-tank Guns (Towed)	4
88mm Flak (Anti-Aircraft Guns)	12
2cm Flak	37
3.7cm Flak	18
SIG (150mm SP Infantry Guns)	12
LIG (75mmTowed Infantry Guns)	26
Light Field Howitzers 105mm (Towed)	12
Heavy Field Howitzers 150mm (Towed)	12
Kanone (Cannon)100mm (Towed)	4
Wespe SP 105mm Howitzers	12
Hummel SP 150mm Howitzers	6
15cm Nebelwerfers (Projectors)	24
Heavy Mortars 120mm	20
Medium Mortars 80mm	52
Machine Guns (All Types)	1493

1.SS Panzer Division
Original German Strength Report
1st June 1944

Verband: 1.SS-Pz.Div. "LSSAH" 27

Meldung vom 1. Juni 1944 Unterstellungsverhältnis: I.SS-Pz.Korps

1. Personelle Lage am Stichtag der Meldung:

a) Personal:

	Soll	Fehl
Offiziere	683	208
Uffz.	4781	2234
Mannsch.	14761	+1070
Hiwi	1251	396
✱ Jnsgesamt	21386	1768

b) Verluste und sonstige Abgänge in der Berichtszeit vom ...... bis ......

	tot	verw.	verm.	krank	sonst.
Offiziere	1			2	3
Uffz. und Mannsch.				63	497
Jnsgesamt	1			65	500

c) in der Berichtszeit eingetroffener Ersatz:

	Ersatz	Genesene
Offiziere	36	3
Uffz. und Mannsch.	302	109

d) über 1 Jahr nicht beurlaubt:

insgesamt: 2435 Köpfe 13 % d. Iststärke

davon:	12 - 18 Monate	19 - 24 Monate	über 24 Monate
	2004	431	–

Platzkarten im Berichtsmonat zugewiesen: –

2. Materielle Lage:

		Gepanzerte Fahrzeuge							Kraftfahrzeuge				
		Stu. Gesch.	III	IV	V	VI	Schtz. Pz. Pz. Sp. Art. Pz. B. (o Pz. Fu. Wg.)	Pak Sf.	Kräder Ketten	Kräder m. angetr. Bwg.	Kräder sonst.	Pkw gel.	Pkw O
Soll (zahlen)		45	21	101	81		364	26		756	1039	1206	402
einsatzbereit	zahlenm.	44	–	42	38		–	–	13	89	47	224	81
	in % des Solls	97,7		41,5	46,9					11,7	4,5	18,5	20,1
in kurzfristiger Jnstandsetzung (bis 3 Wochen)	zahlenm.	1		8	–				3	27	33	118	58
	in % des Solls	22		7,9						3,5	3,1	9,8	20,1

		noch Kraftfahrzeuge							Waffen			
		Maultiere	Lkw gel.	Lkw O	Lkw Tonnage	Ketten-Fahrzeuge Zgkw. *)	Ketten-Fahrzeuge Zgkw. **)	RSO	s Pak	Art.-Gesch.	MG. ()	sonstige Waffen
Soll (Zahlen)		15	1727	2145	11661	283	97	3	31	58	1493	
einsatzbereit	zahlenm.	100	270	700	2910	13	32	–	97 %	60%	30%	
	in % des Solls	666	15,6	32,6	44,3	4,8	32,8				(13%)	
in kurzfristiger Jnstandsetzung (bis 3 Wochen)	zahlenm.	33	197	60	771	7	8	–	3 %	13 %		
	in % des Solls	220	11,4	2,8	6,6	2,4	8,2					

SS K.K.St. 1 (Nr 19c)

*) Zgkw. mit 1-5t, **) Zgkw. mit 8-18t
( ) davon MG. 42

3. Pferdefehlstellen:

Anl. zu Nr. 00656/44 geh.
Gen. Insp. d. Pz. Tr.

Note that the original compiler of this report added up the figures wrongly! – the total manpower figure should read 21,476 NOT 21,386. For an interpretation of this chart see page 40.

1.SS Panzer Division
Organisational Chart
30th May-1st June 1944

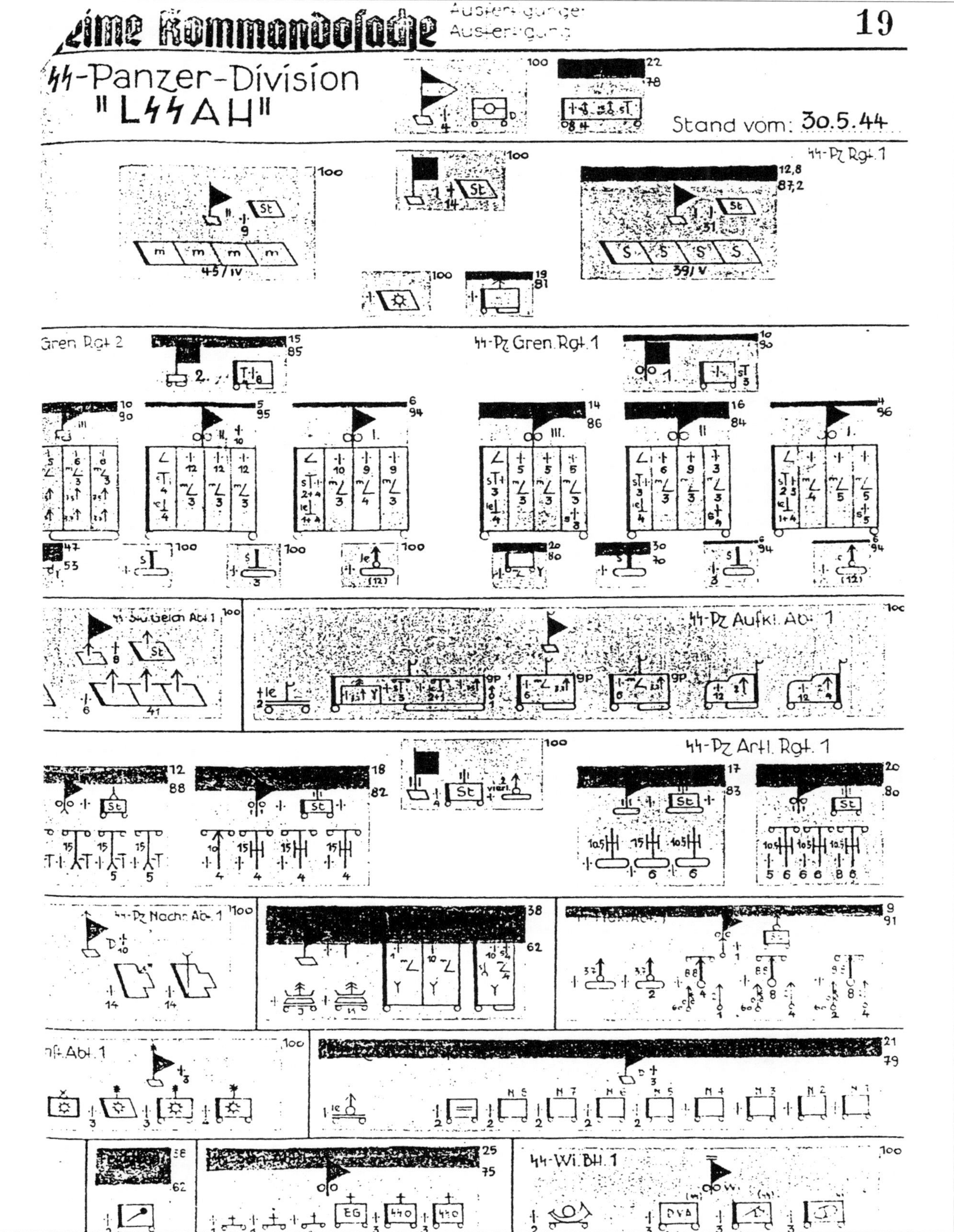

1.SS Panzer Division
Strength Report: 1st June 1944
Under Command of 1.SS Panzer Korps

MANPOWER

	Authorised Strength	Shortages	Actual
Officers	683	208	475
NCOs	4781	2234	2547
Other Ranks	14,761	1070+	15,831
Hiwis	1251	396	855
TOTAL	21,476	1768	19,708

LOSSES FOR PREVIOUS 4 WEEKS

	Dead	Wounded	Missing	Hospital	Other Cases
Officers	1	0	0	2	3
NCOs	0	0	0	63	497
Other Ranks	0	0	0	-	-
TOTAL	1	0	0	65	500

REPLACEMENTS/ARRIVALS

	Replacements	Recovered
Officers	36	3
NCOs	302	109
Other Ranks	-	-

OVER 1 YEAR ABSENT FROM DIVISION (NON-LEAVE)

TOTAL	2435
Of That:	
12 to 18 Months	2004
19 to 24 Months	431

1.SS Panzer Division
Strength Report: 1st June 1944
Material Stocks

ARMOURED VEHICLES

	StuG	Pz III	Pz IV	Pz V	Other AFVs	Sp Pak
Authorised Strength	45	21	101	81	364	26
Ready for Action	44	0	42	38	0	0
Short term repair	1	0	8	0	0	0

MOTOR CYCLES

	Ketten	+Sidecars	Other
Authorised Strength	0	756	1039
Ready for Action	13	89	47
Short term repair	3	27	33

CARS

	Cross country	Normal/Road
Authorised Strength	1206	402
Ready for Action	224	81
Short term repair	118	58

TRUCKS

	Maultiere	Cross country	Normal/Road
Authorised Strength	15	1727	2145
Ready for Action	100	270	700
Short term repair	33	197	60

TRACKED PRIME MOVERS

	1-5 Tons	8-18 Tons	RSOs
Authorised Strength	283	97	3
Ready for Action	13	32	0
Short term repair	7	8	0

WEAPONS

	Heavy Anti-tank Guns	Artillery Guns	MGs
Authorised Strength	31	58	1493
Ready for Action	30	35	448 *(of which 194 are MG42)*
Short term repair	1	8	

1.SS PANZER DIVISION
'Leibstandarte Adolf Hitler'

1st June 1944

- Divisionstab (Divisional HQ)
  100% Manpower
  4 LMG

  Div. Kartenstelle (Mapping Section)
  100% Manpower

  Div. Begleitkompanie (Divisional Security Company)
  78% Manpower
  8 LMG. 4 x 2cm Flak Guns (Towed)

- SS PANZER REGIMENT 1 (Tank Regiment)
  Regimentstab (Regimental HQ)
  100% Manpower
  14 LMG

  1. Panzer Abteilung (1st Tank Battalion)
  87.2% Manpower
  39 *Panthers*. 31 LMG

  2. Panzer Abteilung (2nd Tank Battalion)
  100% Manpower
  50 Pz IV (45 ready for action). 9 LMG

  Pionier Kompanie (Engineer Company)
  81% Manpower

  1 Werkstatt Kompanie (Workshop Company)
  100% Manpower

- SS PANZERGRENADIER REGIMENT 1
  (Motorised Infantry Regiment)
  Regimentstab (Regimental HQ)
  90% Manpower
  3 x 7.5cm Pak (Towed)

  1. Bataillon (Motorised)
  96% Manpower
  3 LMG. 5 HMG. 14 x 81mm Mortars. 1 x 15cm Inf. Gun (Towed). 4 x 7.5cm Inf. Guns (Towed). 2 x 7.5cm Pak (Towed)

  2. Bataillon (Motorised)
  84% Manpower
  18 LMG. 4 HMG. 9 x 81mm Mortars. 4 x 7.5cm Inf. Guns (Towed). 2 x 7.5cm Pak (Towed)

  3. Bataillon (Motorised)
  86% Manpower
  15 LMG. 3 HMG. 9 x 81mm Mortars. 4 x 7.5cm Inf. Guns (Towed). 3 x 7.5cm Pak (Towed)

  Flak Kompanie (Anti-aircraft Company)
  94% Manpower
  12 x 2cm Flak Guns (Towed)

  Infanteriegeschutz Kompanie (Infantry Gun Company)
  94% Manpower
  3 LMG. No heavy weapons

  Panzerjäger Kompanie (Anti-tank Company)
  70% Manpower
  No heavy weapons

  Pionier Kompanie (Engineer Company)
  80% Manpower
  No heavy weapons

- SS PANZERGRENADIER REGIMENT 2
  (Armoured Infantry Regiment)
  Regimentstab (Regimental HQ) (Armoured)
  85% Manpower
  Medium Armoured Halftracks. 8 LMG.
  4 x 5cm Pak (Towed)

  1. Bataillon (Motorised)
  94% Manpower
  32 LMG. 10 x 81mm Mortars. 1 x 15cm Inf. Gun (Towed). 4 x 7.5cm Inf. Guns (Towed). 2 x 7.5cm Pak (Towed). 4 x 5cm Pak (Towed)

  2. Bataillon (Motorised)
  95% Manpower
  46 LMG. 9 x 81mm Mortars. 4 x 7.5cm Inf. Guns (Towed). 4 x 7.5cm Pak (Towed)

3. Bataillon (Armoured)
90% Manpower
Medium Armoured Halftracks. 17 LMG.
6 x 81mm Mortars. 2 x 7.5cm Inf. Guns (Towed).
4 x 7.5cm Pak (Towed)

Flak Kompanie (Anti-aircraft Company)
100% Manpower
12 x 2cm Flak Guns (Towed)

Infanteriegeschutz Kompanie (Infantry Gun Company)
100% Manpower
3 x 15cm SP Infantry Guns

Panzerjäger Kompanie (Anti-tank Company)
100% Manpower
No heavy weapons

Pionier Kompanie (Engineer Company)
53% Manpower
No heavy weapons

- SS AUFKLÄRUNGS ABTEILUNG 1
(Armoured Reconnaissance Battalion)
100% Manpower

1. (Armoured Car) Company
4 x '4-Wheeled' Armoured Cars. (SdKfz 222).
12 LMG

2. (Armoured Car) Company
No Armoured Halftracks. 12 LMG

3.(Armoured Reconnaissance) Company
Light Armoured Halftracks. 6 LMG

4.(Armoured Reconnaissance) Company
Light Armoured Halftracks. 6 LMG

5.(Heavy) Company
Medium Armoured Halftracks. 1 x 15cm Inf. Gun (Towed). 2 x 7.7cm Inf. Guns (Towed). 3 x 7.5cm Pak (Towed). 1 x 2cm Flak Gun (Towed)

Versorgungs Kompanie (Supply Company)
2 LMG

- SS STURMGESCHÜTZ ABTEILUNG 1
(Assault Gun Battalion)
100% Manpower
45 Assault Guns (41 ready for action). 14 LMG

- SS PANZER ARTILLERIE REGIMENT 1
(Armoured Artillery Regiment)
Regimentstab (Regimental HQ)
100% Manpower
4 LMG

1. Abteilung (Towed Battalion)
80% Manpower
18 x 105mm LeFH 18. 19 LMG

2. Abteilung (Armoured Battalion)
83% Manpower
6 *Hummel*. 6 *Wespe*

3. Abteilung (Towed Battalion)
82% Manpower
12 x 150mm SFH 18. 4 x 105mm Kanone

4. Abteilung (Werfer Battalion)
88% Manpower
10 x 15cm Nebelwerfer

- SS FLAKABTEILUNG (Anti-aircraft Battalion)
91% Manpower
20 x 88mm Flak Guns (Towed). 2 x 3.7cm Flak Guns (Towed). 9 x 2cm Flak Guns (Towed).
2 x 60cm Searchlights. 1 LMG

- SS PANZER PIONIER BATAILLON
(Armoured Engineer Battalion)
62% Manpower

1. Kompanie (Armoured)
Medium Armoured Halftracks. 10 LMG. 4 HMG.
4 x 81mm Mortars

2. Kompanie (Motorised)
10 LMG

3. Kompanie (Motorised)
1 LMG

Brucken Kolonne (Bridging Column)

Brucken Kolonne (Bridging Column)

- SS PANZER NACHRICHTEN ABTEILUNG
(Armoured Signals Battalion)
100% Manpower. (Partially Armoured)
Medium Armoured Halftracks. 40 LMG

- SS NACHSCHUBTRUPPEN 1
  (Divisional Supply Battalion)
  79% Manpower
  8 Transportation Companies. 2 Supply Companies.
  11 LMG

- SS INSTADSETZUNGS ABTEILUNG 1
  (Workshop Battalion)
  100% Manpower
  4 Workshop/Repair Companies. 1 Supply Company.
  16 LMG

- SS WIRTSCHAFTS BATAILLON 1
  (Commissary Battalion)
  100% Manpower
  1 Bakery Company. 1 Butcher Company.
  1 Administration Company. 1 Field Post Office.
  11 LMG

- SS SANITÄTS ABTEILUNG 1 (Medical Battalion)
  75% Manpower
  3 Ambulance Columns. 2 Medical Compaies.
  1 Field Hospital. 8 LMG

- SS FELDGENDARMERIE KOMPANIE 1
  (Military Police Company)
  62% Manpower
  2 LMG

- SS KRIEGSBERICHTER ZUG 1
  (War Correspondence Unit)

1.SS Panzer Division Vehicle Stocks
15th June 1944

Throughout the first two weeks of June 1944, LAH continued to build up in strength. By June 15th its stocks of armoured and semi-tracked vehicles had increased substantially. Below is a listing of motorcycles, field cars and tracked vehicles held by the Division on 15th June:

Vehicle Type	Authorised	Actual
Light Motorcycles	33	14
Medium Motorcycles	165	108
Heavy Motorcycles	148	178
Light Field Cars	58	135
Kfz 1 (Kubelwagens)	765	192
Kfz 1/20 (Schwimmwagen)	24	399
Kfz 2 (Radio Vehicle)	3	4
Kfz 2 (Telephone Vehicle)	4	7
Kfz 4 (Light Truck)	-	1
SdKfz 10 (1 Ton Halftrack)	22	18
SdKfz 11 (3 Ton Halftrack)	34	11
SdKfz 6 (5 Ton Halftrack)	33	1
SdKfz 7 (8 Ton Halftrack)	48	37
SdKfz 8 (12 Ton Halftrack)	25	10
SdKfz 9 (18 Ton Halftrack)	10	11
Maultier (Halftrack truck)	77	167
SdKfz 222 (4 Wheeled Armoured Car)	4	-
SdKfz 232 (8 Wheeled Armoured Car)	2	-
SdKfz 234/2 (8 Wheel Armoured Car) *(Puma)*	16	10
Panzer IV	101	78
Panzer V *(Panther)*	81	43
Beobachtungspanzer III (Artillery Observation Vehicle)	-	4
Sturmgeschütz III (Assault Gun)	-	45
Jagdpanzer IV (Tank Destroyer)	31	-
SdKfz 266 (Command Vehicle)	2	-
SdKfz 267 (Command Vehicle)	3	3
SdKfz 268 (Command Vehicle)	6	2
Wespe 105mm SP Gun	12	12
Hummel 150mm SP Gun	6	6
SdKfz 10/4 (2cm Flak on 1 ton Halftrack)	42	2
SdKfz 7/2 (3.7cm Flak on 8 ton Halftrack)	18	-
SdKfz 7/1 (Quad 2cm Flak on 8 ton Halftrack)	10	-
SdKfz 11/5 (Panzerwerfer 42 on 3 ton Halftrack)	28	-

1.SS Panzer Division Vehicle Stocks
15th June 1944

Vehicle Type	Authorised	Actual
ARMOURED HALFTRACKS		
SdKfz 250/1 (Troop Carrier)	22	24
SdKfz 250/2 (Telephone Vehicle)	3	-
SdKfz 250/3 (Radio Vehicle)	7	2
SdKfz 250/5 (Observation Vehicle)	16	-
SdKfz 250/7 (8cm Mortar Carrier)	4	4
SdKfz 250/9 (Reconnaissance Vehicle)	16	-
SdKfz 251/1 (Troop Carrier)	83	55
SdKfz 251/2 (8cm Mortar Carrier)	39	6
SdKfz 251/3 (Radio Vehicle)	54	38
SdKfz 251/5 (Engineer Vehicle)	-	4
SdKfz 251/7 (Engineer Vehicle)	43	41
SdKfz 251/8 (Armoured Ambulance)	10	-
SdKfz 251/9 (7.5cm Gun Mounted Vehicle)	32	-
SdKfz 251/10 (3.7cm Pak Mounted Vehicle)	22	-
SdKfz 251/11 (Telephone Vehicle)	25	8
SdKfz 251/16 (Flamethrower Vehicle)	36	6
SdKfz 251/17 (2cm Flak Mounted Vehicle)	44	16
SdKfz 251/18 (Artillery Observation Vehicle)	12	-

1.SS Panzer Division
Original German Strength Report
1st July 1944

Verband: 1.SS-Pz.Div."LAH" 28

Meldung vom 1. Juli 1944 — Unterstellungsverhältnis: I.SS-Panz.Kps.

1. Personelle Lage am Stichtag der Meldung:

a) Personal:

	Soll	Fehl
Offiziere	647	168
Uffz.	4 185	1 398
Mannsch.	13 229	+ 3 908
Hiwi	1 029	170
Insgesamt	19 090	+ 2 172

b) Verluste und sonstige Abgänge in der Berichtszeit vom 16.6. bis 26.6.44

	tot	verw.	verm.	krank	sonst.
Offiziere	./.	./.	./.	2	./.
Uffz. und Mannsch.	6	12	./.	15	15
Insgesamt	6	12	./.	17	15

c) in der Berichtszeit eingetroffener Ersatz:

	Ersatz	Genesene
Offiziere	./.	3
Uffz. und Mannsch.	19	2

d) über 1 Jahr nicht beurlaubt:

insgesamt: 2769 Köpfe 14 % d. Iststärke

davon:	12 - 18 Monate	19 - 24 Monate	über 24 Monate
	2 222	483	64

Platzkarten im Berichtsmonat zugewiesen: ./.

2. Materielle Lage:

		Gepanzerte Fahrzeuge							Kraftfahrzeuge				
									Kräder			Pkw	
		Stu. Gesch.	III	IV	V	VI	Schtz.Pz. Pz.Sp. Art.Pz.B. (o.Pz.Fu.Wg)	Pak Sf.	Ketten	m. angetr. Bwg.	sonst.	gel.	O
Soll (Zahlen)		./.	2	101	81	./.	534	31	345	148	198	923	28
einsatzbereit	zahlenm.	31	./.	30	25	./.	36	./.	53	103	79	530	101
	in % des Solls	68,8	./.	29,7	30,3	./.	6,7	./.	15,3	69,5	39,8	57,3	360
in kurzfristiger Instandsetzung (bis 3 Wochen)	zahlenm.	14	./.	73	38	./.	224	./.	7	29	19	60	35
	in % des Solls	31,1	./.	72,2	46,9	./.	41,9	./.	2	19,8	9,6	6,4	125

alter . und . auf Marsch

		noch Kraftfahrzeuge							Waffen				
		Lkw				Ketten-Fahrzeuge			s Pak		Art.-Gesch.	MG. ()	sonstige Waffen
		Maultiere	gel.	O	Tonnage	Zgkw. *)	Zgkw. **)	RSO	motz	Sf.			
Soll (Zahlen)		77	1286	856	5550	159	129	./.	25	31	83	1393	./.
einsatzbereit	zahlenm.	110	452	879	3600	10	48	./.	30	./.	50	992 (751)	./.
	in % des Solls	132,8	35,1	102	64,7	6,2	37,1	./.	120	—	60%	71,2 (53,9%)	./.
in kurzfristiger Instandsetzung (bis 3 Wochen)	zahlenm.	45	53	131	570	2	10	./.	—	—	5	./.	./.
	in % des Solls	58,4	4,1	15,3	10,2	1,2	7,8	./.	—	—	6%	./.	./.

SS K.K.St. 1 (Nr 79c)

*) Zgkw. mit 1-5t, **) Zgkw. mit 8-18t
( ) davon MG. 42

3. Pferdefehlstellen:

Die Div. befand sich in der Berichtzeit in der Verlegung, es sind daher bei den einsatzbereiten Kfz. die im neuen Raum noch nicht eingetroffenen Teile nicht erfaßt.

Anl. zu Nr. ...../44 geh.
Gen. Insp. d. Pz. Tr.

1.SS Panzer Division
Original German Theoretical Organisation Chart
1st July 1944

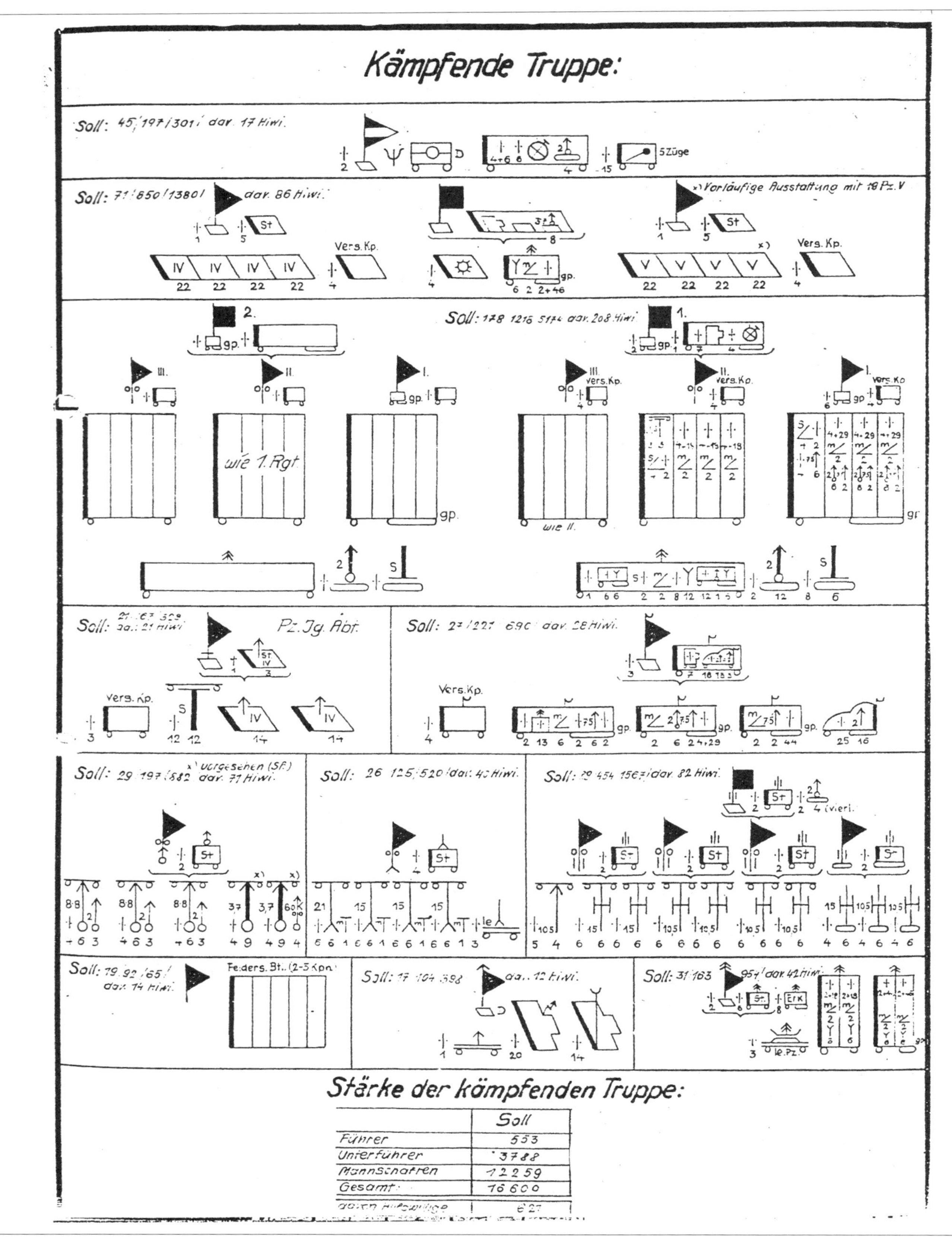

	Soll
Führer	553
Unterführer	3788
Mannschaften	12259
Gesamt:	16600
davon Hilfswillige	627

1.SS Panzer Division
Original German Theoretical Organisation Chart
1st July 1944

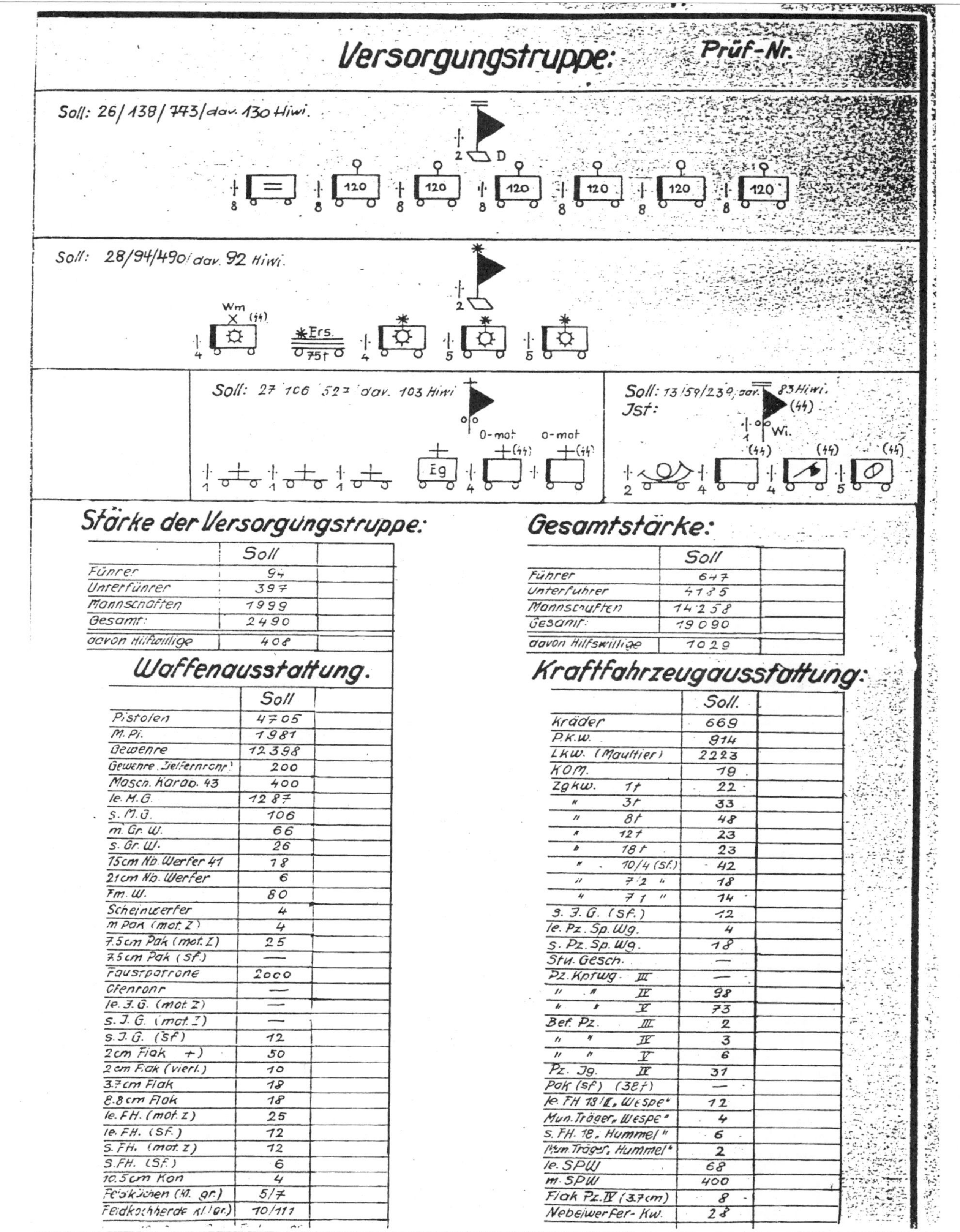

Versorgungstruppe: Prüf-Nr.

Soll: 26/138/743/dav. 130 Hiwi.

Soll: 28/94/490/dav. 92 Hiwi.

Soll: 27/106/527/dav. 103 Hiwi

Soll: 13/59/239/dav. 83 Hiwi.
Jst:

Stärke der Versorgungstruppe:

	Soll	
Führer	94	
Unterführer	397	
Mannschaften	1999	
Gesamt:	2490	
davon Hilfswillige	408	

Gesamtstärke:

	Soll	
Führer	647	
Unterführer	4185	
Mannschaften	14258	
Gesamt:	19090	
davon Hilfswillige	1029	

Waffenausstattung.

	Soll	
Pistolen	4705	
M.Pi.	1981	
Gewehre	12398	
Gewehre (Zielfernrohr)	200	
Masch. Karab. 43	400	
le. M.G.	1287	
s. M.G.	106	
m. Gr. W.	66	
s. Gr. W.	26	
15cm Nb. Werfer 41	18	
21cm Nb. Werfer	6	
Fm. W.	80	
Scheinwerfer	4	
m Pak (mot. Z)	4	
7.5cm Pak (mot. Z)	25	
7.5cm Pak (Sf.)	—	
Faustpatrone	2000	
Ofenrohr	—	
le. J.G. (mot. Z)	—	
s. J.G. (mot. Z)	—	
s. J.G. (Sf)	12	
2cm Flak +)	50	
2cm Flak (vierl.)	10	
3.7cm Flak	18	
8.8cm Flak	18	
le. FH. (mot. Z)	25	
le. FH. (Sf.)	12	
s. FH. (mot. Z)	12	
s. FH. (Sf.)	6	
10.5cm Kan	4	
Feldküchen (kl. gr.)	5/7	
Feldkochherde (kl./gr.)	10/111	

Kraftfahrzeugausstattung:

	Soll.	
Kräder	669	
P.K.W.	914	
Lkw. (Maultier)	2223	
KOM.	19	
Zgkw. 1t	22	
" 3t	33	
" 8t	48	
" 12t	23	
" 18t	23	
" 10/4 (Sf.)	42	
" 7/2 "	18	
" 7/1 "	14	
s. J.G. (Sf.)	12	
le. Pz. Sp. Wg.	4	
s. Pz. Sp. Wg.	18	
Stu. Gesch.	—	
Pz. Kpfwg. III	—	
" " IV	98	
" " V	73	
Bef. Pz. III	2	
" " IV	3	
" " V	6	
Pz. Jg. IV	31	
Pak (Sf) (38 t)	—	
le. FH 18/II „Wespe“	12	
Mun. Träger „Wespe“	4	
s. FH. 18 „Hummel“	6	
Mun. Träger „Hummel“	2	
le. SPW	68	
m. SPW	400	
Flak Pz. IV (3.7cm)	8	
Nebelwerfer-Kw.	28	

1.SS Panzer Division
Original German Actual Organisation Chart
1st July 1944

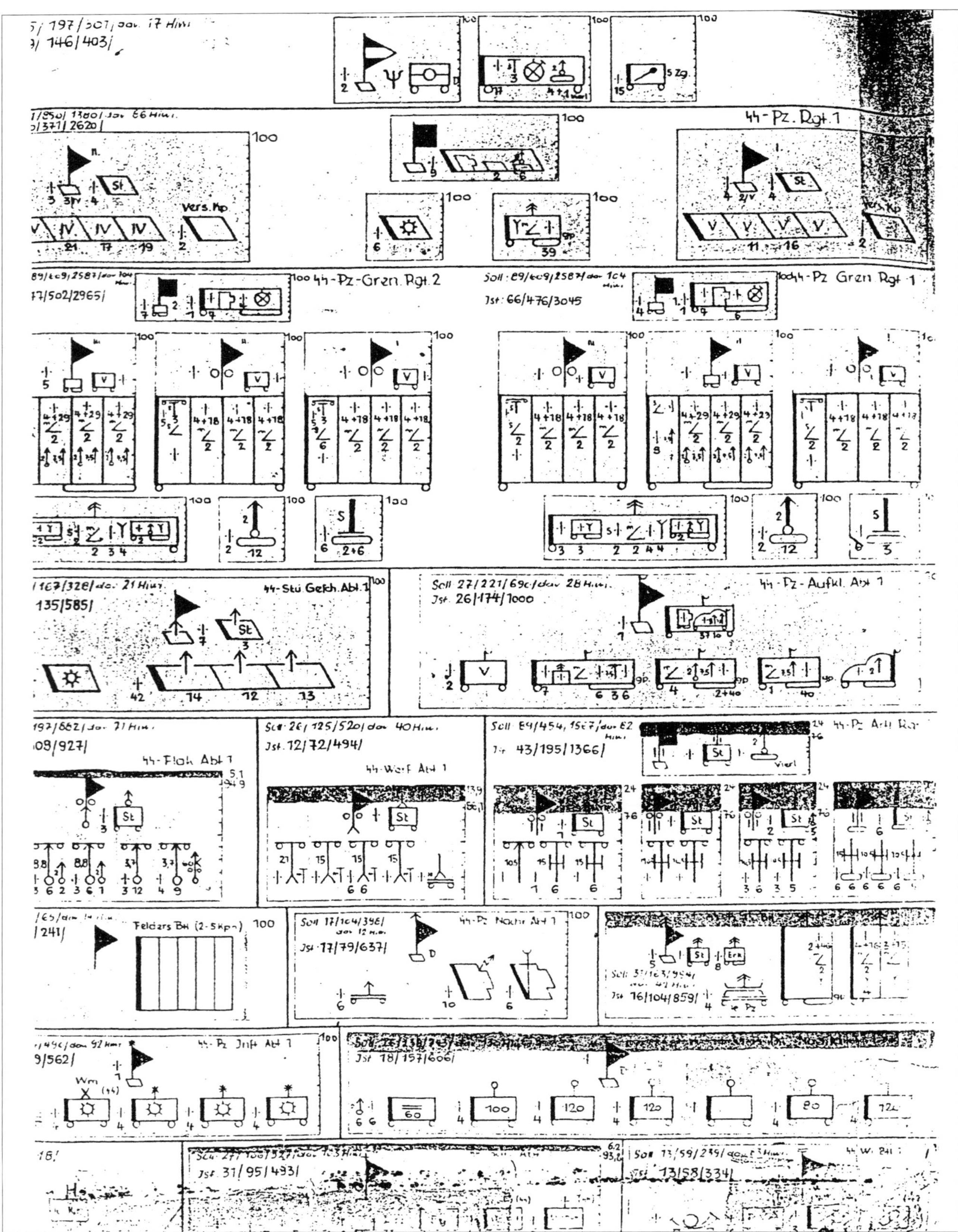

1.SS Panzer Division
Strength Report: 1st July 1944
Under Command of 1.SS Panzer Korps

MANPOWER

	Authorised Strength	Shortages	Actual
Officers	647	168	479
NCOs	4185	1398	2787
Other Ranks	13.229	3908+	17,137
Hiwis	1029	170	859
TOTAL	19,090	2172+	21,262

LOSSES BETWEEN 16/6/44 – 26/6/44

	Dead	Wounded	Missing	Hospital	Other Cases
Officers	0	0	0	2	0
NCOs }	6	12	0	15	15
Other Ranks }	-	-	-	-	-
TOTAL	6	12	0	17	15

REPLACEMENTS/ARRIVALS

	Replacements	Recovered
Officers	0	3
NCOs }	19	2
Other Ranks }	-	-

OVER 1 YEAR ABSENT FROM DIVISION (NON-LEAVE)

TOTAL	2769
Of That:	
12 to 18 Months	2,222
19 to 24 Months	483
Over 24 Months	64

1.SS Panzer Division
Strength Report 1st July 1944
Material Stocks

ARMOURED VEHICLES

	StuG	Pz III	Pz IV	Pz V	Other AFVs	Jagd IV
Authorised strength	0	2	101	81	534	31
Ready for action	31	0	30	25	36	0
Short term repair	14	0	73	38	224	0

MOTORCYCLES

	Ketten	+Sidecar	Other
Authorised strength	345	148	198
Ready for action	53	103	79
Short term repair	7	29	19

CARS

	Cross-country	Normal/Road
Authorised strength	923	28
Ready for action	530	101
Short term repair	60	35

TRUCKS

	Maultier	Cross-country	Normal/Road
Authorised strength	77	1286	856
Ready for action	110	452	879
Short term repair	45	53	131

TRACKED PRIME MOVERS

	1-5 Tons	8-18 Tons
Authorised strength	159	129
Ready for action	10	48
Short term repair	2	10

WEAPONS

	Heavy Anti-Tank Guns	Artillery Guns	MGs
Authorised strength	25	83	1393
Ready for action	30	50	992
Short term repair	0	5	*(Of which 757 are MG42)*

1.SS PANZER DIVISION
'Leibstandarte Adolf Hitler'

1st July 1944

- Divisionstab (Divisional HQ)
100% Manpower
2 LMG

Div. Kartenstelle (Mapping Section)
100% Manpower

Div. Begleitkompanie (Divisional Security Company)
100% Manpower
17 LMG. 4 x SdKfz 10/4 2cm Flak (SP). 1 x SdKfz 7/1 Quad 2cm Flakwagen. 3 x 7.5cm Pak (Towed)

Feldgendarmerie Kompanie (Military Police Company)
100% Manpower
15 LMG. 5 Zug (Platoons)

- SS PANZER REGIMENT 1 (Tank Regiment)
Regimentstab (Regimental HQ)
100% Manpower
3 x *Panther* Command Vehicles (2 ready for action). 11 x (2cm) Flakpanzer 38(t) (6 ready for action)

1. Panzer Abteilung (1st Tank Battalion)
100% Manpower
63 *Panthers,* including 2 Command Vehicles (29 ready for action). 10 LMG

2. Panzer Abteilung (2nd Tank Battalion)
100% Manpower
103 Pz IV, including 5 Command Vehicles (60 ready for action). 9 LMG

Pionier Kompanie (Engineer Company) (Armoured)
100% Manpower
Medium Armoured Halftracks. 39 LMG

1 Werkstatt Kompanie (Workshop Company)
100% Manpower
6 LMG

- SS PANZERGRENADIER REGIMENT 1
(Motorised Infantry Regiment)
Regimentstab (Regimental HQ)
100% Manpower
Medium Armoured Halftracks. 18 LMG

1. Bataillon (Motorised)
100% Manpower
54 LMG. 12 HMG. 6 x 81mm Mortars. 2 x 120mm Mortars (Towed)

2. Bataillon (Partially Armoured)
100% Manpower
Medium Armoured Halftracks
95 LMG. 12 HMG. 6 x 81mm Mortars

3. Bataillon (Motorised)
100% Manpower
54 LMG. 12 HMG. 6 x 81mm Mortars. 2 x 120mm Mortars (Towed)

Flak Kompanie (Anti-aircraft Company)
100% Manpower
12 x 2cm Flak Guns (Most towed, a few SP).
2 LMG

Infanteriegeschutz Kompanie (Infantry Gun Company)
100% Manpower
3 x 15cm Infantry Guns (Towed). 6 LMG

Pionier Kompanie (Engineer Company) (Armoured)
100% Manpower
Medium Armoured Halftracks. 12 LMG. 2 HMG.
2 x 81mm Mortars. 4 Flamethrowers

- SS PANZERGRENADIER REGIMENT 2
(Armoured Infantry Regiment)
Regimentstab (Regimental HQ) (Armoured)
100% Manpower
Medium Armoured Halftracks. 19 LMG

1. Bataillon (Motorised)
100% Manpower
59 LMG. 12 HMG. 6 x 81mm Mortars. 6 x 120mm Mortars. 3 x 7.5cm Pak (Towed)

2. Bataillon (Armoured)
100% Manpower
59 LMG. 12 HMG. 6 x 81mm Mortars. 3 x 7.5cm Pak (Towed)

3. Bataillon (Armoured)
100% Manpower
Medium Armoured Halftracks (including 6 x SdKfz 251/2). 108 LMG. 12 HMG. 6 x 81mm Mortars (Halftrack mounted)

Flak Kompanie (Anti-aircraft Company)
100% Manpower
12 x 2cm Flak Guns (Mostly towed, a few SP).
2 LMG

Infanteriegeschutz Kompanie (Infantry Gun Company)
100% Manpower
6 x 15cm SP Infantry Guns. 2 x 7.5cm Infantry Guns (Towed)

Pionier Kompanie (Engineer Company) (Armoured)
100% Manpower
Medium Armoured Halftracks. 9 LMG. 2 HMG.
2 x 81mm Mortars. 4 Flamethrowers

- SS AUFKLÄRUNGS ABTEILUNG 1
(Armoured Reconnaissance Battalion)
100% Manpower
Abteilungstab (HQ Company)
16 *Puma* Armoured Cars (10 ready for action).
38 LMG

1. Kompanie (Armoured Car Company)
No armoured vehicles or heavy weapons

2. Kompanie (Armoured Reconnaissance Company)
Light Armoured Halftracks (including 1 x SdKfz 250/7). 40 LMG. 2 HMG. 1 x 81mm Mortars (Halftrack mounted)

3. Kompanie (Armoured Reconnaissance Company)
Light Armoured Halftracks (including 4 x SdKfz 250/7). 40 LMG. 2 HMG. 4 x 81mm Mortars (Halftrack mounted)

4. Kompanie (Heavy Company)
Medium Armoured Halftracks. 19 LMG.
3 x 7.5cm Pak (Towed)

Versorgungs Kompanie (Supply Company)
2 LMG

- SS STURMGESCHÜTZ ABTEILUNG 1
(Assault Gun Battalion)
100% Manpower
45 Assault Guns (42 ready for action). 52 LMG

- SS PANZER ARTILLERIE REGIMENT 1
(Armoured Artillery Regiment)
Regimentstab (Regimental HQ)
76% Manpower

1. Abteilung (Armoured Battalion)
76% Manpower
6 *Hummel* Munitions Carriers. 12 *Wespe* (11 ready for action). 4 *Wespe* Munitions Carrier.
24 LMG. 4 x 2cm Flak Guns (Towed)

2. Abteilung (Towed Battalion)
76% Manpower
12 x 105mm LeFH 18 (11 ready for action). 8 LMG.
3 x 2cm Flak Guns (Towed)

3. Abteilung (Towed Battalion)
76% Manpower
No heavy weapons

4. Abteilung (Towed Battalion)
76% Manpower
12 x 150mm SFH 18. 2 LMG

- SS WERFER ABTEILUNG
(Rocket Projector Battalion)
86.1% Manpower
6 x 15cm Nebelwerfer. 6 LMG

- SS FLAKABTEILUNG (Anti-aircraft Battalion)
94.9% Manpower
18 x 88mm Flak Guns (Towed). 21 x 3.7cm Flak Guns (Mostly towed, some SdKfz 7/2). 6 x 2cm Flak Guns (Towed). 19 LMG

- SS PANZER PIONIER BATAILLON
  85% Manpower
  Stabs Kompanie (Partially Armoured)
  Medium Armoured Halftracks. 13 LMG

  1. Kompanie (Motorised)
  15 LMG. 3 HMG

  2. Kompanie (Motorised)
  16 LMG. 4 HMG. 2 x 81mm Mortars.
  4 Flamethrowers

  3. Kompanie (Armoured)
  Medium Armoured Halftracks (including 2 x SdKfz 251/2). 46 LMG. 2 HMG. 2 x 81mm Mortars (Halftrack mounted)

  Brucken Kolonne (Light Bridging Column) (Motorised)
  4 LMG

- SS PANZER NACHRICHTEN ABTEILUNG
  (Armoured Signals Battalion)
  100% Manpower. (Partially Armoured)
  Medium Armoured Halftracks. 22 LMG

- SS FELDERS BATAILLON (Replacement Battalion)
  100% Manpower.
  No heavy weapons

- SS NACHSCHUBTRUPPEN 1
  (Divisional Supply Battalion)
  86% Manpower
  6 Transportation Companies (540 Tonnes capacity).
  1 Supply Company (60 Tonnes capacity).
  26 LMG. 6 x 2cm Flak Guns (Towed)

- SS INSTADSETZUNGS ABTEILUNG 1
  (Workshop Battalion)
  100% Manpower
  4 Workshop/Repair Companies. 1 Supply Company.
  17 LMG

- SS WIRTSCHAFTS BATAILLON 1
  (Commissary Battalion)
  100% Manpower
  1 Bakery Company. 1 Butcher Company.
  1 Administration Company. 1 Field Post Office.
  11 LMG

- SS SANITÄTS ABTEILUNG 1 (Medical Battalion)
  93.8% Manpower
  3 Ambulance Columns. 2 Medical Compaies.
  1 Field Hospital. 12 LMG

- SS KRIEGSBERICHTER ZUG 1
  (War Correspondence Unit)
  16 Officers. 18 NCOs (Not included in Divisional manpower strengths)

1.SS Panzer Division
Strength Report: 1st July 1944

DIVISIONAL UNIT MANPOWER STRENGTHS

	Authorised Strength			Actual Strength		
	Officers	NCOs	Other Ranks	Officers	NCOs	Other Ranks
Division Stab	45	197	301	29	146	403
Panzer Regiment	71	850	1380	80	371	2620
Panzer Gren. Regt. 1	89	609	2587	66	476	3045
Panzer Gren. Regt. 2	89	609	2587	77	502	2965
Panzer Aufkl. Abt.	27	221	690	26	174	1000
Sturmgeschütz Regt.	89	454	1567	43	195	1366
Werfer Abt.	26	125	520	12	72	494
Flak Abt.	29	197	882	17	108	927
Pionier Bn.	31	163	954	16	104	859
Nachrichten Abt.	17	104	398	17	79	637
Felders Bn.	19	92	65	2	16	241
Div. Nachschub.	26	138	743	18	157	606
Instand. Abt.	28	94	490	17	99	562
Wirtschafts Bn.	13	59	239	31	95	334
Sanitäts Abt.	27	106	527	31	95	493
Hiwis (Russian Helpers)						859
TOTAL	647	4,185	14,258	479	2,787	17,996
COMBINED TOTALS		19,090			21,262	

1.SS Panzer Division
Original German List of Vehicle Stocks
1st July 1944

Einheit: 1. SS-Pz.-Div. L SS A H ~~Kraftfahrzeuge~~ 24

Geheime Kommandosache
270/44 g. Kdos.

Kfz.-Art	Soll	Ist	im Zuf.
le. Krad	35	14	-
m. Krad	165	110	-
s. Krad	148	164	1
[illegible]dder	545	66	6
le. Pkw.	58	225	-
Kfz. 1	768	191	-
" 1/20 schwf.Wag.	24	302	-
" 2Sa	3	4	-
" 2 Fu	4	8	-
" 2/40	46	20	-
" 4		1	-
" 11	19	1	-
" m. Pkw.	28	66	2
" 12	15	9	-
" 15	29	47	-
" 15 Na.	7	12	-
" 15 Fu.	5	3	1
" 17 Fu.	5	13	-
" 17 Fe.	-	1	-
s. Pkw.	-	1	-
s.gl. Pkw. (Kfz.21)	1	-	-
Kfz. 23 Fe.	2	5	-
Kdr.-Kfz.	-	1	1
Kfz. 81	-	1	-
le. Lkw.	35	33	-
le. Lkw. geschl.	-	2	-
Kfz. 31	73	51	-
Fu.-Kw.	-	1	-
le.gl.Lkw. Kfz.2/40	-	14	-
Kfz. 12	-	26	-
Kfz. 18 Fu	-	9	-
Kfz. 15 Na	-	4	-
Kfz. 17 Fu.	-	17	-
le.gl. Lkw.	460	3	-
Kfz.62 [illegible]-Kw.	-	1	-
Kfz.69 Protz-Kw.	-	172	-
Kfz.70 Mannsch.-Kw.	[illegible]	13	-

Kfz.-Art	Soll	Ist	im Zuf.
Sammler-Kw.42	3	3	-
Kfz.42 Na.Wa.	2	2	-
m.Lkw. geschl.	15	3	-
Kfz. 305	-	5	-
m.gl. Lkw.	545	346	5
" geschl.	6	-	-
Kfz.79 So.Kw.	12	8	-
Werkst.Ger.Kw.	36	23	-
Kfz. 14 Wasser	4	-	-
Kühlwagen	2	-	-
s. Lkw.	61	161	-
s. " geschl.	1	4	-
s.gl.Lkw.	37	48	-
Vulk.-Kw.	2	2	-
I-Staffel	14	6	8
m.Lkw.Kesselwg.	-	1	-
s.Werkst.Zug	-	1	-
Kfz. 74	-	1	-
Radschlepper	-	3	(davon 2 ital.)
Sd.-Kfz. 10	22	19	-
" 11	34	9	20
" 6	33	-	-
" 7	48	41	6
" 8	25	10	4
" 9	22	9	1
" 3	71	161	66
Maultier 4,5t	6	-	-
9/1 Drehkran	2	1	-
Kfz.100	3	4	(davon 3 behelfsm.)
le. Kom.	3	2	-
m. Kom.	16	42	-
s. Kom.	2	3	-
Befehls-Kom	1	6	-
Sd.-Kfz.222	4	-	-
Sd.-Kfz.232	2	-	-

1.SS Panzer Division
Original German List of Vehicle Stocks
1st July 1944

Kfz.-Art	Soll	Ist	in Zuf.
Pz.-Kpfwg. V	79	61	-
Beo.Pz.III	6	4	-
Zf. 10/4	42	9	-
7/2	18	11	-
7/1	10	5	-
11/5	28	1	-
7/6	-	4	-
6/2	-	1	-
Bergewannen Pz.III	4	-	-
" V	(2)	2	-
Stu.-Gesch.	-	45	-
5 cm KwK 2 Bef.Fg.	4	-	-
7,5 cm KwK L 48 Bef.Fg.	-	5	-
7,5 cm KwK L 70/ V	-	5	1
38 to 2 cm Flak	-	11	1
Pz.Jgr.IV Sd.Kfz. 2	51	-	-
le.F.H. 18/II Wespe	12	12	-
s.F.18 Hummel	6	6	-
Grillen	12	6	-

Kfz.-Art	Soll	Ist	in Zuf.
Sd.-Kfz.250/1	22	24	-
" 250/2	3	-	22
" 250/3	4	2	-
" 250/5	16	-	9
" 250/7	4	4	-
" 250/8	2	-	-
" 250/9	16	-	-
" 251/1	83	61	59
" 251/2	45	6	10
" 251/3	54	38	16
" 251/5	-	4	-
" 251/6	6	-	-
" 251/7	43	41	7
" 251/8	8	-	-
" 251/9	32	-	14
" 251/11	25	8	10
" 251/16	30	6	6
" 251/17	44	2[illegible]	1
" 251/19	12	-	-
Beob.Pz.Wg.253	1		

1.SS Panzer Division Vehicle Stocks
1st July 1944

Vehicle Type	Authorised	Actual	In Process of Delivery
MOTORCYCLES			
Light Motorcycles	33	14	
Medium Motorcycles	165	110	
Motorcycle Combinations	148	164	1
Kettenkrads	345	66	6
CARS			
Light Road Cars	58	225	
Kfz 1 (Kubelwagens)	768	191	
Kfz 1/20 (Schwimmwagen)	24	392	
Kfz 2	3	4	
Kfz 2 (Radio Vehicle)	4	8	
Kfz 2/40	46	20	
Kfz 4 (Light Truck)	-	1	
Kfz 11	19	1	
Medium Road Cars	28	66	2
Kfz 12	15	9	
Kfz 15	29	47	
Kfz 15 (Na)	7	12	
Kfz 15 (Fu)	5	3	1
Kfz 17 (Fu)	3	13	
Kfz 17 (Fe)	-	1	
Heavy Road Cars	-	1	
Kfz 21	1	-	
Kfz 23 (Fe)	2	5	
Kdr Kfz	-	1	1
Kfz 81	-	1	
TRUCKS			
Light Trucks	35	33	
Light Trucks (geschi)	-	2	
Kfz 31	78	51	
Fu LKW	-	1	
Kfz 2/40 (Light Truck)	-	14	
Kfz 12	-	26	
Kfz 15 (Fu)	-	9	
Kfz 15 (Na)	-	4	
Kfz 17 (Fu)	-	17	
Light Trucks (Cross-country type)	460	3	
Kfz 62	-	1	
Kfz 69 (Protze kw)	-	172	
Kfz 70 (Mannsch Kw)	-	13	
Kfz 81 (Mannsch Fl. Kw)	-	3	
Medium Road Trucks	745	1205	
Sammler- Kw 42	3	3	
Kfz 42 (Na We)	2	2	

1.SS Panzer Division Vehicle Stocks
1st July 1944

Vehicle Type	Authorised	Actual	In Process of Delivery
TRUCKS			
Kfz 305	-	5	
Medium Trucks (Cross-country type)	543	346	5
Medium Truck (geschl.)	6	-	
Kfz 79 (Fe. Kw)	12	8	
Werkst. Kw.	36	23	
Kfz 94 (Water Vehicle)	4	-	
Kahlwagen	2	-	
Heavy Road Trucks	61	161	
Heavy Trucks (geschl.)	1	4	
Heavy Trucks (Cross-country type)	87	48	
Vulk Kw	-	2	
I. Staffel	14	6	
Medium Kesselwg.	-	1	
S. Werkst. Zug	-	1	
Kfz 74	-	1	
Radschlepper	-	3 *(Includes 2 Italian vehicles)*	
SdKfz 3 (Maultier)	71	161	66
Maultier (4.5 tons)	6	-	
Kfz 100	3	4	
Light Command Truck	3	2	
Medium Command Truck	16	42	
Heavy Command Truck	2	3	
Befehl Command Truck	1	6	
HALFTRACKS			
SdKfz 10 (1 Ton)	22	19	
SdKfz 11 (3 Ton)	34	9	20
SdKfz 6 (5 Ton)	33	-	
SdKfz 7 (8 Ton)	48	41	6
SdKfz 8 (12 Ton)	25	10	4
SdKfz 9 (18 Ton)	22	9	1
SdKfz 9/1 (18 Ton with Crane)	2	1	
ARMOURED VEHICLES			
Pz IV	101	98	1
Panther	79	61	
Pz III (Observation Tank)	6	4	
Pz IV (Command Tank)	-	5	
Panther (Command Tank)	-	5	1
Pz III (Command Tank)	4	-	
Bergepanzer III	4	-	
Bergepanther	2	2	
Sturmgeschütz III	-	45	
Jagdanzer IV	31	-	
Flakpanzer 38(t)	-	11	1

1.SS Panzer Division Vehicle Stocks
1st July 1944

Vehicle Type	Authorised	Actual	In Process of Delivery
ARMOURED VEHICLES			
Wespe (SP 105 mm Light Field Howitzer)	12	12	
Hummel (SP 150mm Heavy Field Howitzer)	6	6	
Grille (SP 150mm Infantry Gun)	12	6	
SdKfz 10/4 (2cm Flak on 1 ton Halftrack)	42	9	
SdKfz 7/2 (3.7cm Flak on 8 ton Halftrack)	18	11	
SdKfz 7/1 (Quad 2cm Flak on 8 ton Halftrack)	10	5	
SdKfz 11/5 (Panzerwerfer 42 on 3 ton Halftrack)	28	1	
SdKfz 7/6	-	4	
SdKfz 6/2	-	1	
Beob. Pz Wg 253	1	-	
ARMOURED CARS			
SdKfz 222 (4 Wheeled Armoured Car)	4	-	
SdKfz 232 (8 Wheeled Armoured Car)	2	-	
SdKfz 234/2 (8 Wheel Armoured Car) *(Puma)*	-	16	
ARMOURED HALFTRACKS			
SdKfz 250/1 (Troop Carrier)	22	24	
SdKfz 250/2 (Telephone Vehicle)	3	-	22
SdKfz 250/3 (Radio Vehicle)	4	2	
SdKfz 250/5 (Observation Vehicle)	16	-	9
SdKfz 250/7 (8cm Mortar Carrier)	4	4	
SdKfz 250/8 (7.5cm Gun)	2	-	
SdKfz 250/9 (Reconnaissance Vehicle)	16	-	
SdKfz 251/1 (Troop Carrier)	83	61	59
SdKfz 251/2 (8cm Mortar Carrier)	45	6	10
SdKfz 251/3 (Radio Vehicle)	54	38	16
SdKfz 251/5 (Engineer Vehicle)	-	4	
SdKfz 251/6 (Command Vehicle)	6	-	
SdKfz 251/7 (Engineer Vehicle)	43	41	7
SdKfz 251/8 (Armoured Ambulance)	8	-	
SdKfz 251/9 (7.5cm Gun Mounted Vehicle)	32	-	14
SdKfz 251/11 (Telephone Vehicle)	25	8	10
SdKfz 251/16 (Flamethrower Vehicle)	30	6	6
SdKfz 251/17 (2cm Flak Mounted Vehicle)	44	20	1
SdKfz 251/19 (Telephone Exchange Vehicle)	12	-	

1.SS Panzer Division
Original German List of Weapon and Equipment Stocks
1st July 1944

Geheime Kommandosache

Waffen und Gerät Anlage 26

Einheit: 1.SS-Panzer Division "LSSAH" 1. 7. 1944

Waffenart	Soll	Ist	In Zuführung	Bemerkung
Seitengewehre 84/98	12398	13359		
Karabiner 98 k	12398	13057		
Pistole	4705	6652		
M.P.	1981	1138		
Gr.B.39	—	—		
Gew.Gr.Gerät	332	332		
Karabiner m.Zilfernrohr	200	200		
Gewehr 41 u. 43	400	1483		Der Überbestand rechnet a.d.Ist [illegible]
le. M.G.	1287	997		
s. M.G.	106	106		
8 cm Gr.W.34	66	74		
12 cm Gr.W.	26	—		
10 cm Nb.W.35	—	—		
15 cm Nb.W.41	18	10	8	
21 cm Nb.W.42	6	—		
Wurfrahmen 40	36	—		
[illegible]	80	68		
M.G. m.Pzm. i.Pz.Kpfw.	369	348		
Geschütze:				
s.Pz.B.41	—	6		
5 cm Pak 38	4	5		
7,5 cm Pak	25	31		
7,5 cm Pak 40 (Sf.)	31	—		
7,62cm Pak 36	—	—		
8,8 cm Pak 43	—	—		
le.J.G.18	—	27		
s. J.G.33	—	4		
2 cm Flak 38	50	64		
2 cm Flak Vierl.	10	10		
2 cm Geb.Flak	—	—		
3,7 cm Flak 18	—	—		
3,7 cm Flak 36 u. 37	18	20		

1.SS Panzer Division
Original German List of Weapon and Equipment Stocks
1st July 1944

Waffenart	Soll	Ist	In Zuführung	Bemerkung
noch Geschütze:				
8,8 cm Flak 37	18	18		
7,5 cm Geb.K.15	—	—		
7,5 cm Geb.Gesch.36	—	—		
le.F.H.18	25	25		
le.F.H.18/1 (Sf.)	12	12		
le.F.H.40	—	—		
s. F.H.18	12	12		
s. F.H.18/1 (Sf.)	6	6		
s. 10 cm K.18	4	4		
Gerät:				
Kl.Feldküche od.Kl.Feldk.H.	15	51		
gr.Feldküche od.gr.Feldk.H.	118	107		
Brück.Kol. B (mot)	—	—		
Brück.Kol. C (mot)	—	—		
Brück.Kol. K (mot)	1	1		
Kdo.Gerät	3	3		
Kdo. Mi.Gerät	—	—		
Em 4 m R	3	3		
Backanhänger	6	6		
Masch.Satz 220 V 6,5 Kw.	1	1		
Teigknetanhänger	1	1		
Satz Bäckereigerät	1	1		
Satz Schlächt.Masch.Satz a	1	-		
Masch.Satz 25 KVA	-	-		
Schlächt.Gerät Satz a	1	1		
Minensuchgeräte	41	39		
Scheinwerfer	4	6		

1.SS Panzer Division
Original German Strength Report
1st August 1944

Geheime Kommandosache

Meldung vom 1. 8. 194~~3~~4

Verband: 1.SS-Pz.Div. "LSSAH" 16
Unterstellungsverhältnis: I.SS-Panz.Korps

Anlg. 5 Ia/1182/44 g.Kdos. 38

1. Personelle Lage am Stichtag der Meldung:

a) Personal:

	Soll	Fehl
Offiziere	647	182
Uffz.	4185	1354
Mannsch.	13229	+ 3011
Hiwi	1029	170
Insgesamt	19090	+ 1305

b) Verluste und sonstige Abgänge in der Berichtszeit vom 16.7. bis 1.8.1944

	tot	verw.	verm.	krank	sonst.
Offiziere	6	19	3	3	10
Uffz. und Mannsch.	237	728	99	137	171
Insgesamt	243	747	102	140	181

c) in der Berichtszeit eingetroffener Ersatz: 29

	Ersatz	Genesene
Offiziere	7	–
Uffz. und Mannsch.	1	5

d) über 1 Jahr nicht beurlaubt:

insgesamt: 3783 Köpfe 19 % d. Iststärke

davon:

72 - 18 Monate	19 - 24 Monate	über 24 Monate
2870	725	88

Platzkarten im Berichtsmonat zugewiesen: —

2. Materielle Lage:

		Gepanzerte Fahrzeuge							Kraftfahrzeuge				
									Kräder			Pkw	
		Stu. Gesch.	III	IV	V	VI	Schtz. Pz. Pz. Sp. Art. Pz. B. (o. Pz. Fu. Wg.)	Pak Sf.	Ketten	m. angetr. Bwg.	sonst.	gel.	O
Soll (Zahlen)		–	4	101	81	–	472	31	345	148	198	877	86
einsatzbereit	zahlenm.	23	–	61	40	–	261	–	59	109	131	521	152
	in % des Solls	–	–	60,3	48,7	–	55,2	–	17,1	72,9	66,1	59,4	176,7
in kurzfristiger Instandsetzung (bis 3 Wochen)	zahlenm.	–	–	14	14	–	11	–	2	22	21	75	35
	in % des Solls	–	–	13,8	17,0	–	25,4	–	95	14,8	1,6	8,5	4,6

		noch Kraftfahrzeuge							Waffen			
		Lkw				Ketten-Fahrzeuge						
		Maultiere	gel.	O	Tonnage	Zgkw. *)	Zgkw. **)	RSO	s Pak	Art.-Gesch.	MG. ( )	sonstige Waffen
Soll (Zahlen)		77	1309	861	5617	159	129	–	56	83	1393	–
einsatzbereit	zahlenm.	120	534	930	3960	22	54	–	17	36	787 (566)	–
	in % des Solls	155,8	40,7	108,0	70,4	13,8	41,8	–	28,6	43,3	56,5 (40,6)	–
in kurzfristiger Instandsetzung (bis 3 Wochen)	zahlenm.	15	78	115	208	7	11	–	3	7	–	–
	in % des Solls	19,4	5,9	13,3	3,6	5,5	7,2	–	5,3	8,2	–	–

SS K.K.St. 1 (Nr. 19c)

*) Zgkw. mit 1-5t, **) Zgkw. mit 8-18t
( ) davon MG. 42

3. Pferdefehlstellen:

Anl. zu Nr. 00940 .44 geh.
Gen. Insp. d. Pz. Tr.

1.SS Panzer Division
Original German Theoretical Organisation Chart
3rd August 1944

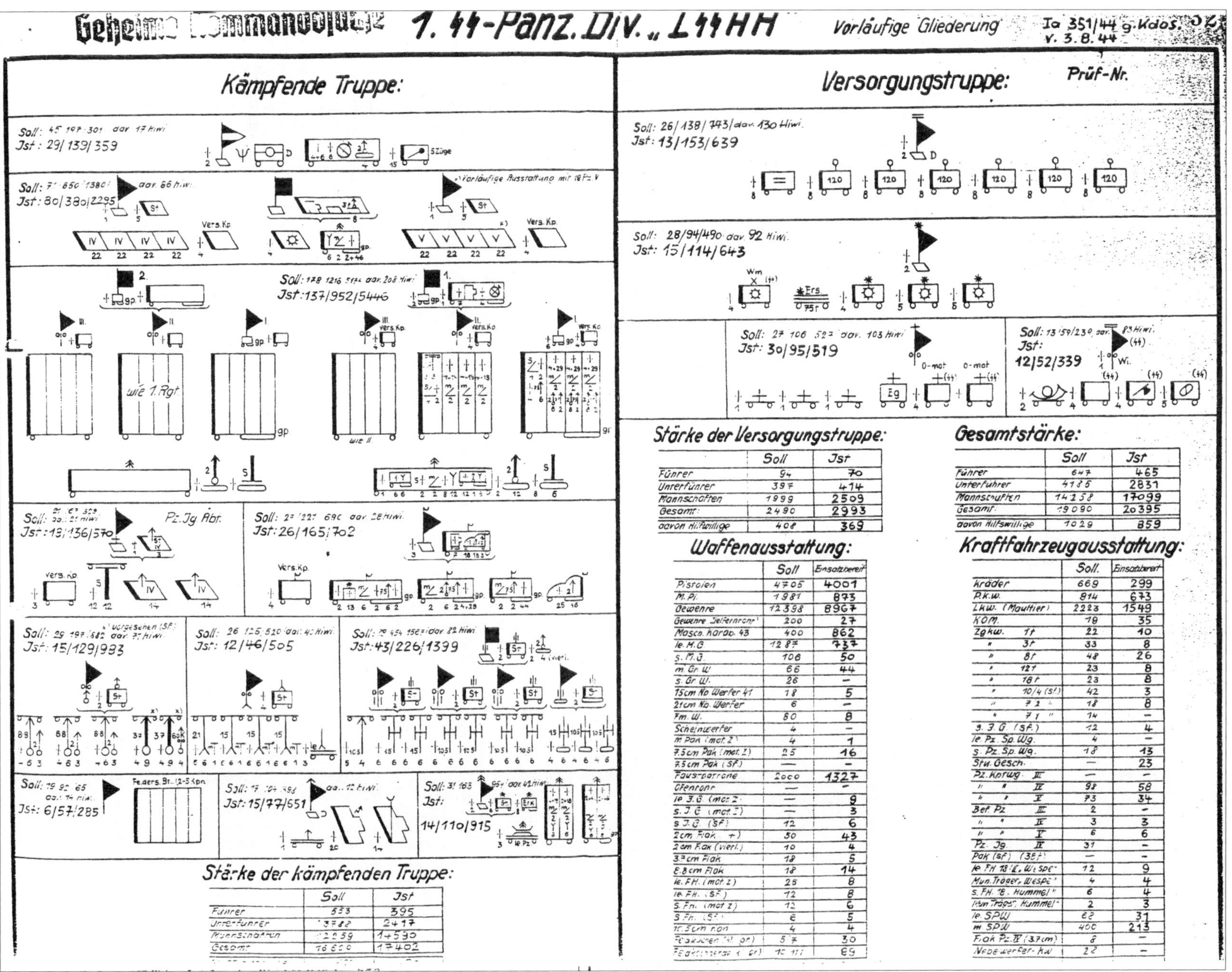

Stärke der kämpfenden Truppe:

	Soll	Jst
Führer	553	395
Unterführer	3782	2417
Mannschaften	12259	14590
Gesamt	16600	17402

Stärke der Versorgungstruppe:

	Soll	Jst
Führer	94	70
Unterführer	397	414
Mannschaften	1999	2509
Gesamt:	2490	2993
davon Hilfswillige	408	369

Gesamtstärke:

	Soll	Jst
Führer	647	465
Unterführer	4185	2831
Mannschaften	14258	17099
Gesamt:	19090	20395
davon Hilfswillige	1029	859

Waffenausstattung:

	Soll	Einsatzbereit
Pistolen	4705	4001
M.Pi.	1981	873
Gewehre	12398	8967
Gewehre Zielfernrohr	200	27
Masch. Karab. 43	400	862
le. M.G.	1287	737
s. M.G.	106	50
m. Gr. W.	66	44
s. Gr. W.	26	–
15cm Nb. Werfer 41	18	5
21cm Nb. Werfer	6	–
Fm. W.	80	8
Scheinwerfer	4	–
m. Pak (mot. Z)	4	1
7.5cm Pak (mot. Z)	25	16
7.5cm Pak (Sf.)	—	–
Faustpatrone	2000	1327
Ofenrohr	—	–
le. J.G. (mot. Z)	—	9
s. J.G. (mot. Z)	—	3
s. J.G. (Sf)	12	6
2cm Flak	50	43
2cm Flak (vierl.)	10	4
3.7cm Flak	18	5
8.8cm Flak	18	14
le. F.H. (mot. Z)	25	8
le. F.H. (Sf.)	12	8
s. F.H. (mot. Z)	12	6
s. F.H. (Sf.)	6	5
10.5cm Kan.	4	4
[illegible]	57	30
[illegible]	[illegible]	69

Kraftfahrzeugausstattung:

	Soll.	Einsatzbereit
Kräder	669	299
P.K.W.	814	673
LKW. (Maultier)	2223	1549
KOM.	18	35
Zgkw. 1t	22	10
" 3t	33	8
" 8t	48	26
" 12t	23	8
" 18t	23	8
" 10/4 (Sf.)	42	3
" 7 2 "	18	8
" 7 1 "	14	–
s. J.G. (Sf.)	12	4
le. Pz. Sp. Wg.	4	–
s. Pz. Sp. Wg.	18	13
Stu. Gesch.	—	23
Pz. Kpfwg. III	—	–
" " IV	98	58
" " V	73	34
Bef. Pz. III	2	–
" " IV	3	3
" " V	6	6
Pz. Jg. IV	31	–
Pak (Sf) (38t)	—	–
le. FH 18/II „Wespe“	12	9
Mun. Träger „Wespe“	4	4
s. FH. 18 „Hummel“	6	4
Mun. Träger „Hummel“	2	3
le. SPW	62	31
m. SPW	400	213
Flak Pz. IV (3.7cm)	8	–
Nebelwerfer-Kw	22	–

1.SS Panzer Division
Original German Actual Organisation Chart
3rd August 1944

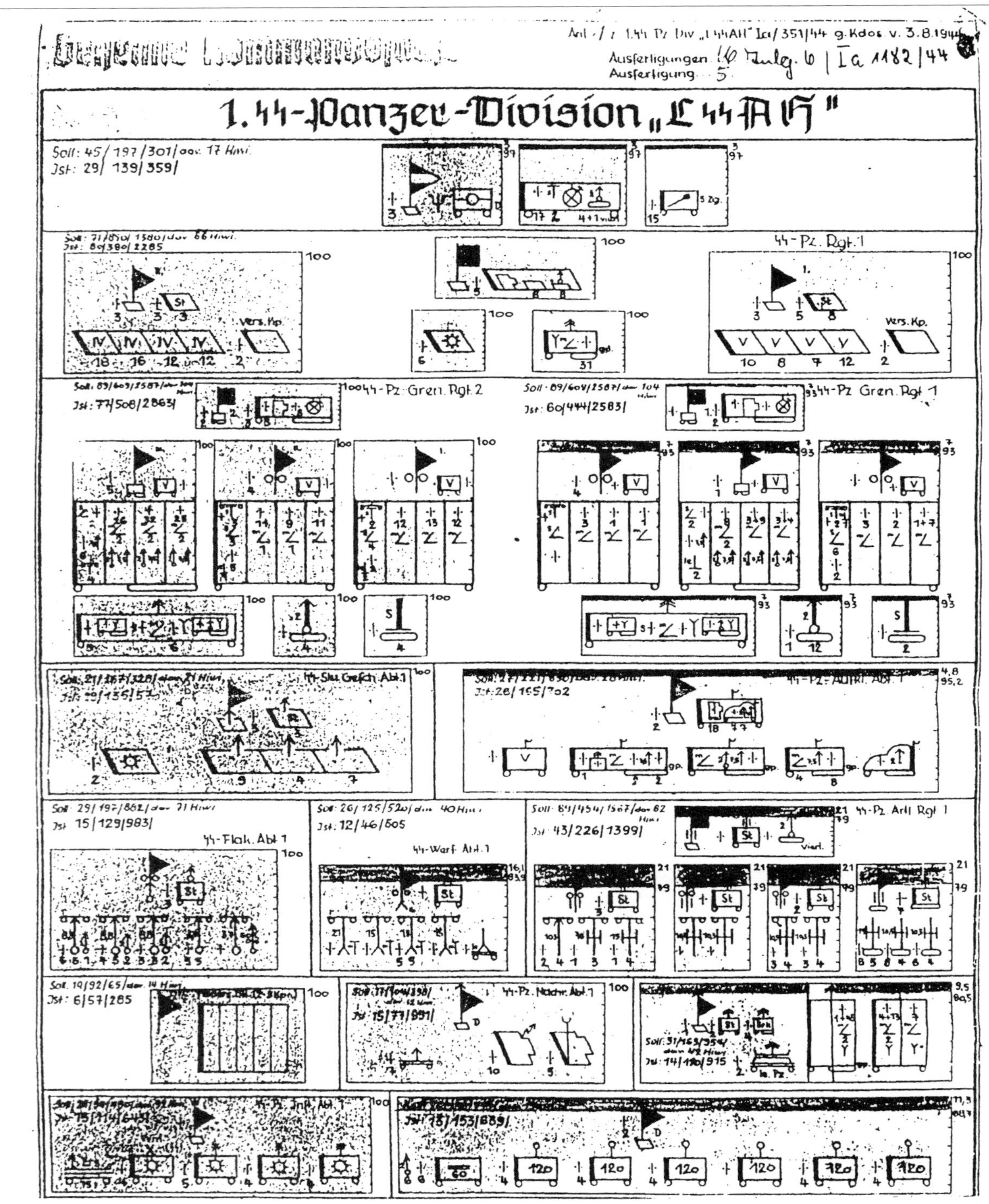

The Division had several units still absent from its Order of Battle. These units were still in the process of reforming and had yet to receive their vehicles and weapons.

The missing units were:
3. Battalion Artillery Regiment
3 Batteriesof 4th (Werfer) Battalion Artillery Regiment
1st (Panzerspahwagen) Company.
Reconnaissance Battalion

1.SS Panzer Division
Strength Report: 1st August 1944
Under Command of 1.SS Panzer Korps

MANPOWER

	Authorised Strength	Shortages	Actual
Officers	647	182	465
NCOs	4185	1354	2831
Other Ranks	13,229	3011+	16,240
Hiwis	1029	170	859
TOTAL	19,090	1305+	20,395

LOSSES FOR PREVIOUS 4 WEEKS

	Dead	Wounded	Missing	Hospital	Other Cases
Officers	6	19	3	3	10
NCOs / Other Ranks	237	728	99	137	171
TOTAL	243	747	102	140	181

REPLACEMENTS/ARRIVALS

	Replacements	Recovered
Officers	7	-
NCOs / Other Ranks	1	5

OVER 1 YEAR ABSENT FROM DIVISION (NON-LEAVE)

TOTAL	3783
Of That:	
12 to 18 Months	2870
19 to 24 Months	725
Over 24 Months	88

1.SS Panzer Division
Strength Report: 1st August 1944
Material Stocks

ARMOURED VEHICLES

	StuG	Pz III	Pz IV	Pz V	Other AFVs	Jagd IV
Authorised Strength	0	4	101	81	472	31
Ready for Action	23	0	61	40	261	0
Short term repair	0	0	14	14	11	0

MOTOR CYCLES

	Ketten	+Sidecars	Other
Authorised Strength	345	148	198
Ready for Action	59	109	131
Short term repair	2	22	21

CARS

	Cross country	Normal/Road
Authorised Strength	877	86
Ready for Action	521	152
Short term repair	75	35

TRUCKS

	Maultiere	Cross country	Normal/Road
Authorised Strength	77	1309	861
Ready for Action	120	534	930
Short term repair	15	78	115

TRACKED PRIME MOVERS

	1-5 Tons	8-18 Tons
Authorised Strength	159	129
Ready for Action	22	54
Short term repair	7	11

WEAPONS

	Heavy Anti-tank Guns	Artillery Guns	MGs
Authorised Strength	56	83	1393
Ready for Action	17	36	787 *(of which 566 are MG42)*
Short term repair	3		

1.SS PANZER DIVISION
'Leibstandarte Adolf Hitler'

1st August 1944

- Divisionstab (Divisional HQ)
  97% Manpower
  3 LMG

  Div. Kartenstelle (Mapping Section)
  97% Manpower

  Div. Begleitkompanie (Divisional Security Company)
  97% Manpower
  17 LMG. 4 x SdKfz 10/4 2cm Flak (SP). 1 x SdKfz 7/1 Quad 2cm Flakwagen. 2 x 7.5cm Pak (Towed)

  Feldgendarmerie Kompanie (Military Police Company)
  97% Manpower
  15 LMG. 5 Zug (Platoons)

- SS PANZER REGIMENT 1 (Tank Regiment)
  Regimentstab (Regimental HQ)
  100% Manpower
  6 *Panthers* (Including 3 Command Vehicles).
  8 x (2cm) Flakpanzer 38(t). 5 LMG

  1. Panzer Abteilung (1st Tank Battalion)
  100% Manpower
  40 *Panthers* ready for action (14 in short term repair). 10 LMG

  2. Panzer Abteilung (2nd Tank Battalion)
  100% Manpower
  61 Pz IV, ready for action (14 in short term repair).
  8 LMG

  Pionier Kompanie (Engineer Company) (Armoured)
  100% Manpower
  Medium Armoured Halftracks. 31 LMG

  1Werkstatt Kompanie (Workshop Company)
  100% Manpower
  6 LMG

- SS PANZERGRENADIER REGIMENT 1
  (Motorised Infantry Regiment)

  Regimentstab (Regimental HQ)(Armoured)
  93% Manpower
  Medium Armoured Halftracks. 2 LMG

  1. Bataillon (Motorised)
  93% Manpower
  14 LMG. 1 HMG. 6 x 120mm Mortars (Towed).
  1 x 7.5cm Infantry Gun (Towed). 2 x 7.5cm Pak (Towed)

  2. Bataillon (Partially Armoured)
  93% Manpower
  Medium Armoured Halftracks
  22 LMG. 6 HMG. 2 x 81mm Mortars.
  2 x 7.5cmInfantry Guns (Towed).
  2 x 120mm Mortars (Towed)

  3. Bataillon (Motorised)
  93% Manpower
  9 LMG

  Flak Kompanie (Anti-aircraft Company)
  93% Manpower
  12 x 2cm Flak Guns (Towed). 1 LMG

  Infanteriegeschutz Kompanie (Infantry Gun Company)
  93% Manpower
  2 x 15cm Infantry Guns (SP)

  Pionier Kompanie (Engineer Company) (Armoured)
  93% Manpower
  Medium Armoured Halftracks. No heavy weapons

- SS PANZERGRENADIER REGIMENT 2
  (Armoured Infantry Regiment)
  Regimentstab (Regimental HQ) (Armoured)
  100% Manpower
  Medium Armoured Halftracks. 11 LMG

  1. Bataillon (Motorised)
  100% Manpower
  39 LMG. 2 x 7.5cm Infantry Guns (Towed).
  2 x 7.5cm Pak (Towed). 4 x 120mm Mortars

(Towed)

2. Bataillon (Motorised)
100% Manpower
40 LMG. 2 x 81mm Mortars. 3 x 120mm Mortars (Towed). 1 x 7.5cm Infantry Gun (Towed). 3 x 7.5cm Pak (Towed)

3. Bataillon (Armoured)
100% Manpower
Medium Armoured Halftracks (including 6 x SdKfz 251/2). 94 LMG. 6 x 81mm. Mortars (Halftrack mounted). 4 x 7.5cm Pak (Towed)

Flak Kompanie (Anti-aircraft Company)
100% Manpower
4 x 2cm Flak Guns (Towed)

Infanteriegeschutz Kompanie (Infantry Gun Company)
100% Manpower
4 x 15cm SP Infantry Guns

Pionier Kompanie (Engineer Company) (Armoured)
100% Manpower
Medium Armoured Halftracks. 11 LMG

- SS AUFKLÄRUNGS ABTEILUNG 1
(Armoured Reconnaissance Battalion)
95.2% Manpower
Abteilungstab (HQ Company)
13 Puma Armoured Cars (7 ready for action). 9 LMG

1. Kompanie (Armoured Car Company)
No armoured vehicles or heavy weapons

2. Kompanie (Armoured Reconnaissance Company)
Light Armoured Halftracks (including 4 x SdKfz 250/7). 8 LMG. 2 HMG. 4 x 81mm Mortars (Halftrack mounted)

3. Kompanie (Armoured ReconnaissanceCompany)
Light Armoured Halftracks. No heavy weapons

4. Kompanie (Heavy Company)
Medium Armoured Halftracks. 5 LMG.

Versorgungs Kompanie (Supply Company)
0 LMG

- SS STURMGESCHÜTZ ABTEILUNG 1
(Assault Gun Battalion)
100% Manpower
23 Assault Guns (23 ready for action). 5 LMG

- SS PANZER ARTILLERIE REGIMENT 1
(Armoured Artillery Regiment)
Regimentstab (Regimental HQ)
79% Manpower

1. Abteilung (Armoured Battalion)
79% Manpower
5 *Hummel* (4 ready for action). 3 *Hummel* Munitions Carriers. 9 *Wespe* (8 ready for action). 4 *Wespe* Munitions Carrier. 29 LMG

2. Abteilung (Towed Battalion)
79% Manpower
8 x 105mm LeFH 18. 8 LMG

3. Abteilung (Towed Battalion)
79% Manpower
No heavy weapons

4. Abteilung (Towed Battalion)
79% Manpower
7 x 150mm SFH 18 (6 ready for action). 4 x 105mm Kanone. 7 LMG

- SS WERFER ABTEILUNG 1
(Rocket Projector Battalion)
83.9% Manpower
5 x 15cm Nebelwerfers. 5 LMG

- SS FLAKABTEILUNG 1 (Anti-aircraft Battalion)
100% Manpower
14 x 88mm Flak Guns (Towed)(13 ready for action). 5 x 3.7cm Flak Guns (Towed). 5 x 2cm Flak Guns (Towed). 20 LMG

- SS PANZER PIONIER BATAILLON 1
(Armoured Engineer Battalion)
90.5% Manpower
Stabs Kompanie (Partially Armoured)
Medium Armoured Halftracks. 7 LMG

1. Kompanie (Motorised)
7 LMG

2. Kompanie (Motorised)
13 LMG. 4 HMG. 2 x 81mm Mortars

3. Kompanie (Armoured)
Medium Armoured Halftracks (including 2 x SdKfz 251/2). 45 LMG. 1 HMG. 2 x 81mm Mortars

(Halftrack mounted)
Brucken Kolonne (Light Bridging Column)
(Motorised)
2 LMG

- SS PANZER NACHRICHTEN ABTEILUNG
(Armoured Signals Battalion)
100% Manpower. (Partially Armoured)
Medium Armoured Halftracks. 22 LMG

- SS FELDERS BATAILLON (Replacement Battalion)
100% Manpower.
No heavy weapons

- SS NACHSCHUBTRUPPEN 1
(Divisional Supply Battalion)
88.7% Manpower
6 Transportation Companies. 1 Supply Company.
28 LMG. 6 x 2cm Flak Guns (Towed)

- SS INSTADSETZUNGS ABTEILUNG 1
(Workshop Battalion)
100% Manpower
4 Workshop/Repair Companies. 1 Supply Company.
17 LMG

- SS WIRTSCHAFTS BATAILLON 1
(Commissary Battalion)
100% Manpower
1 Bakery Company. 1 Butcher Company.
1 Administration Company. 1 Field Post Office.
11 LMG

- SS SANITÄTS ABTEILUNG 1 (Medical Battalion)
100% Manpower
3 Ambulance Columns. 2 Medical Compaies.
1 Field Hospital. 9 LMG

1.SS Panzer Division
Strength Report: 1st August 1944

DIVISIONAL UNIT MANPOWER STRENGTHS

	Authorised Strength			Actual Strength		
	Officers	NCOs	Other Ranks	Officers	NCOs	Other Ranks
Division Stab	45	197	301	29	139	359
Panzer Regiment	71	850	1380	80	380	2285
Panzer Gren. Regt. 1	89	609	2587	60	444	2583
Panzer Gren. Regt. 2	89	609	2587	77	508	2863
Panzer Aufkl. Abt.	27	221	690	26	165	702
Sturmgeschütz Regt.	21	167	328	18	136	570
Panzer Art. Regt.	89	454	1567	43	226	1399
Werfer Abt.	26	125	520	12	46	505
Flak Abt.	29	197	882	15	129	983
Pionier Bn.	31	163	954	14	110	915
Nachrichten Abt.	17	104	398	15	77	651
Felders Bn.	19	92	65	6	57	285
Div. Nachschub.	26	138	743	13	153	639
Instand. Abt.	28	94	490	15	114	643
Wirtschafts Bn.	13	59	239	12	52	339
Sanitäts Abt.	27	106	527	30	95	519
Hiwis (Russian Helpers)						859
TOTAL	647	4,185	14,258	465	2,831	17,099
COMBINED TOTALS		19,090			20,395	

2.SS PANZER DIVISION

'Das Reich'

In February 1944 the bulk of 2.SS Panzer Division was transferred from the Eastern Front to the south of France for reast and refitting. A Divisional Battlegroup was retained in the east until April when it rejoined the rest of the Division.

'Das Reich' began its move to Normandy in early June, although it did not see any action until the end of that month.

On 1st June 1944, the 2.SS Panzer Division had the following units on strength:

- Stab der Division
- SS Panzer Regiment 2
- SS Panzer Grenadier Regiment 3 'Deutschland'
- SS Panzer Grenadier Regiment 4 'Der Führer'
- SS Panzer Aufklärungs Abteilung 2
- SS Sturmgeschütz Abteilung 2
- SS Panzer Atillerie Regiment 2
- SS Flak Abteilung 2
- SS Panzer Pionier Bataillon 2
- SS Panzer Nachrichten Abteilung 2
- SS Divisionsnachschubtruppen 2
- SS Panzer Instandsetzungs Abteilung 2
- SS Wirtschafts Bataillon 2
- SS Sanitäts Abteilung 2
- SS Feldgendarmerie Kompanie 2

- SS Panzer Regiment 2

1. *(Panther)* Abteilung began equipping with new vehicles in February 1944. The refit was expected to be completed by 10th June 1944.

Tanks received by I. Abteilung

Delivered between 27/3-31/5/44	37 Pz V
Delivered between 1/6-6/6/44	41 Pz V
TOTAL	78 Pz V

(Including 6 Command Panthers)

Tanks received by II. Abteilung

Delivered between 27/3-10/6/44	54 Pz IV
Delivered on 16/6/44	24 Pz IV
Delivered March/April 1944	3 Pz IV*
TOTAL	81 Pz IV

**Command Tanks*

13 StuGs delivered by 31/5/44
(Assigned to II Abteilung)

Also received in the same period
6 SdKfz 7/1 Quad 2cm Flakwagens
(formed into 9 Kompanies)
10 Medium armoured halftracks (SdKfz 251)

By 23/7/44 the Regiment had been reduced to the following:
41 Pz V (including 6 Command *Panthers*)
37 Pz IV (including 2 Command Tanks)

By October 1944 the Regiment had:
1 Pz V
5 Pz IV
1 StuG

SS Sturmgeschütze Abteilung 2

Delivered by 31/5/44	29 StuG

25 StuGs were still on strength on 23/7/44

SS Panzer Regiment 2
Tank Strengths September 1942 – April 1943

30/9/42 — PANZER ABTEILUNG 'DAS REICH'

	Pz II	Pz III	Pz IV	Pz VI	Bef Pz	TOTAL
a: Ready for action	-	35	10	-	-	45
b: Under repair	-	1	-	-	-	1
c: In the process of delivery	-	1	4	-	-	-

30/11/42 — PANZER REGIMENT 'DAS REICH'

	Pz II	Pz III	Pz IV	Pz VI	Bef Pz	TOTAL
a: Ready for action	10	34	10	-	-	54
b: Under repair	-	2	-	-	-	2
c: In the process of delivery	-	44	10	-	-	-

15/12/42	Pz II	Pz III	Pz IV	Pz VI	Bef Pz	TOTAL
a: Ready for action	10	35	7	-	-	52
b: Under repair	-	1	3	-	-	4
c: In the process of delivery	-	44	10	-	-	-

30/12/42	Pz II	Pz III	Pz IV	Pz VI	Bef Pz	TOTAL
a: Ready for action	10	35	7	-	-	52
b: Under repair	-	1	3	-	-	4
c: In the process of delivery	-	45	10	-	-	-

15/1/43	Pz II	Pz III	Pz IV	Pz VI	Bef Pz	TOTAL
a: Ready for action (on strength)	10	78	20	-	-	108

31/1/43	Pz II	Pz III	Pz IV	Pz VI	Bef Pz	TOTAL
a: Ready for action (on strength)	10	91	21	10	-	132

17/2/43	Pz II	Pz III	Pz IV	Pz VI	Bef Pz	TOTAL
a: Ready for action	2	29	3	3	7	44
b: Under repair	4	32	12	6	3	57

28/3/43	Pz II	Pz III	Pz IV	Pz VI	Bef Pz	TOTAL
a: Ready for action	-	-	-	-	-	-
b: Under repair	5	70	13	9	8	105

10/4/43	Pz II	Pz III	Pz IV	Pz VI	Bef Pz	TOTAL
a: Ready for action	-	34	7	-	5	46
b: Under repair	1	36	5	8	5	56

20/4/43	Pz II	Pz III	Pz IV	Pz VI	Bef Pz	TOTAL
a: Ready for action	-	36	6	7	10	59
b: Under repair	1	32	6	1	-	40
c: In the process of delivery	-	-	-	10	-	10

30/4/43	Pz II	Pz III	Pz IV	Pz VI	Bef Pz	TOTAL
a: Ready for action	-	31	8	6	10	55
b: Under repair	1	34	4	2	-	41
c: In the process of delivery	-	-	-	6	-	6

SS Panzer Regiment 2
Tank Strengths May 1943 – September 1943

10/5/43	Pz II	Pz III	Pz IV	Pz VI	Bef Pz	TOTAL
a: Ready for action	-	49	12	3	8	72
b: Under repair	1	16	-	5	2	24
c: In the process of delivery	-	-	21	6	-	27

31/5/43	Pz II	Pz III	Pz IV	Pz VI	Bef Pz	Pz Beo III	TOTAL
a: Ready for action	-	44	8 + 15	8	6	-	5
b: Under repair	1	20	5	6	4	-	20
c: In the process of delivery	-	-	6	-	-	-	6

20/6/43	Pz II	Pz III	Pz IV	Pz VI	Bef Pz	Pz Beo III	TOTAL
a: Ready for action	-	39	28	8	6	-	81
b: Under repair	1	25	5	6	4	-	41
c: In the process of delivery	-	-	-	-	-	9*	9

* *Assigned to Pz. Art. Rgt.*

30/6/43	Pz II	Pz III	Pz IV	Pz VI	Bef Pz	Pz Beo III	TOTAL
a: Ready for action	-	51	31	12	10	9	113
b: Under repair	1	11	2	2	-	-	16

10/7/43	Pz II	Pz III	Pz IV	Pz VI	Bef Pz	Pz Beo III	TOTAL
a: Ready for action	-	36	18	9	10	9	82
b: Under repair	1	26	14	5	-	-	46

20/7/43	Pz II	Pz III	Pz IV	Pz VI	Bef Pz	Pz Beo III	TOTAL
a: Ready for action	-	47	19	8	5	8	87
b: Under repair	1	13	8	5	5	1	33

31/7/43	Pz II	Pz III	Pz IV	Pz VI	Bef Pz	Pz Beo III	TOTAL
a: Ready for action	-	39	16	3	7	5	70
b: Under repair	1	28	48	19	3	4	103

10/8/43	Pz II	Pz III	Pz IV	Pz VI	Bef Pz	Pz Beo III	TOTAL
a: Ready for action	-	18	38	3	6	2	67
b: Under repair	1	30	23	19	4	7	84
c: In the process of delivery	-	-	10	-	-	-	10

20/8/43	Pz II	Pz III	Pz IV	Pz V	Pz VI	Bef Pz	Pz Beo III	TOTAL
a: Ready for action	-	18	38	-	3	6	2	67
b: Under repair	1	30	23	-	19	4	7	84
c: In the process of delivery	-	-	10	71	-	-	-	81

31/8/43	Pz II	Pz III	Pz IV	Pz V	Pz VI	Bef Pz	Pz Beo III	TOTAL
a: Ready for action	-	3	10	21	2	6	3	45
b: Under repair	1	39	45	40	15	3	6	149

10/9/43	Pz II	Pz III	Pz IV	Pz V	Pz VI	Bef Pz	Pz Beo III	TOTAL
a: Ready for action	-	7	20	18	5	6	5	61
b: Under repair	1	35	35	41	14	2	4	132
c: In the process of delivery	-	-	10	8	-	-	-	18

SS Panzer Regiment 2
Tank Strengths September 1943 – April 1944

20/9/43	Pz II	Pz III	Pz IV	Pz V	Pz VI	Bef Pz	Pz Beo III	TOTAL
a: Ready for action	-	6	13	8	7	4	6	44
b: Under repair	1	36	40	51	11	3	3	145
c: In the process of delivery	-	-	13	-	-	-	-	-

30/9/43	Pz II	Pz III	Pz IV	Pz V	Pz VI	Bef Pz	Pz Beo III	TOTAL
a: Ready for action	-	2	3	46	-	2	4	37
b: Under repair	1	16	50	12	8	4	5	96
c: In the process of delivery	-	-	3	-	-	-	-	3

20/10/43	Pz II	Pz III	Pz IV	Pz V	Pz VI	Bef Pz	Pz Beo III	TOTAL
a: Ready for action	-	9	14	6	4	4	2	39
b: Under repair	1	20	35	47	14	2	7	126
c: In the process of delivery	-	-	3	-	-	-	-	3

31/10/43	Pz III	Pz IV	Pz V	Pz VI	Bef Pz	Pz Beo III	TOTAL
a: Ready for action	3	8	-	3	3	2	19
b: Under repair	25	38	52	16	3	7	141
c: In the process of delivery	-	3	-	-	-	-	3

10/11/43	Pz III	Pz IV	Pz V	Pz VI	Bef Pz	Pz Beo III	TOTAL
a: Ready for action	2	15	-	5	4	2	28
b: Under repair	20	30	50	14	2	7	123
c: In the process of delivery	-	10	-	-	-	-	10

31/11/43	Pz III	Pz IV	Pz V	Pz VI	Bef Pz	Pz Beo III	TOTAL
a: Ready for action	5	6	16	3	3	2	35
b: Under repair	12	43	28	13	3	7	106

10/12/43	Pz III	Pz IV	Pz V	Pz VI	Bef Pz	Pz Beo III	TOTAL
a: Ready for action	-	3	3	3	2	2	13
b: Under repair	14	47	41	13	4	6	125

20/12/43	BATTLE GROUP 'DAS REICH'			
	Pz IV	Pz V	Pz VI	Bef Pz
a: Ready for action	15	10	4	2
b: Under repair	7	10	4	-

1/3/44	Pz IV	Pz V	Pz VI
a: Ready for action	6	4	5
b: Under repair	3	-	-

1/4/44	2nd SS Pz. Div. 'DAS REICH'		
	Pz III	Pz IV	Pz V
a: Ready for action	-	1	3
b: Under repair	6	4	3

15/4/44	Pz III	Pz IV	Pz V
a: Ready for action	1	48	32
b: Under repair	3	6	5

2.SS Panzer Division
Original German Strength Report
1st June 1944

29

21 Ausfertigungen
14. Ausfertigung

Anlage zu Ia 253/44 g.Kdos.

Meldung vom 1. Juni 1944

2. SS-Panzer-Division „Das Reich"
Unterstellungsverhältnis: LVIII. Pz. Korps

1. Personelle Lage am Stichtag der Meldung:

a) Personal:

	Soll	Fehl
Offiziere	645	151
Uffz.	4440	1339
Mannsch.	14512	
Hiwi	(1074)	
insgesamt	19598	

c) in der Berichtszeit eingetroffener Ersatz:

	Ersatz	Genesene
Offiziere	3	–
Uffz. und Mannsch.	71 343	7 30

b. Verluste und sonstige Abgänge in der Berichtszeit vom .... bis ....

	tot	verw.	verm.	krank	sonst
Offiziere	–	–	–	7	–
Uffz. und Mannsch.	3	1	–	259	–
Insgesamt	3	1	–	266	–

d) über ein Jahr nicht beurlaubt:

insgesamt: 20 Köpfe [illegible] % d.Iststärke

davon:	12–18 Monate	19–24 Monate	über 24 Monate
	[illegible]	5	2
Platzkarten im Berichtsmonat zugewiesen:	–		

2. Materielle Lage:

		Gepanzerte Fahrzeuge							Kraftfahrzeuge				
									Kräder			Pkw	
		Stu. Gesch.	III	IV	V	VI	Schtz.Pz. Pz.Sp. Art.Pz.B. (o.Pz.FuWg.)	Art. SF.	Ketten	m. angelr. Bwg.	sonst.	gel.	O
Soll (Zahlen)		75	7	57	99	–	314	[illegible]	151	310	302	784	104
einsatzbereit	zahlenm.	33	–	44	25	–	235	[illegible]	–	8	76	155	27
	in % des Solls	44	–	77	25	–	75	77	–	2	25	20	5
In kurzfristiger Instandsetzung (bis 3 Wochen)	zahlenm.	9	–	11	12	–	14	–	–	–	[illegible]	11	5
	in % des Solls	12	–	20	12	–	4	–	–	–	4	2	5

		noch Kraftfahrzeuge							Waffen		
		Lkw				Kettenfahrzeuge					
		Maultiere	gel.	O	Tonnage	Zgkw.		RSO	s.Pak	Art. Gesch.	MG. ( )
Soll (Zahlen)		56	1312	1000	67435	*176	**117	–	31	41	[illegible]
einsatzbereit	zahlenm.	10	98	501	1827	20	16	–	21	[illegible]	[illegible]
	in % des Solls	18	7	50	28	11	14	–	66	54	[illegible]
in kurzfristiger Instandsetzung (bis 3 Wochen)	zahlenm.	–	21	25	138	–	–	–	–	–	–
	in % des Solls	–	2	2	2	–	–	–	–	–	–

*) Zgkw. mit 1-5t, **) Zgkw. mit 8-18t, ( ) davon MG.42

sonstige Waffen:	Soll	Ist	% d.Solls
Karabiner 98k	12426	12100	96
[illegible] 38/40	1255	1155	92
5 cm G.r.W. 34	91	61	66
le.J.G. 18	25	17	80
2 cm Flak 38	47	36	80
3,7 cm Flak 37	9	9	100

sonstige Waffen:	Soll	Ist	% d.Solls
8,8 cm Flak 37	12	12	100
le.F.H. 18	13	14	100
s.F.H. 18	12	4	33
10 cm Kan.	4	4	100

Anl. zu Nr. 00736/44 geh.

Gen. Insp. d. Pz. Tr.

Druck: Div.-Kartenstelle

2.SS Panzer Division
Original German Theoretical Organisation Chart
1st June 1944

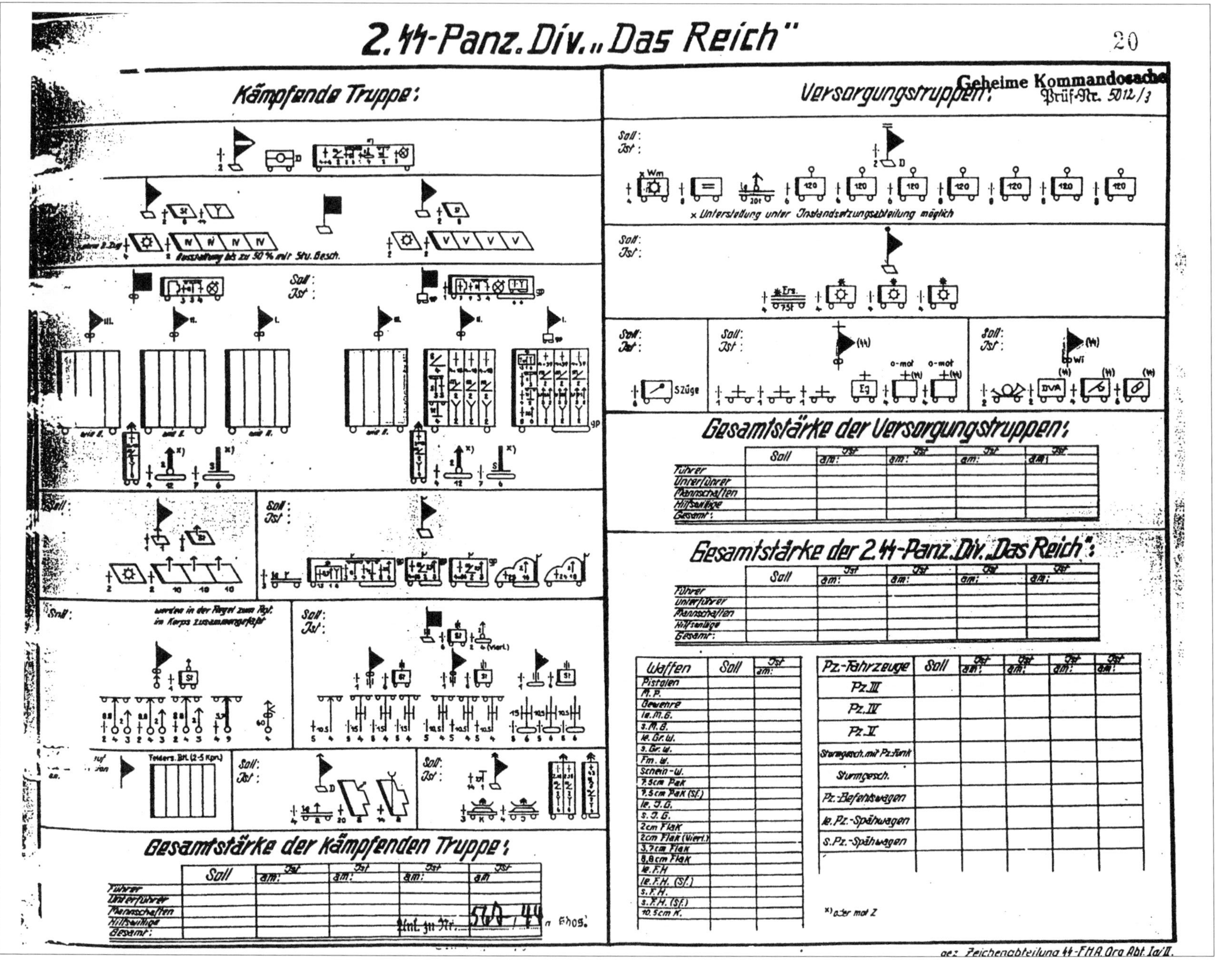

2.SS Panzer Division
Original German Actual Organisation Chart
3rd June 1944

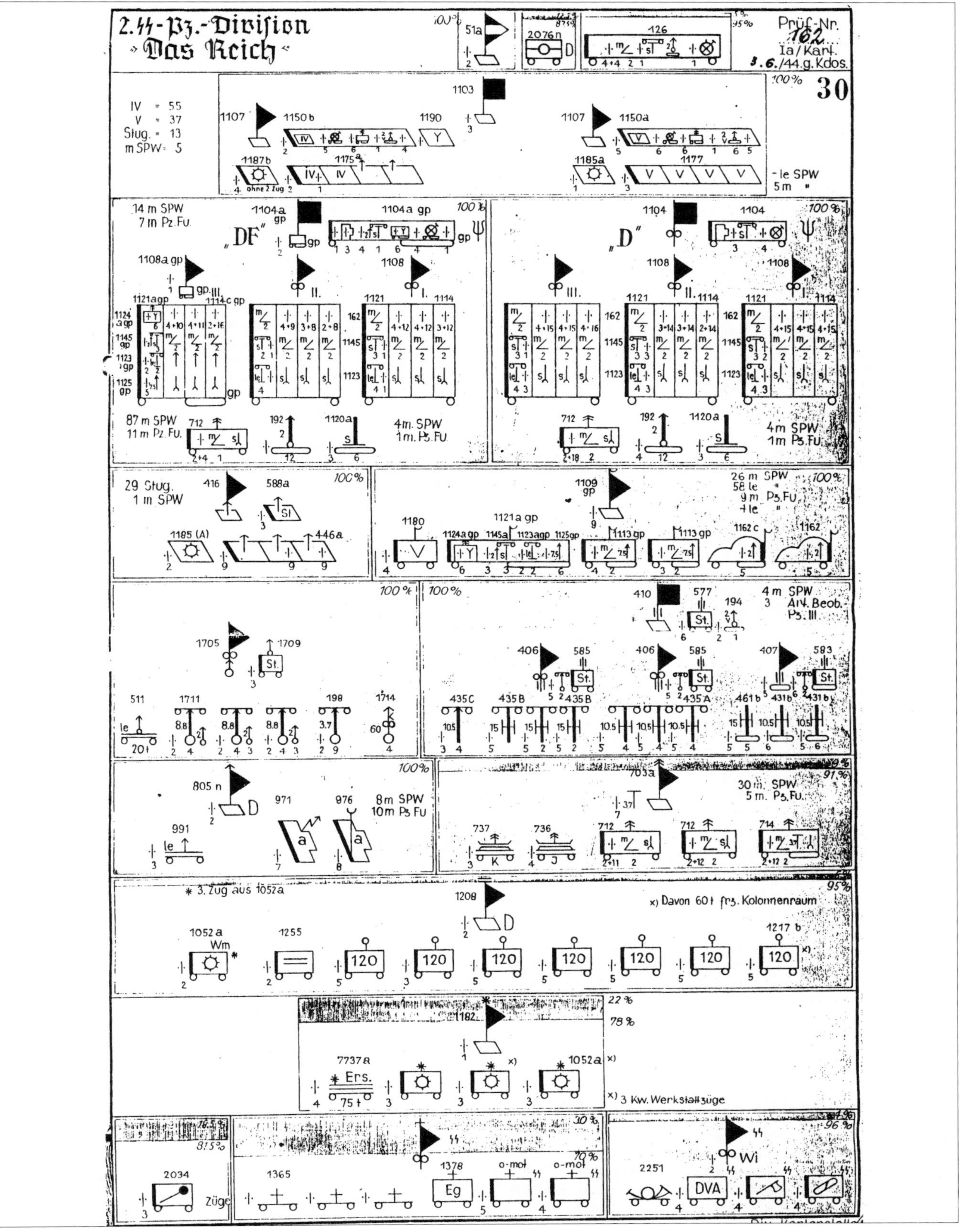

2.SS Panzer Division
Strength Report 1st June 1944
Under Command of 58 Panzer Korps

MANPOWER

	Authorised Strength	Shortages	Actual
Officers	646	151	495
NCOs	4440	1339	3101
Other Ranks	14,512	-	14,500 (approx)
Hiwis	1074	-	-
TOTAL	19,598	-	18,000 (approx)

LOSSES FOR PREVIOUS 4 WEEKS

	Dead	Wounded	Missing	Hospital	Other Cases
Officers	0	0	0	7	0
NCOs / Other Ranks	3	1	0	259	-
TOTAL	3	1	0	266	0

REPLACEMENTS/ARRIVALS

	Replacements	Recovered
Officers	6	0
NCOs	71	7
Other Ranks	343	30

OVER 1 YEAR ABSENT FROM DIVISION (NON-LEAVE)

TOTAL	80
Of That:	
12 to 18 Months	73
19 to 24 Months	5
Over 24 Months	2

2.SS Panzer Division
Strength Report: 1st June 1944
Material Stocks

ARMOURED VEHICLES

	StuG	Pz III	Pz IV	Pz V	Other AFVs	Art (SP)
Authorised Strength	75	7	57	99	314	30
Ready for Action	33	0	44	25	235	23
Short term repair	9	0	11	12	14	0

MOTOR CYCLES

	Ketten	+Sidecars	Other
Authorised Strength	131	310	362
Ready for Action	0	8	76
Short term repair	0	0	14

CARS

	Cross country	Normal/Road
Authorised Strength	784	104
Ready for Action	156	27
Short term repair	11	5

TRUCKS

	Maultiere	Cross country	Normal/Road
Authorised Strength	56	1312	1099
Ready for Action	10	98	501
Short term repair	0	21	25

TRACKED PRIME MOVERS

	1-5 Tons	8-18 Tons
Authorised Strength	176	117
Ready for Action	20	16
Short term repair	0	0

WEAPONS	Authorised Strength	Actual Strength MGs
Heavy Anti-tank Guns	31	21
Artillery Guns	41	22
MG (MG 42)	1055 (166)	1050 (151)
Rifle Kar 98	12,426	12,100
M. Pistol 38/40	1255	1155
8cm Mortar	91	61
Light Infantry Gun	25	17
2cm Flak 38	47	36
3.7cm Flak 37	9	9
88mm Flak 37	12	12
Light Artillery Gun 18	13	14
Heavy Artillery Gun	12	4
10cm Kanone	4	4

2.SS PANZER DIVISION
'Das Reich'

1st June 1944

- Divisionstab (Divisional HQ)
  100% Manpower
  2 LMG

  Div. Kartenstelle (Mapping Section)
  87.5% Manpower

  Div. Begleitkompanie (Divisional Security Company)
  95% Manpower
  6 LMG. 4 HMG. 2 x 81mm Mortars

- SS PANZER REGIMENT 2 (Tank Regiment)
  Regimentstab (Regimental HQ)
  100% Manpower
  3 LMG

  1. Panzer Abteilung (1st Tank Battalion)
  100% Manpower
  37 *Panthers*. 6 x SdKfz 7/1 Quad 2cm Flakwagens. 5 x Medium Armoured Halftracks. (2 x SdKfz 251/8; 3 x SdKfz 251/7). 27 LMG

  2. Panzer Abteilung (2nd Tank Battalion)
  100% Manpower
  55 Pz IV. 13 StuGs. 25 LMG

- SS PANZERGRENADIER REGIMENT 3 'DEUTSCHLAND'
  (Motorised Infantry Regiment)
  Regimentstab (Regimental HQ)
  100% Manpower
  7 LMG

  1. Bataillon (Partially Motorised)
  100% Manpower
  50 LMG. 12 HMG. 8 x 81mm Mortars. 4 x 7.5cm Inf. Guns (Towed). 3 x 7.5cm Pak (Towed)

  2. Bataillon (Partially Motorised)
  100% Manpower
  48 LMG. 8 HMG. 8 x 81mm Mortars. 4 x 7.5cm Inf. Guns (Towed). 3 x 7.5cm Pak (Towed)

  3. Bataillon (Partially Motorised)
  100% Manpower
  50 LMG. 12 HMG. 8 x 81mm Mortars. 4 x 7.5cm Inf. Guns (Towed). 3 x 7.5cm Pak (Towed)

  Flak Kompanie (Anti-aircraft Company)
  100% Manpower
  12 x 2cm Flak Guns (Towed). 4 LMG

  Infanteriegeschutz Kompanie (Infantry Gun Company)
  100% Manpower
  6 x 15cm SP Infantry Guns. 5 x Medium Armoured Halftracks. (4 x SdKfz 251/1; 1 x SdKfz 251/3). 3 x LMG

  Pionier Kompanie (Engineer Company)
  100% Manpower
  18 LMG. 2 HMG. 2 x 81mm Mortars

- SS PANZERGRENADIER REGIMENT 4 'DER FÜHRER'
  (Armoured Infantry Regiment)
  Regimentstab (Regimental HQ) (Armoured)
  100% Manpower
  21 Medium Armoured Halftracks (including 7 x SdKfz 251/3). 20 LMG. 1 x 7.5cm Pak (Towed)

  1. Bataillon (Partially Motorised)
  100% Manpower
  38 LMG. 11 HMG. 8 x 81mm Mortars. 4 x 7.5cm Inf. Guns (Towed). 3 x 7.5cm Pak (Towed)

  2. Bataillon (Partially Motorised)
  100% Manpower
  27 LMG. 9 HMG. 8 x 81mm Mortars. 4 x 7.5cm Inf. Guns (Towed). 2 x 7.5cm Pak (Towed)

  3. Bataillon (Armoured)
  100% Manpower
  98 Medium Armoured Halftracks (including 11 x SdKfz 251/3; 6 x SdKfz 251/2). 45 LMG. 10 HMG. 6 x 81mm Mortars. 2 x 7.5cm Inf. Guns (Towed). 3 x 7.5cm Pak (Towed). 6 Flamethrowers

Flak Kompanie (Anti-aircraft Company)
100% Manpower
12 x 2cm Flak Guns (Towed)

Infanteriegeschutz Kompanie (Infantry Gun Company)
100% Manpower
6 x 15cm SP Infantry Guns. 5 Medium Armoured Halftracks (4 x SdKfz 251/1; 1 x 251/3). 3 LMG

Pionier Kompanie (Engineer Company)
100% Manpower
4 LMG. 2 HMG. 1 x 81mm Mortar

- SS PANZER AUFKLÄRUNGS ABTEILUNG 2
(Armoured Reconnaissance Battalion)
100% Manpower
35 Medium Armoured Halftracks. 62 Light Armoured Halftracks

Abteilungstab (HQ Company)
9 LMG

1. Kompanie (Armoured Car Company)
No Armoured Cars. 5 LMG

2. Kompanie (Armoured Car Company)
No Armoured Cars. (250/9). 5 LMG

3. Kompanie (Armoured Reconnaissance Company)
Light Armoured Halftracks. 3 LMG. 2 x 81mm Mortars

4. Kompanie (Armoured Reconnaissance Company)
Light Armoured Halftracks. 4 LMG. 2 x 81mm Mortars

5. Kompanie (Heavy Company)
Medium Armoured Halftracks. 11 LMG. 6 x 7.5cm KwK L/24. (Halftrack mounted). 2 x 7.5cm Inf. Guns (Towed). 3 x 7.5cm Pak (Towed)

Versorgungs Kompanie (Supply Company)
4 LMG

- SS STURMGESCHÜTZ ABTEILUNG 2
(Assault Gun Battalion)
100% Manpower
29 Assault Guns (7.5cm). 1 Medium Armoured Halftrack. 32 LMG

- SS PANZER ARTILLERIE REGIMENT 2
(Armoured Artillery Regiment)
Regimentstab (Regimental HQ)
100% Manpower
8 LMG. 1 x SdKfz 7/1 Quad 2cm Flakwagen

1. Abteilung (Armoured Battalion)
100% Manpower
5 *Hummel*. 6 *Wespe*. 3 Pz III Observation Tanks. 4 Medium Armoured Halftracks. 2 x 2cm Flak Guns (Towed). 27 LMG

2. Abteilung (Towed Battalion)
100% Manpower
12 x 105mm LeFH 18. 20 LMG. 2 x 2cm Flak Guns (Towed)

3. Abteilung (Towed Battalion)
100% Manpower
4 x 150mm SFH 18. 4 x 105mm Kanone. 23 LMG. 2 x 2cm Flak Guns (Towed)

- SS FLAKABTEILUNG 2 (Anti-aircraft Battalion)
100% Manpower
12 x 88mm Flak Guns (Towed). 9 x 3.7cm Flak Guns (Towed). 6 x 2cm Flak Guns (Towed). 4 x 60cm Searchlights. 11 LMG

- SS PANZER PIONIER BATAILLON
(Armoured Engineer Battalion)
91% Manpower
Stabs Kompanie (Company HQ)(Partially Armoured)
10 Medium Armoured Halftracks. 7 LMG

1. Kompanie (Armoured)
25 Medium Armoured Halftracks. 12 LMG. 2 HMG. 2 x 81mm Mortars

2. Kompanie (Motorised)
12 LMG. 2 HMG. 2 x 81mm Mortars

3. Kompanie (Motorised)
11 LMG. 2 HMG. 2 x 81mm Mortars

Brucken Kolonne 'J' (Bridging Column)
4 LMG

Brucken Kolonne 'K' (Bridging Column)
3 LMG

- SS PANZER NACHRICHTEN ABTEILUNG 2
  (Armoured Signals Battalion)
  100% Manpower
  18 Medium Armoured Halftracks (including
  10 x SdKfz 251/3). 20 LMG

- SS NACHSCHUBTRUPPEN 2
  (Divisional Supply Battalion)
  95% Manpower
  7 Transportation Companies. 1 Supply Company.
  1 Workshop Company. 39 LMG

- SS INSTADSETZUNGS ABTEILUNG 2
  (Workshop Battalion)
  78% Manpower
  3 Workshop/Repair Companies. 1 Supply Company.
  14 LMG

- SS WIRTSCHAFTS BATAILLON 2
  (Commissary Battalion)
  96% Manpower
  1 Bakery Company. 1 Butcher Company.
  1 Administration Company. 1 Field Post Office.
  14 LMG

- SS SANITÄTS ABTEILUNG 2 (Medical Battalion)
  70% Manpower
  3 Ambulance Columns. 2 Medical Companies.
  1 Field Hospital. 9 LMG

- SS FELDGENDARMERIE KOMPANIE 2
  (Military Police Company)
  81.5% Manpower
  3 LMG

2.SS Panzer Division
Original German Strength Report
1st July 1944

19. Ausfertigung 32

Meldung vom 1.7. 1944

Verband: 2.SS-Pz.Div."DAS REICH"
AOK 7
Unterstellungsverhältnis: ______

1. Personelle Lage am Stichtag der Meldung:

a) Personal:

	Soll	Fehl
Offiziere	6[illegible]6	85
Uffz.	3331	444
Mannsch.	13272	–
Hiwi	(949)	—
Insgesamt	17 3[illegible]9	529

c) in der Berichtszeit eingetroffener Ersatz:

	Ersatz	Genesene
Offiziere	–	–
Uffz. und Mannsch.	354	–

b) Verluste und sonstige Abgänge in der Berichtszeit vom ______ bis 1.7.44

	tot	verw.	verm.	krank	sonst.
Offiziere	4	12	1	14	–
Uffz. und Mannsch.	114	4[illegible]1	24	265	29
Insgesamt	118	413	25	279	29

d) über 1 Jahr nicht beurlaubt:

insgesamt	Köpfe		% d. Iststärke
davon	12-18 Monate	19-24 Monate	über 24 Monate
	37	8	5
Platzkarten im Berichtsmonat zugewiesen	–		

2. Materielle Lage:

		Gepanzerte Fahrzeuge							Kraftfahrzeuge				
								Art. Pak SF	Kräder			Pkw	
		Stu. Gesch.	III	IV	V	VI	Schtz.Pz. Pz.Sp. Art.Pz.B. (o.Pz.Fu.Wg.)		Ketten	m.angek. Bwg.	sonst.	gel.	o
Soll (Zahlen)		51	2	1[illegible]1	79	–	297	3[illegible]	3[illegible]6	14[illegible]	175	757	84
einsatzbereit	zahlenm.	56	–	50	26	–	227	23	2[illegible]	14	62	345	28
	in % des Solls	10[illegible]	–	50	30	–	73	77	[illegible]	10	4[illegible]	45	34
in kurzfristiger Instandsetzung (bis 3 Wochen)	zahlenm.	3	–	25	46	–	18	–	–	1	22	62	5
	in % des Solls	10	–	24	32	–	7	–	–	1	13	8	6

		noch Kraftfahrzeuge							Waffen			
		Lkw				Ketten-Fahrzeuge						
		Maultiere	gel.	o	Tonnage	Zgkw.		RSO	s.Pak	Art.-Gesch.	M.G. ( )	sonstige Waffen
Soll (Zahlen)		1[illegible]	1046	877	6138	*) 98	**) 1[illegible]4	–	28	41	1102 (102)	
einsatzbereit	zahlenm.	4	192	672	2[illegible]4	21	30	–	21	22	1056 (98)	
	in % des Solls	4	18	79	39	20	36	–	75	53	95 (96)	
in kurzfristiger Instandsetzg. (bis 3 Wochen)	zahlenm.	–	17	22	117	2	3	–	–	–		
	in % des Solls	–	2	3	2	2	3	–	–	–		

*) Zgkw. mit 1-5t **) Zgkw. mit 8-18t
( ) ~~davon MG. 42~~ s.M.G.

3. Pferdefehlstellen:

sonst. Waffen	Soll	Ist	%
Karab.98 K	11685	11991	100
M.P.38/40	1712	1[illegible]09	94
8 cm Gr.W.	62	61	99
2 cm Flak 38	50	36	72
2 cm Fla-Vierl.	10	7	70
3,7 cm Flak 37	9	9	100
8,8 cm Flak 37	18	12	66

Anl. zu Nr. 00868 /44 geh.
Gen. Insp. d. Pz. Tr.

2.SS Panzer Division
Original German Theoretical Organisation Chart
1st July 1944

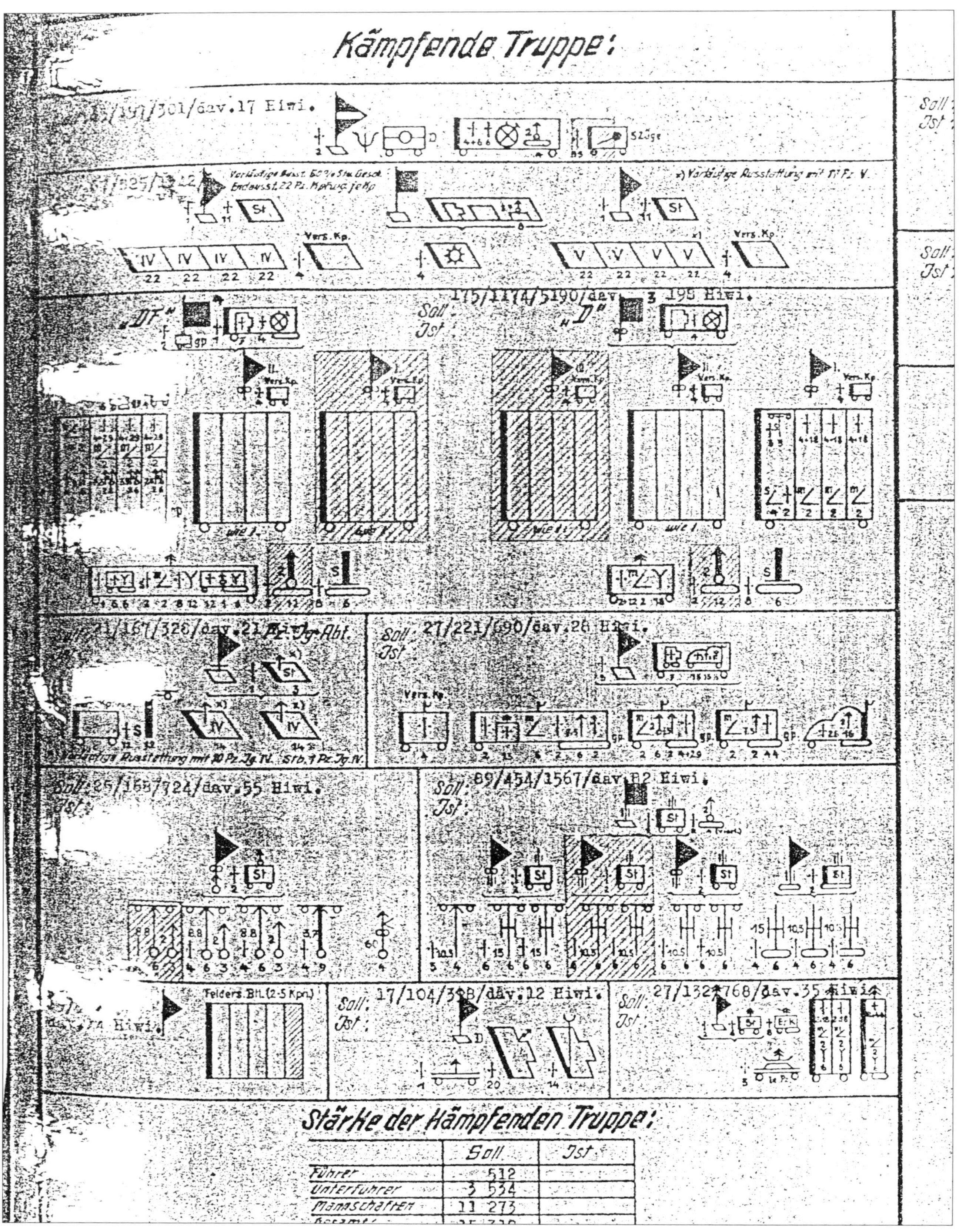

	Soll	Ist
Führer	512	
Unterführer	3 534	
Mannschaften	11 273	
Gesamt		

2.SS Panzer Division
Original German Theoretical Organisation Chart
1st July 1944

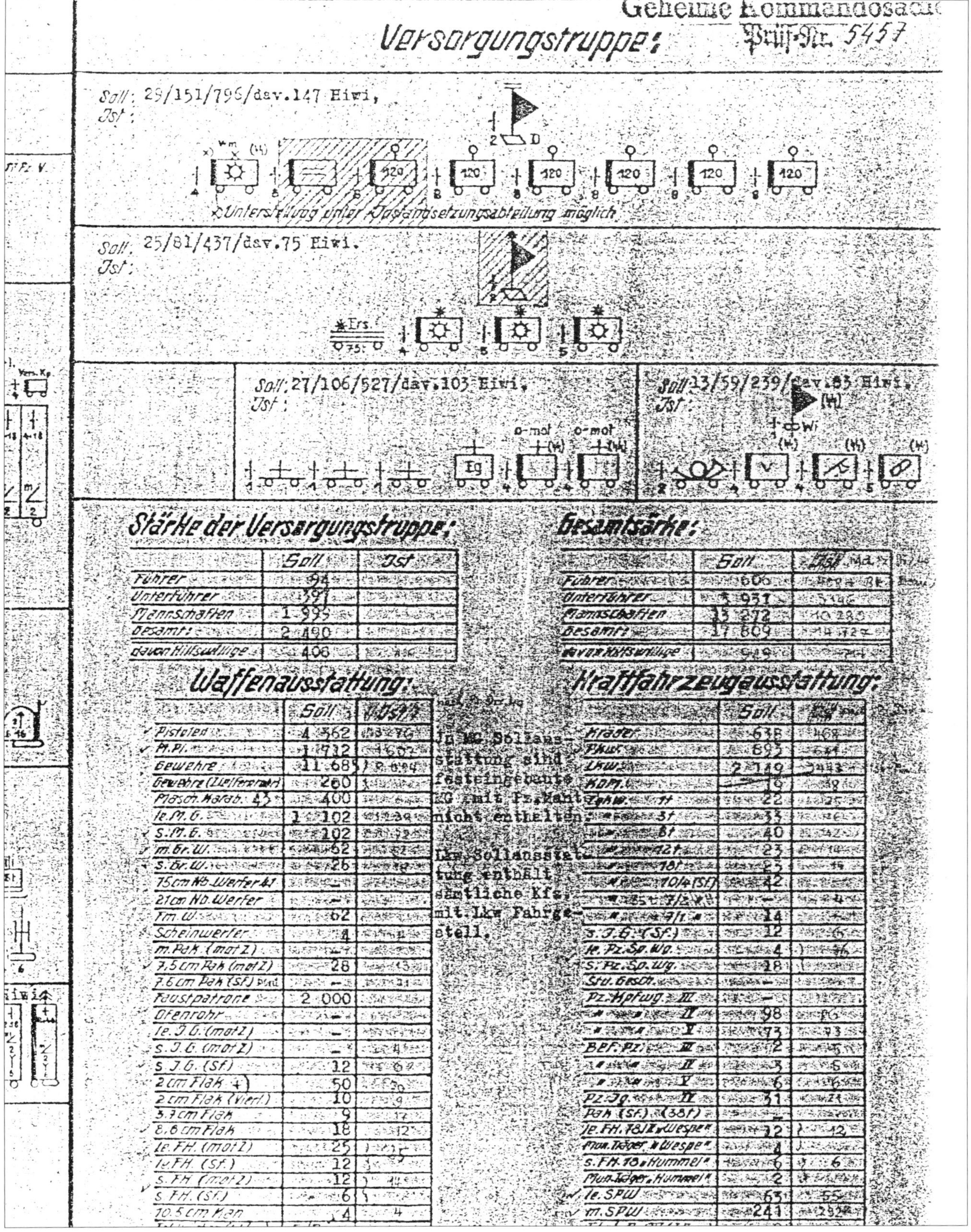

Geheime Kommandosache
Prüf-Nr. 5457

Versorgungstruppe:

Soll: 29/151/796/dav.147 Hiwi,
Ist:

x) Unterstellung unter Instandsetzungsabteilung möglich

Soll: 25/81/437/dav.75 Hiwi.
Ist:

Soll: 27/106/527/dav.103 Hiwi.
Ist:

Soll: 13/59/239/dav.83 Hiwi.
Ist:

Stärke der Versorgungstruppe:

	Soll	Ist
Führer	94	
Unterführer	397	
Mannschaften	1 999	
Gesamt:	2 490	
davon Hilfswillige	406	

Gesamtstärke:

	Soll	Ist
Führer	606	
Unterführer	3 931	3 146
Mannschaften	13 272	10 283
Gesamt:	17 809	14 727
davon Hilfswillige	949	

Waffenausstattung:

	Soll	Ist
Pistolen	4 362	[illegible]
M.Pi.	1 732	[illegible]
Gewehre	11 685	8 694
Gewehre (Zielfernrohr)	260	
Masch. Karab. 43	400	
le.M.G.	1 102	[illegible]
s.M.G.	102	[illegible]
m.Gr.W.	62	[illegible]
s.Gr.W.	26	[illegible]
7.5cm Nb.Werfer 41	–	
21cm Nb.Werfer	–	
Fm.W.	62	
Scheinwerfer	4	
m.Pak (mot Z)	–	
7.5cm Pak (mot Z)	28	13
7.5cm Pak (Sf)	–	31
Faustpatrone	2 000	
Ofenrohr	–	
le.J.G. (mot Z)	–	
s.J.G. (mot Z)	–	4
s.J.G. (Sf)	12	6
2cm Flak (+)	50	30
2cm Flak (Vierl.)	10	9
3.7cm Flak	9	17
8.8cm Flak	18	12
le.F.H. (mot Z)	25	25
le.F.H. (Sf.)	12	
s.F.H. (mot Z)	12	44
s.F.H. (Sf.)	6	
10.5cm Kan.	4	4

In MG Sollausstattung sind festeingebaute MG mit Pz.Kant nicht enthalten.

Lkw Sollausstattung enthält sämtliche Kfz. mit Lkw Fahrgestell.

Kraftfahrzeugausstattung:

	Soll	Ist
Kräder	638	468
Pkw	895	[illegible]
Lkw	2 149	2443
Kom.	16	8
Zgkw. 1t	22	25
" 3t	33	36
" 8t	40	42
" 12t	23	14
" 18t	25	15
" 10/4 (Sf)	42	
" 3t 7/2	–	4
" 7/1	14	
s.J.G. (Sf.)	12	6
le.Pz.Sp.Wg.	4	36
s.Pz.Sp.Wg.	18	
Stu.Gesch.	–	
Pz.Kpfwg. III	–	
" IV	98	76
" V	73	73
Bef.Pz. III	2	3
" IV	3	5
" V	6	6
Pz.Jg. IV	31	21
Pak (Sf.) (38t)	–	
le.F.H. 18/II "Wespe"	12	12
Mun.Träger "Wespe"	4	
s.F.H. 18 "Hummel"	6	6
Mun.Träger "Hummel"	2	
le.SPW	63	55
m.SPW	241	292

2.SS Panzer Division
Original German Actual Organisation Chart
1st July 1944

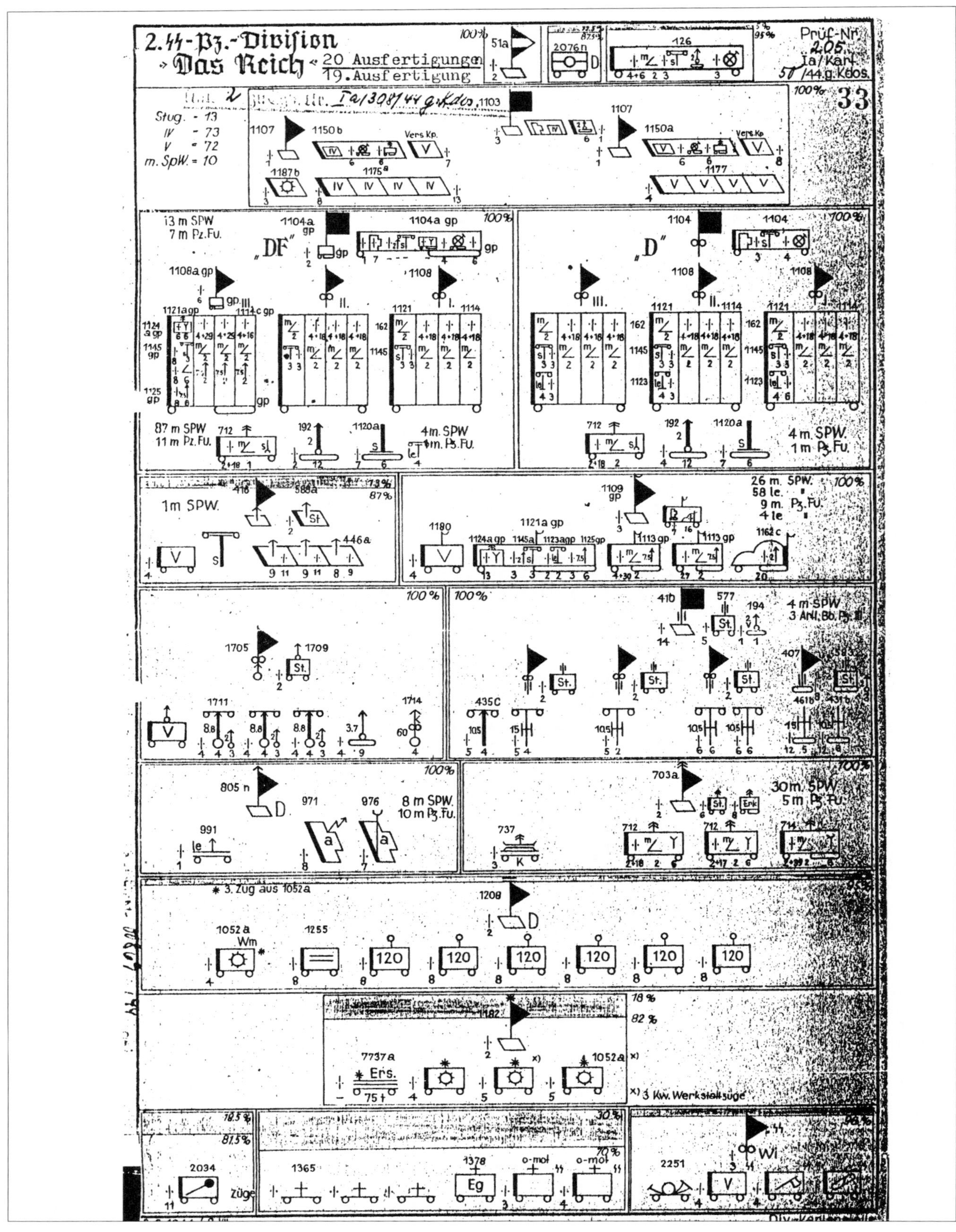

2.SS Panzer Division
Strength Report 1st July 1944
Under Command of 7. Armee

MANPOWER

	Authorised Strength	Shortages	Actual
Officers	606	85	521
NCOs	3931	444	3487
Other Ranks	13,272	-	-
Hiwis	(949)	-	-
TOTAL	17,809	329	18,138 (approx)

LOSSES between 1/6/44 – 1/7/44

	Dead	Wounded	Missing	Hospital	Other Cases
Officers	4	12	1	14	-
NCOs / Other Ranks	114	401	24	265	29
TOTAL	118	413	25	279	29

REPLACEMENTS/ARRIVALS

	Replacements	Recovered
Officers	-	-
NCOs / Other Ranks	354	-

OVER 1 YEAR ABSENT FROM DIVISION (NON-LEAVE)

TOTAL	110
Of That:	
12 to 18 Months	97
19 to 24 Months	8
Over 24 Months	5

2.SS Panzer Division
Strength Report: 1st July 1944
Material Stocks

ARMOURED VEHICLES

	StuG	Pz III	Pz IV	Pz V	Other AFVs	Art (SP)
Authorised Strength	31	2	101	79	297	30
Ready for Action	36	-	50	26	227	23
Short term repair	3	-	23	46	18	

MOTOR CYCLES

	Ketten	+Sidecars	Other
Authorised Strength	338	140	173
Ready for Action	20	14	62
Short term repair		1	22

CARS

	Cross country	Normal/Road
Authorised Strength	767	84
Ready for Action	345	28
Short term repair	62	5

TRUCKS

	Maultiere	Cross country	Normal/Road
Authorised Strength	125	1046	877
Ready for Action	4	192	572
Short term repair	-	17	22

TRACKED PRIME MOVERS

	1-5 Tons	8-18 Tons
Authorised Strength	98	104
Ready for Action	21	33
Short term repair	2	3

WEAPONS	Authorised Strength	Actual Strength	MGs
Heavy Anti-tank Guns	28	21	
Artillery Guns	41	22	
MG (MG 42)	1102 (102)	1036 (98)	
Rifle Kar 98	11,685	11,991	
M. Pistol 38/40	1712	1609	
8cm Mortar	62	61	
2cm Flak 38	50	36	
2cm Flakvierl	10	7	
3.7cm Flak 37	9	9	
88mm Flak 37	18	12	

2.SS PANZER DIVISION
'Das Reich'

1st July 1944

- Divisionstab (Divisional HQ)
  100% Manpower
  2 LMG

  Div. Kartenstelle (Mapping Section)
  87.5% Manpower

  Div. Begleitkompanie (Divisional Security Company)
  95% Manpower
  12 LMG. 4 HMG. 2 x 81mm Mortars

- SS PANZER REGIMENT 2 (Tank Regiment)
  Regimentstab (Regimental HQ)
  100% Manpower
  3 *Panthers*. 5 Pz IV. 6 x SdKfz 7/1 Quad 2cm Flakwagens. 4 LMG

  1. Panzer Abteilung (1st Tank Battalion)
  100% Manpower
  69 *Panthers*. 5 x Medium Armoured Halftracks (2 x SdKfz 251/8; 3 x SdKfz 251/7). 25 LMG

  2. Panzer Abteilung (2nd Tank Battalion)
  100% Manpower
  68 Pz IV. 13 StuGs. 5 Medium Armoured Halftracks (2 x SdKfz 251/8; 3 x SdKfz 251/7).
  44 LMG

- SS PANZERGRENADIER REGIMENT 3 DEUTSCHLAND'
  (Motorised Infantry Regiment)
  Regimentstab (Regimental HQ)
  100% Manpower
  7 LMG

  1. Bataillon (Partially Motorised)
  100% Manpower
  63 LMG. 12 HMG. 8 x 81mm Mortars. 4 x 7.5cm Inf. Guns (Towed). 3 x 7.5cm Pak (Towed)

  2. Bataillon (Partially Motorised)
  100% Manpower
  60 LMG. 12 HMG. 8 x 81mm Mortars. 4 x 7.5cm Inf. Guns (Towed). 3 x 7.5cm Pak (Towed)

  3. Bataillon (Partially Motorised)
  100% Manpower
  60 LMG. 12 HMG. 8 x 81mm Mortars. 4 x 7.5cm Inf. Guns (Towed). 3 x 7.5cm Pak (Towed)

  Flak Kompanie (Anti-aircraft Company)
  100% Manpower
  12 x 2cm Flak Guns (Towed). 4 LMG

  Infanteriegeschutz Kompanie (Infantry Gun Company)
  100% Manpower
  6 x 15cm SP Infantry Guns. 5 Medium Armoured Halftracks (4 x SdKfz 251/1; 1 x SdKfz 251/3).
  7 LMG

  Pionier Kompanie (Engineer Company)
  100% Manpower
  18 LMG. 2 HMG. 2 x 81mm Mortars

- SS PANZERGRENADIER REGIMENT 4 'DER FÜHRER'
  (Armoured Infantry Regiment)
  Regimentstab (Regimental HQ) (Armoured)
  100% Manpower
  20 Medium Armoured Halftracks (including 7 x SdKfz 251/3). 20 LMG

  1. Bataillon (Partially Motorised)
  100% Manpower
  57 LMG. 12 HMG. 8 x 81mm Mortars. 3 x 7.5cm Pak (Towed)

  2. Bataillon (Partially Motorised)
  100% Manpower
  57 LMG. 12 HMG. 8 x 81mm Mortars. 3 x 7.5cm Pak (Towed)

3. Bataillon (Armoured)
100% Manpower
98 Medium Armoured Halftracks (including 11 x SdKfz 251/3; 12 x SdKfz 251/9; 12 x SdKfz 251/2).
110 LMG. 12 HMG. 12 x 81mm Mortars.
12 x 7.5cm KwK L/24 (Halftrack mounted).
3 x 7.5cm Pak (Towed). 6 Flamethrowers

Flak Kompanie (Anti-aircraft Company)
100% Manpower
12 x 2cm Flak Guns (Towed). 2 LMG

Infanteriegeschutz Kompanie (Infantry Gun Company)
100% Manpower
6 x 15cm SP Infantry Guns. 4 x 7.5cm Infantry Guns (Towed). 5 Medium Armoured Halftracks (4 x SdKfz 251/1; 1 x 251/3). 37 LMG

Pionier Kompanie (Engineer Company)
100% Manpower
18 LMG. 2 HMG. 1 x 81mm Mortar

- SS AUFKLÄRUNGS ABTEILUNG 2
(Armoured Reconnaissance Battalion)
100% Manpower
35 Medium Armoured Halftracks. 62 Light Armoured Halftracks

Abteilungstab (Company HQ)
Medium Armoured Halftracks. 9 LMG

1. (Armoured Car) Company
No Armoured Cars. 20 LMG

2. (Armoured Reconnaissance) Company
Light Armoured Halftracks. 27 LMG. 2 x 81mm Mortars

3.(Armoured Reconnaissance) Company
Light Armoured Halftracks. 30 LMG. 4 HMG.
2 x 81mm Mortars

4.(Heavy) Company
Medium Armoured Halftracks. 21 LMG. 6 x 7.5cm KwK L/24 (Halftrack mounted). 2 x 7.5cm Infantry Guns (Towed). 3 x 7.5cm Pak (Towed)

Versorgungs Kompanie (Supply Company)
4 LMG

- SS STURMGESCHÜTZ ABTEILUNG 2
(Assault Gun Battalion)
87% Manpower
26 Assault Guns (7.5cm). 33 LMG

- SS PANZER ARTILLERIE REGIMENT 2
(Armoured Artillery Regiment)
Regimentstab (Regimental HQ)
100% Manpower
20 LMG. 1 SdKfz 7/1 Quad 2cm Flakwagon

1. Abteilung (Armoured Battalion)
100% Manpower
5 *Hummel*. 6 *Wespe*. 3 Pz III Observation Tanks.
4 Medium Armoured Halftracks. 3 x 2cm Flak Guns (Towed). 32 LMG

2. Abteilung (Towed Battalion)
100% Manpower
12 x 105mm LeFH 18. 14 LMG

3. Abteilung (Towed Battalion)
100% Manpower
2 x 105mm LeFH 18. 7 LMG

4. Abteilung (Towed Battalion)
100% Manpower
4 x 150mm SFH 18. 4 x 105mm Kanone. 12 LMG

- SS FLAKABTEILUNG (Anti-aircraft Battalion)
100% Manpower
12 x 88mm Flak Guns (Towed). 9 x SdKfz 7/2 3.7cm Flakwagons. 9 x 2cm Flak Guns (Towed).
4 x 60cm Searchlights. 18 LMG

- SS PANZER PIONIER BATAILLON
(Armoured Engineer Battalion)
100% Manpower
Stabs Kompanie (Company HQ)(Partially Armoured)
10 Medium Armoured Halftracks. 16 LMG

1. Kompanie (Armoured)
25 Medium Armoured Halftracks. 39 LMG.
2 HMG. 2 x 81mm Mortars. 6 Flamethrowers

2. Kompanie (Motorised)
17 LMG. 2 HMG. 2 x 81mm Mortars.
6 Flamethrowers

3. Kompanie (Motorised)
18 LMG. 2 HMG. 2 x 81mm Mortars.
6 Flamethrowers

Brucken Kolonne 'K' (Bridging Column – Motorised)
3 LMG

- SS PANZER NACHRICHTEN ABTEILUNG 2
(Armoured Signals Battalion)
100% Manpower
18 Medium Armoured Halftracks (including
10 x SdKfz 251/3). 16 LMG

- SS NACHSCHUBTRUPPEN 2
(Divisional Supply Battalion)
95% Manpower
6 Transportation Companies. 1 Supply Company.
1 Workshop Company. 62 LMG

- SS INSTADSETZUNGS ABTEILUNG 2
(Workshop Battalion)
82% Manpower
3 Workshop/Repair Companies. 1 Supply Company.
16 LMG

- SS WIRTSCHAFTS BATAILLON 2
(Commissary Battalion)
96% Manpower
1 Bakery Company. 1 Butcher Company.
1 Administration Company. 1 Field Post Office.
15 LMG

- SS SANITÄTS ABTEILUNG 2 (Medical Battalion)
70% Manpower
3 Ambulance Columns. 2 Medical Compaies.
1 Field Hospital. 7 LMG

- SS FELDGENDARMERIE KOMPANIE 2
(Military Police Company)
81.5% Manpower
11 LMG

9.SS PANZER DIVISION
'Hohenstaufen'

Formed in early 1943, 'Hohenstaufen' spent the next twelve months in France training and equipping. Initially a Panzer-Grenadier unit, it converted to a Panzer Division in the autumn of 1943.

In March 1944, as part of II.SS Panzer Korps, 9.SS Panzer Division transferred to the Eastern Front. It remained in the east until June 1944 when it was ordered to Normandy, arriving there towards the end of that month.

On 1st June 1944, 9.SS Panzer Division had the following units on strength:

Stab der Division
SS Panzer Regiment 9*
SS Panzer Grenadier Regiment 19
SS Panzer Grenadier Regiment 20
SS Panzer Aufklärungs Abteilung 9
SS Panzer Artillerie Regiment 9
SS Flak Abteilung 9
SS Panzer Pionier Bataillon 9
SS Panzer Nachrichten Abteilung 9
SS Felders Bataillon 9
SS Divisionsnachschubtruppen 9
SS Panzer Instandsetzungs Abteilung 9
SS Wirtschafts Bataillon 9
SS Sanitäts Abteilung 9
SS Feldgendarmerie Kompanie 9
SS Kriegsberichter Zug 9

- SS Panzer Regiment 9

* On this date the Panzer regiment was without its I. (Panther) Abteilung as it was still equipping at Mailly-le-Camp. It joined up with the Division en-route to Normandy.

I. Abteilung began equipping with *Panther* tanks in January 1944. The unit was expected to be up to full strength by 30/6/44.

Tanks received by I. Abteilung

Delivered by 1/6/44	40 Pz V*
Delivered between 1/6/44-8/6/44	39 Pz V*
TOTAL	79 Pz V

(Including 6 Command Tanks)

Tanks/Assault Guns on strength with II. Abteilung

	48 Pz IV
Delivered by 1/6/44 {	40 StuG
	3 Pz III*
TOTAL	9 Panzers/StuGs

**Command Tank*

Also on strength in the same period

SdKfz 7/1 Quad 2cm Flakwagen	6
Bergepanther (Recovery Tanks)	2
Medium armoured halftracks	6 (SdKfz 251)

On 28/6/44 SS Panzer Regiment 9 had the following vehicles on strength:

73 Pz V (including 2 Command Tanks)
48 Pz IV
40 StuG
6 Pz III Command Tanks
2 *Bergepanther* (Recovery Tanks)
4 SdKfz 7/1 Quad 2cm Flakwagons
6 Medium Armoured Haltftracks

- SS Panzerjäger Abteilung 9

On 1st June SS Panzerjäger Abteilung 9 was still awaiting delivery of its Jagdpanzer IV's. It did not become operational until late summer.

SS Panzer Regiment 9
Tank Strengths 1st July 1944 – 15th August 1944

Between 1/7/44 and 15/8/44, SS Panzer Regiment 9 had the following Panzers and StuGs ready for action:

Date	Pz V	Pz IV	StuG	Bef Pz
1/7/44	27	9	22	
8/7/44	50	19	25	5
12/7/44	35	13	12	4
14/7/44	38	19	16	4
15/7/44	41	19	22	4
19/7/44	24	22	17	
20/7/44	8	19	16	
21/7/44	8	19	19	
23/7/44	10	22	13	
24/7/44	10	22	19	
26/7/44	18	18	11	
27/7/44	26	18	11	
28/7/44	26	22	22	
31/7/44*	29	22	27	
2/8/44	23	15	23	
3/8/44	18	7	9	
7/8/44	7	9	7	
10/8/44	11	9	8	
12/8/44	13	10	15	
15/8/44	15	11	14	

**On this date Funk Lenk Kompanie 9 (Radio-controlled Vehicles), was temporarily attached to the division*

9.SS Panzer Division
Original German Strength Report
1st June 1944

...me Kommandosache

...ung vom 1. Juni 1944

Anlage 1 Ia 592/44 g.Kdos

Verband: 9.SS-Panzer-Division "Hohenstaufen"

Unterstellungsverhältnis: II.SS-Pz.Korps.

31

12 Ausfertigungen

7. Ausfertigung

Gen. Kdo. II.SS-Pz. Kps. Umlauf

Ia Nr. 384/44 g.Kdos. 31

...nelle Lage am Stichtag der Meldung

...sonal:

	Soll	Fehl
	619	161
	4232	852
	14020	268
	1055	1003
...gesamt	18871	1281

c) Seit der Berichtszeit eingetroffener Ersatz

	Ersatz	Genesene
Offiziere	11	7
Uffz. und Mannsch.	236	123

...Verluste und sonstige Abgänge: in der Berichtszeit vom 16.5. bis 31.5.1944

	tot	verw.	verm.	krank	sonst.
...iziere	1	-	-	7	18
...Uffz. und Mannsch.	11	5	4	230	315
...gesamt	12	5	4	237	333

d) über 1 Jahr nicht beurlaubt:

insgesamt: 198 Köpfe 1,05 % d. Iststärke

daron:	12–18 Monate	18–24 Monate	über 24 Monate
	190	6	2

Platzkarten im Berichtsmonat zugewiesen: 648

2. Materielle Lage:

		Gepanzerte Fahrzeuge							Kraftfahrzeuge				
									Kräder			Pkw	
		Stu. Gesch.	III	IV	V	VI	Schtz.Pz. Pz.Sp. Art.Pz.B. (o.Pz.Fu.Wg)	Art. Pak Sf	Ketten	mit angetr. Bwg	Sonst.	gel.	o
Soll (Zahlen)		40	12	58	-	-	335	25	117	251	343	785	93
[illegible]	Zahlenm.	38	4	41	-	-	259	24	6	124	391	698	37
	in % des Solls	95	33,3	71	-	-	77,2	96	5,1	49,9	114	88,8	398
kurzfristiger Instandsetzung (bis 3 Wochen)	Zahlenm.	2	2	5	-	-	34	-	-	39	161	118	94
	in % des Solls	5	16,6	8,6	-	-	10,8	-	-	15,5	52,9	15	1oo,1

		noch Kraftfahrzeuge							Waffen			
		Lkw				Ketten-Fahrzeuge						
		Maultier	gel.	O	Tonnage	Zgkw.		RSO	s. Pak	Art. Gesch	M.G. x)	Sonstig. Waffen
Soll (Zahlen)		78	1096	868	5024	156 [*)]	99 [**)]	-	31	47	988	-
einsatzbereit	Zahlenm.	69	345	967	2901	80	49	1	27	47	(949)	-
	in % des Solls	88,5	32,4	111,8	57,8	45,4	49,6	-	87	100	96	100
in kurzfristiger Instandsetzung bis 3 Woch.	Zahlenm.	23	53	199	578	22	32	6	-	-	-	-
	in % des Solls	29,6	4,8	23	11,4	14,1	32,4	-	-	-	-	-

ohne I./SS-Pz.Rgt.9

x) ohne eingebaute M.G.

eingebaute M.G.: Soll = 547

Ist = 479 (336)

*) Zugkw. mit 1–5 t **) Zugkw. mit 8–18 t

( ) davon MG 42

RH10/318

9.SS Panzer Division
Original German Organisation Chart
1st June 1944

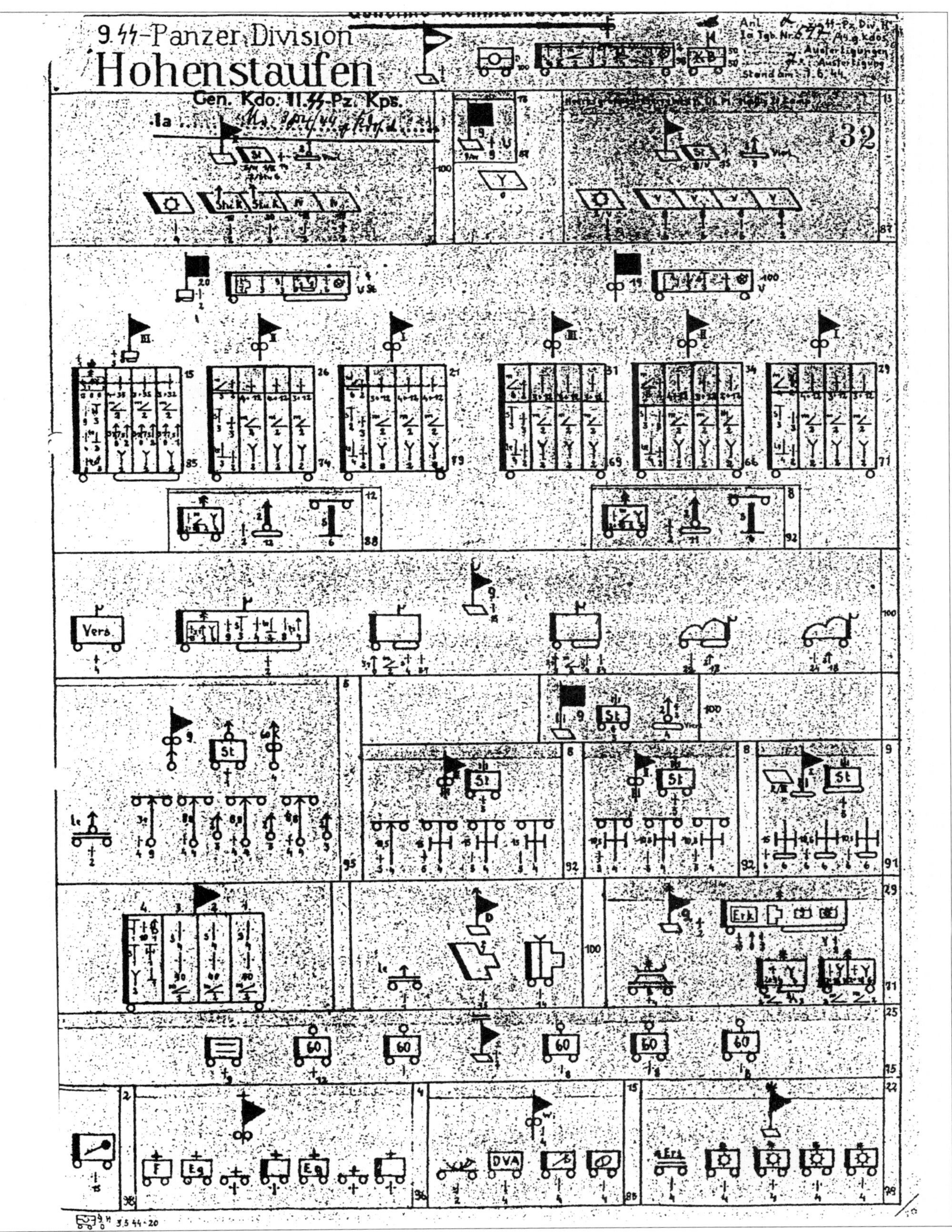

9.SS Panzer Division
Strength Report: 1st June 1944
Under Command of II.SS Panzer Korps

MANPOWER

	Authorised Strength	Shortages	Actual
Officers	619	161	458
NCOs	4232	852	3380
Other Ranks	14,020	268	13,752
Hiwis	1055	1003	52
TOTAL	18,871	1281	17,590

LOSSES BETWEEN 16/5/44 – 31/5/44

	Dead	Wounded	Missing	Hospital	Other Cases
Officers	1	-	-	7	18
NCOs / Other Ranks	11	5	4	230	315
TOTAL	12	5	4	237	333

REPLACEMENTS/ARRIVALS

	Replacements	Recovered
Officers	11	7
NCOs / Other Ranks	236	123

OVER 1 YEAR ABSENT FROM DIVISION (NON-LEAVE)

TOTAL	198
Of That:	
12 to 18 Months	190
19 to 24 Months	6
Over 24 Months	2
Places allocated in Monthly Report	648

9.SS Panzer Division
Strength Report: 1st June 1944
Material Stocks

ARMOURED VEHICLES

	StuG	Pz III	Pz IV	Other AFVs	Art (SP)
Authorised Strength	40	12	58	335	25
Ready for Action	38	4	41	259	24
Short term repair	2	2	5	34	0

MOTOR CYCLES

	Ketten	+Sidecars	Other
Authorised Strength	117	251	343
Ready for Action	6	124	391
Short term repair	0	39	161

CARS

	Cross country	Normal/Road
Authorised Strength	785	93
Ready for Action	698	37
Short term repair	118	94

TRUCKS

	Maultiere	Cross country	Normal/Road
Authorised Strength	78	1096	868
Ready for Action	69	345	967
Short term repair	23	53	199

TRACKED PRIME MOVERS

	1-5 Tons	8-18 Tons	RSO
Authorised Strength	156	99	0
Ready for Action	80	49	1
Short term repair	22	32	6

WEAPONS	Heavy Anti-tank Guns	Artillery Guns	MG
Authorised Strength	31	47	988
Ready for Action	27	47	(949) *Installed MGs 479*
Short term Repair	0	0	

1. (Panther) Abteilung
9.SS Panzer Division
Original German Strength Report: 1st June 1944

Ia Tgb. Nr. / geh. 50

Meldung vom 1. Juni 1944

Verband: I./SS-Panzer-Regiment "Hohenstaufen"

Unterstellungsverhältnis:

1. **Personelle Lage** am Stichtag der Meldung:

a) **Personal:**

	Soll	Fehl
Offiziere	34	8
Uffz.	353	186
Mannsch.	597	+ 236
Hiwi.	–	–
Insgesamt	984	+ 42

b) **Verluste und sonstige Abgänge** in der Berichtszeit vom 16.5. bis 31.5.44

	tot.	verw.	verm.	krank	sonst.
Offiziere					1
Uffz. und Mannsch.	1				
Insgesamt	1				1

c) **In der Berichtszeit eingetroffener Ersatz:**

	Ersatz	Genesene
Offiziere	–	–
Uffz. und Mannsch.	1o	5

d) **über 1 Jahr nicht beurlaubt:**

insgesamt: – Köpfe – % d. Iststärke

davon:	12-18 Monate	19-24 Monate	über 24 Monate

Platzkarten im Berichtsmonat zugewiesen:

2. **Materielle Lage:**

		Gepanzerte Fahrzeuge							Krafttahrzeuge				
		Sd.Kfz. 251/7	Berge Pz	Befehls Pz	V	Sd.Kfz 251/8	Schtz. Pz. Pz. Sp. Art. Pz. B. (o. Pz. Fu. Wg.)	Pak SF	Kräder Ketten	Kräder m. angetr. Bwg.	Kräder m	Pkw gel.	Pkw O
Soll (Zahlen)		3	2	3	73	2	3	–	16	–	5	37	–
einsatzbereit	zahlenm.	3	2	3	27	–	3	–	5	–	27	26	–
	in % des Solls	100	100	100	37	–	100	–	31	–	540	70	–
In kurzfristiger Instandsetzung (bis 3 Wochen)	zahlenm.	–	–	–	4	–	–	–	–	–	–	–	–
	in % des Solls	–	–	–	5	–	–	–	–	–	–	–	–

		noch Kraftfahrzeuge							Waffen			
		Maultiere	Kfz.1bc + Lkw gel.	Kom. Lkw O	Tonnage	Ketten-Fahrzeuge Zgkw.*	Ketten-Fahrzeuge Zgkw.**	Ketten-Fahrzeuge [illegible]	s Pak	Art.-Gesch. Kw.K.	MG. ( )	sonstige Waffen
Soll (Zahlen)		8	2+97	[illegible]	351	9	3+7	4	–	76	172 (15)	Karb. - 436 Pist. - 418 M.Pi. - 137
einsatzbereit	zahlenm.	15	– 56	–	195	9	3+2	1	–	36	101 (32)	Karb. - 513 Pist. - 640 M.Pi. - 37
	in % des Solls	188	– 58	–	56	100	50	25	–	46	59 (213)	Karb. - 118 Pist. - 153 M.Pi. - 27
in kurzfristiger Instandsetzung (bis 3 Wochen)	zahlenm.	–	–	–	–	–	–	–	–	–	–	Karb. - 4 Pist. - 5 M.Pi. - 0
	in % des Solls	–	–	–	–	–	–	–	–	–	–	Karb. - 1 Pist. - 1 M.Pi. - 0

*) Zgkw. mit 1–5 t, **) Zgkw. mit 8–18 t
( ) davon MG. 42

3. **Pferdefehlstellen:**

Anl. zu Nr. 00234 /44 g.
Gen. Insp. d. Pz. Tr.

1 (Panther) Abteilung
9.SS Panzer Division
Strength Report: 1st June 1944

MANPOWER

	Authorised Strength	Shortages	Actual
TOTAL	984	-	1026

LOSSES BETWEEN 16/5/44 – 31/5/44

	Dead	Wounded	Missing	Hospital	Other Cases
Officers	-	-	-	-	1
NCOs / Other Ranks	1	-	-	-	-
TOTAL	1				1

REPLACEMENTS/ARRIVALS

	Replacements	Recovered
NCOs / Other Ranks	10	5

ARMOURED VEHICLES	Bef Pz	BergePz	Pz V	MSPW	Other AFVs
Authorised Strength	3	2	73	5	3
Ready for Action	3	2	27	3	3
Short term repair	-	-	4	-	-

MOTOR CYCLES	Ketten	Medium
Authorised Strength	16	5
Ready for Action	5	27
Short term repair	-	-

CARS	Cross country	Normal/Road
Authorised Strength	37	-
Ready for Action	26	-
Short term repair	-	-

TRUCKS	Maultiere	Kfz 100	Cross country	Command
Authorised Strength	8	2	97	1
Ready for Action	15	-	56	-
Short term repair	-	-	-	-

TRACKED PRIME MOVERS	1-5 Tons	8-18 Tons	Combat Trailers
Authorised Strength	9	3+7	4
Ready for Action	9	3+2	1
Short term repair	-	-	-

WEAPONS	MG	MG 42	Rifle Kar 98	M. Pistol	Pistol
Authorised Strength	172	15	436	137	418
Actual Strength	101	32	513	37	645

9.SS Panzer Division
Original German Weapons Stocks List
1st June 1944

Deutsche Waffen in Kriegsgliederung nicht enthalten.

11 393	Karabiner 98 k
165	Gewehre 41
5 187	Pistolen
1 035	M.Pi. 38/40
322	M.Pi. 38/40 in gp. Kfz.
205	Karabiner m.Zielfernrohr
540	Gewehrgranatgerät

9.SS PANZER DIVISION
'Hohenstaufen'

1st June 1944

- Divisionstab (Divisional HQ)
  100% Manpower
  2 LMG

  Div. Kartenstelle (Mapping Section)
  100% Manpower

  Div. Begleitkompanie (Divisional Security Company)
  96% Manpower
  15 LMG. 4 HMG. 2 x 81mm Mortars. 3 x 5cm Pak (Towed). 4 x SdKfz 10/4 2cm Flak (SP)

  Kriegsberichter (Divisional War Correspondence Unit)
  50% Manpower

- SS PANZER REGIMENT 9 (Tank Regiment)
  Regimentstab (Regimental HQ)
  87% Manpower
  7 Pz IV. 9 LMG

  1. Panzer Abteilung (1st Tank Battalion)
  87% Manpower
  40 *Panthers*. 2 *Bergpanthers*. 3 x SdKfz 7/1 Quad 2cm Flakwagens. 37 LMG

  2. Panzer Abteilung (2nd Tank Battalion)
  100% Manpower
  41 Pz IV. 40 StuGs. 1 Pz III. 3 x SdKfz 7/1 Quad 2cm Flakwagens. 26 LMG

- SS PANZERGRENADIER REGIMENT 19
  (Motorised Infantry Regiment)
  Regimentstab (Regimental HQ)
  100% Manpower
  3 x 7.5cm Pak (Towed). 9 LMG

  1. Bataillon (Motorised)
  71% Manpower
  43 LMG. 10 HMG. 10 x 81mm Mortars. 4 x 7.5cm Inf. Guns (Towed). 3 x 7.5cm Pak (Towed).
  6 Flamethrowers

  2. Bataillon (Motorised)
  66% Manpower
  43 LMG. 9 HMG. 11 x 81mm Mortars. 4 x 7.5cm Inf. Guns (Towed). 3 x 7.5cm Pak (Towed)

  3. Bataillon (Motorised)
  69% Manpower
  43 LMG. 9 HMG. 12 x 81mm Mortars. 4 x 7.5cm Inf. Guns (Towed). 3 x 7.5cm Pak (Towed).
  6 Flamethrowers

  Flak Kompanie (Anti-aircraft Company)
  92% Manpower
  11 x SdKfz 10/4 2cm Flak (SP). 2 LMG

  Infanteriegeschutz Kompanie (Infantry Gun Company)
  92% Manpower
  6 x 15cm Infantry Guns (Towed)

  Pionier Kompanie (Engineer Company)
  92% Manpower
  18 LMG. 2 HMG. 2 x 81mm Mortars.
  6 Flamethrowers

- SS PANZERGRENADIER REGIMENT 20
  (Armoured Infantry Regiment)
  Regimentstab (Regimental HQ) (Armoured)
  96% Manpower
  About 20 Medium Armoured Halftracks. 19 LMG. 3 x 7.5cm Pak (Towed). 1 Flamethrower

  1. Bataillon (Motorised)
  79% Manpower
  43 LMG. 11 HMG. 12 x 81mm Mortars. 4 x 7.5cm Inf. Guns (Towed). 2 x 7.5cm Pak (Towed)

  2. Bataillon (Partially Motorised)
  74% Manpower
  43 LMG. 11 HMG. 11 x 81mm Mortars. 3 x 7.5cm Inf. Guns (Towed). 3 x 7.5cm Pak (Towed).
  6 Flamethrowers

3. Bataillon (Armoured)
85% Manpower
About 90 Medium Armoured Halftracks (including 8 x SdKfz 251/9; 6 x SdKfz 251/2). 136 LMG. 10 HMG. 6 x 81mm Mortars. 8 x 7.5cm KwK L/24 (Halftrack mounted). 3 x 7.5cm Inf. Guns (Towed). 3 x 7.5cm Pak (Towed). 6 Flamethrowers

Flak Kompanie (Anti-aircraft Company)
88% Manpower
12 x SdKfz 10/4 2cm Flak (SP). 2 LMG

Infanteriegeschutz Kompanie (Infantry Gun Company)
88% Manpower
6 x 15cm Infantry Guns (Towed)

Pionier Kompanie (Engineer Company)
88% Manpower
18 LMG. 2 HMG. 2 x 81mm Mortars. 4 Flamethrowers

- SS AUFKLÄRUNGS ABTEILUNG 9
(Armoured Reconnaissance Battalion)
100% Manpower

Abteilungstab (HQ Company)
Medium Armoured Halftracks. 15 LMG

1. Kompanie (Armoured Car Company)
12 x '4 Wheeled' Armoured Cars (including SdKfz 221, 222, 223). 6 x '8 Wheeled' Armoured Cars (including SdKfz 231, 232). 24 LMG. 18 x 2cm KwK (Armoured Car mounted)

2. Kompanie (Armoured Car Company)
Light Armoured Halftracks (including 13 x 250/9). 22 LMG. 13 x 2cm KwK (Armoured Car mounted)

3. Kompanie (Armoured Reconnaissance Company)
Light Armoured Halftracks. 54 LMG. 4 HMG. 2 x 81mm Mortars. 3 x 3.7cm Pak

4. Kompanie (Armoured Reconnaissance Company)
Light Armoured Halftracks. 57 LMG. 4 HMG. 2 x 81mm Mortars

5. Kompanie (Heavy Company)
Medium Armoured Halftracks. 36 LMG. 4 x 7.5cm KwK L/24 (Halftrack mounted). 2 x 7.5cm Infantry Guns (Towed). 3 x 7.5cm Pak (Towed). 1 x 3.7cm Pak (Halftrack mounted). 6 Flamethrowers

Versorgungs Kompanie (Supply Company)
4 LMG

- SS PANZER ARTILLERIE REGIMENT 9
(Armoured Artillery Regiment)
Regimentstab (Regimental HQ)
100% Manpower
7 LMG. 4 x SdKfz 7/1 Quad 2cm Flakwagens

1. Abteilung (Armoured Battalion)
91% Manpower
6 *Hummel*. 12 *Wespe*. 2 Pz III Observation Tanks. 23 LMG

2. Abteilung (Towed Battalion)
92% Manpower
12 x 105mm LeFH 18. 20 LMG.

3. Abteilung (Towed Battalion)
92% Manpower
12 x 150mm SFH 18. 4 x 105mm Kanone. 25 LMG

- SS FLAKABTEILUNG 9 (Anti-aircraft Battalion)
95% Manpower
12 x 88mm Flak Guns (Towed). 9 x 3.7cm Flak Guns (Towed). 9 x 2cm Flak Guns (Towed). 4 x 60cm Searchlights. 19 LMG

- SS PANZER PIONIER BATAILLON 9
(Armoured Engineer Battalion)
71% Manpower
Stabs Kompanie (Company HQ)(Partially Armoured)
Medium Armoured Halftracks. 17 LMG

1. Kompanie (Motorised)
18 LMG. 2 HMG. 2 x 81mm Mortars. 6 Flamethrowers

2. Kompanie (Motorised)
18 LMG. 2 HMG. 2 x 81mm Mortars. 6 Flamethrowers

3. Kompanie (Armoured)
Medium Armoured Halftracks. 46 LMG. 2 HMG. 2 x 81mm Mortars. 6 Flamethrowers. 3 Panzerbüchse

Brucken Kolonne (Bridging Column – Motorised)
4 LMG

- SS PANZER NACHRICHTEN ABTEILUNG 9
  (Armoured Signals Battalion)
  100% Manpower
  30 LMG

- SS FELDERS BATAILLON 9 (Replacement Battalion)
  130 LMG. 12 HMG. 5 x 81mm Mortars.
  2 Flamethrowers. 1 x 105mm LeFH 18 (ITowed).
  1 x 7.5cm Pak (Towed). 1 x 5.0cm Pak (Towed).
  1 x 7.5cm Inf. Gun (Towed). 1 x 2cm Flak Gun (Towed)

- SS NACHSCHUBTRUPPEN 9
  (Divisional Supply Battalion)
  75% Manpower
  6 Transportation Companies. 1 Supply Company.
  53 LMG

- SS INSTADSETZUNGS ABTEILUNG 9
  (Workshop Battalion)
  78% Manpower
  4 Workshop/Repair Companies. 1 Supply Company.
  20 LMG

- SS WIRTSCHAFTS BATAILLON 9
  (Commissary Battalion)
  85% Manpower
  1 Bakery Company. 1 Butcher Company.
  1 Administration Company. 1 Field Post Office.
  18 LMG

- SS SANITÄTS ABTEILUNG 9 (Medical Battalion)
  96% Manpower
  2 Ambulance Columns. 2 Medical Companies.
  2 Field Hospitals.

- SS FELDGENDARMERIE KOMPANIE 9
  (Military Police Company)
  98% Manpower
  15 LMG

9.SS PANZER DIVISION
'Hohenstaufen'

28th June 1944

In early June the Panzer Regiment's II Abteilung underwent a change of organisation:
StuGs moved from 7 & 8 Companies to 5 & 6 Companies.
Pz IVs moved from 5 & 6 Companies to 7 & 8 Companies (changes did not actually occur).

SS PANZER REGIMENT 9. 28.6.44

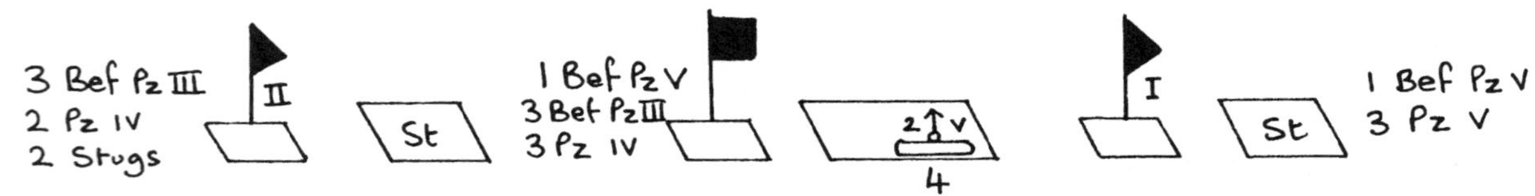

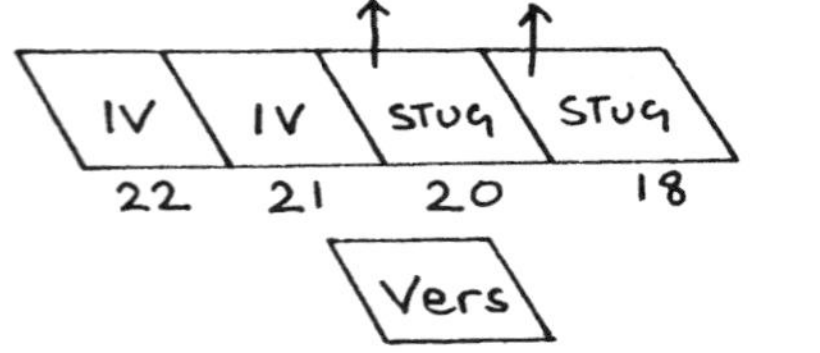

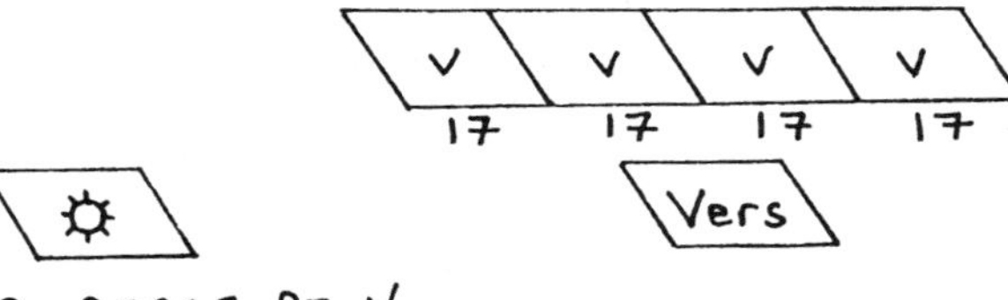

2 BERGE PZ V

NOTE.

IN EARLY JUNE THE REGIMENT'S II ABTEILUNG UNDERWENT A CHANGE OF ORGANIZATION –

STUGS MOVED FROM 7 + 8 COMPANIES TO 5 + 6 COMPANIES.
MK IV S MOVED FROM 5 + 6 COMPANIES TO 7 + 8 COMPANIES.

10.SS PANZER DIVISION
'Frundsberg'

'Frundsberg' was formed in early 1943 as a Panzer-Grenadier Division. It converted to a Panzer Division in the autumn of that year. Its first twelve months were spent training and equipping in France.

In March 1944 it transferred to the Eastern Front as part of II.SS Panzer Korps. Within three months it was again transferred, this time to Normandy, where it arrived in late June.

On 1st June 1944, 10.SS Panzer Division had the following units on strength:

Stab der Division
SS Panzer Regiment 10*
SS Panzer Grenadier Regiment 21
SS Panzer Grenadier Regiment 22
SS Panzer Aufklärungs Abteilung 10
SS Panzer Artillerie Regiment 10
SS Flak Abteilung 10
SS Panzer Pionier Bataillon 10
SS Panzer Nachrichten Abteilung 10
SS Felders Bataillon 10
SS Divisionsnachschubtruppen 10
SS Panzer Instandsetzungs Abteilung 10
SS Wirtschafts Bataillon 10
SS Sanitäts Abteilung 10
SS Feldgendarmerie Kompanie 10
SS Kriegsberichter Zug 10

- SS Panzer Regiment 1*0*

* SS Panzer Regiment 10 fought throughout the Normandy Campaign without its I *(Panther)* Abteilung which was equipping at Mailly-le-Camp.

Tanks received by I. Abteilung

Delivered by 1/6/44	4 Pz V
Delivered in July 1944	1 Pz III*
Delivered in July 1944	6 Pz V
TOTAL	10 Pz V 1 Pz III

**Command Tank*

Tanks/Assault Guns on strength by II. Abteilung

Delivered by 1/6/44 {	39 Pz IV 38 StuG 3 Pz III*
TOTAL	80 Panzers/StuGs

**Command Tanks*

Also on strength in the same period

SdKfz 7/1 Quad 2cm Flakwagen	6
Light Armoured Halftracks	2 (SdKfz 250)
Medium armoured halftracks	6 (SdKfz 251)

- SS Panzerjäger Abteilung1*0*

SS Panzerjäger Abteilung 10 was still awaiting delivery of its Jagdpanzer IVs and it did not become operational until August 1944

SS Panzer Regiment 10
Tank Strengths: 2nd July 1944 – 7th August 1944

Between 2/7/44 and 7/8/44, SS Panzer Regiment 10 had the following Panzers and StuGs ready for action:

Date	Pz IV	StuG	Bef Pz III
27/44	20	25	2
8/7/44	27	25	1
11/7/44	18	10	1
13/7/44	16	10	1
15/7/44	16	12	1
16/7/44	17	13	1
17/7/44	10	9	2
18/7/44	12	6	2
19/7/44	12	12	1
207/44	14	14	1
26/7/44	14	11	0
29/7/44	16	16	0
4/8/44	20	8	1
7/8/44	5	5	3

10.SS Panzer Division
Original German Strength Report
1st June 1944

Meldung vom 1. 6. 1943 [illegible] **Verband:** 10. SS-Panzer-Division

Unterstellungsverhältnis: II. SS-Pz.Korps

35

Soll-Stärken ohne [illegible] Flak-Zug sowie I./Pz.Rgt.10, jedoch mit [illegible] Abt.10,

1. Personelle Lage am Stichtag der Meldung:

a) Personal:

	Soll	Fehl
Offiziere	595	169
Uffz.	3 874	1 442
Mannsch.	13 526	373
Hiwi	(1 004)	([illegible]93)
Insgesamt	17 995	1 984

\+ [illegible] Hiwi-Anwärter.

b) Verluste und sonstige Abgänge in der Berichtszeit vom 1. 5. bis 1. 6. 44

	tot	verw.	verm.	krank	sonst.
Offiziere	1	2	-	1	6
Uffz. und Mannsch.	21	17		203	345
Insgesamt	22	19	-	204	351

c) In der Berichtszeit eingetroffener Ersatz:

	Ersatz	Genesene
Offiziere	1	1
Uffz. und Mannsch.	331	142

Gen. Kdo. II.SS-Pz. Kps.

Ia [illegible]

d) Über 1 Jahr nicht beurlaubt:

insgesamt: 287 Köpfe 1,7 % d. Iststärke

davon:	12-18 Monate	19-24 Monate	über 24 Monate
	284	3	-

Plankarten im Berichtsmonat zugewiesen: 615

2. Materielle Lage: Ausstattung I. Pz.Rgt.10, Flak-Zug und [illegible]

In Abänderung der vom SS-F.H.A. befohlenen Sollstärken, der Kfz.-[illegible] vom II.SS-Pz.Korps befohlen

		Gepanzerte Fahrzeuge: Stu. Gesch.	III	IV	V	VI (Hummel) (OSt)	Schtz.Pz. Pz.Sp. Art.Pz.B.	Pak SF	Krafttfahrzeuge: Kräder: Ketten	m. angetr. Bwg.	sonst.	Pkw: gel.	O
Soll (Zahlen)		44	3	54	3	9 (16)	349	-	111	-	566	733	92
einsatzbereit	zahlenm.	34	3	32	-	7 (12)	287	-	6	88	369	663	70
	in % des Solls	77,3	100	59,1	-	77,8 (75)	32,2	-	5,4	15,7	65,2	91,1	76,1
in kurzfristiger Instandsetzung (bis 3 Wochen)	zahlenm.	1	-	1	-	1 (2)	10	-	-	21	52	20	37
	in % des Solls	2,3	-	1,9	-	11,1 (12,5)	2,9	-	-	5,7	9,2	2,7	40,2

		noch Kraftfahrzeuge: Lkw: Maultiere	gel.	O	Tonnage	Ketten-Fahrzeuge: Zgkw.*	Zgkw.**	RSO	Waffen: s.Pak	Art.-Gesch.	MG. ( )	sonstige Waffen
Soll (Zahlen)		71	982	883	4241,3	147	85	-	31([illegible]) 24([illegible])	29	1549 (1248)	-
einsatzbereit	zahlenm.	105	171	1124	3713	100	68	2	24	29	1411 (1256)	-
	in % des Solls	147,3	17,4	126,8	87,5	68	80	-	77	100	91	-
in kurzfristiger Instandsetzung (bis 3 Wochen)	zahlenm.	6	27	38	390	9	2	-	-	-	-	-
	in % des Solls	8,5	2,7	11	9,2	6,1	2,4	-	-	-	-	-

*) Zgkw. mit 1–5 t. **) Zgkw. mit 8–18 t

( ) davon MG. 42

3. Pferdefehlstellen:

1.) Division befindet sich seit 27.3.44 auf [illegible] [illegible] nach dem [illegible] ([illegible] 1262/44 g.Kdos. vom 26.3.44).-

2.) [illegible] zwecks Ausstattung mit [illegible] und [illegible] um verbleiben.-
Unterstellung : [illegible]
[illegible] und
versorgungsmäßig : [illegible]
[illegible] 26.3.44 .

3.) [illegible] von 3.6.44 [illegible] der 17. SS-Pz.Gren.Div. "Götz v.Berlichingen" unterstellt.-

10.SS Panzer Division
Original German Organisation Chart
1st June 1944

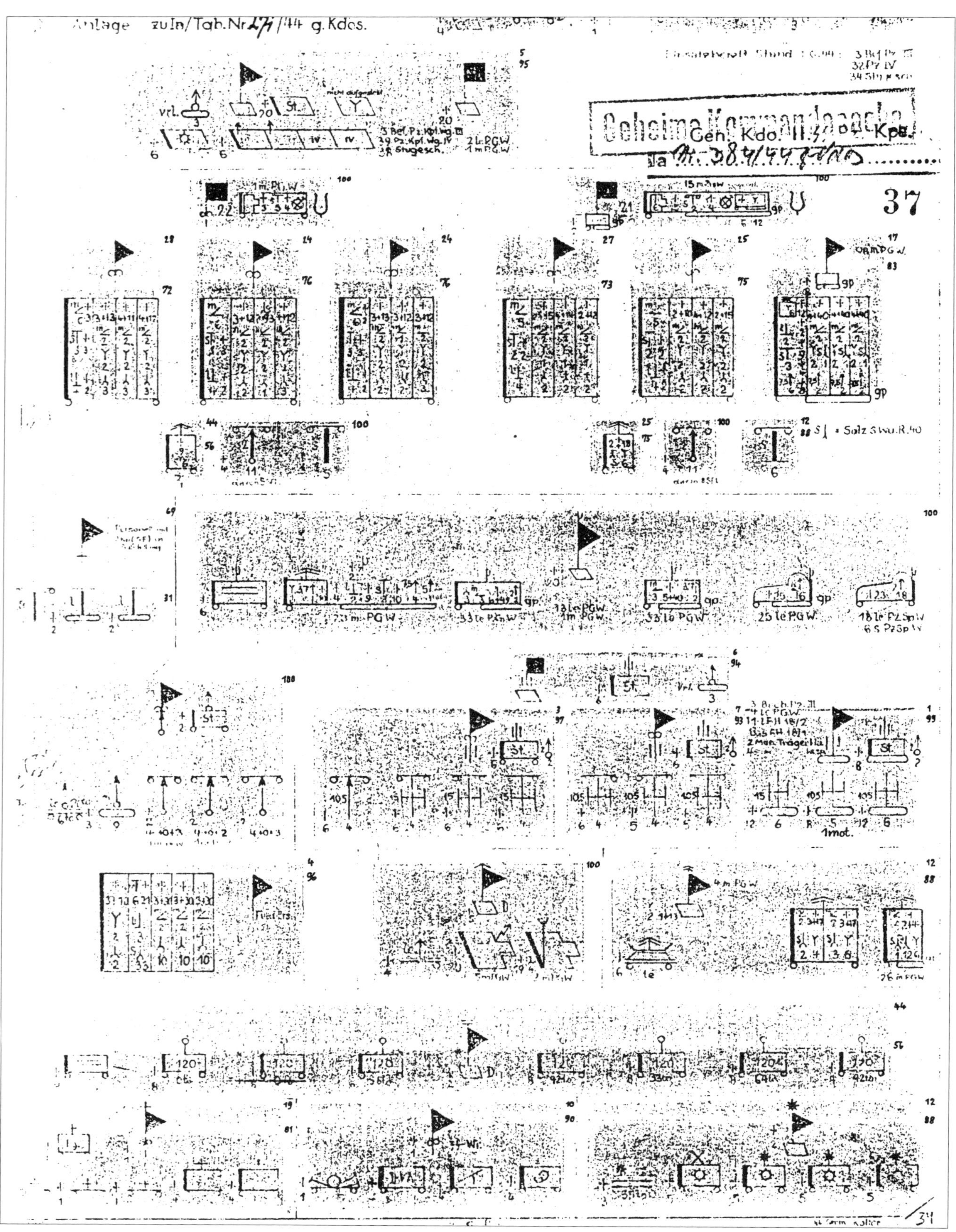

10.SS Panzer Division
Strength Report: 1st June 1944
Under Command of II.SS Panzer Korps

MANPOWER

	Authorised Strength	Shortages	Actual
Officers	595	169	426
NCOs	3874	1442	2432
Other Ranks	13,526	573	12,953
Hiwis	(1004)	(493)	511
TOTAL	17,995	1984	15,811

LOSSES BETWEEN 1/5/44 – 1/6/44

	Dead	Wounded	Missing	Hospital	Other Cases
Officers	1	2	-	1	6
NCOs / Other Ranks	21	17	-	203	345
TOTAL	22	19	-	204	351

REPLACEMENTS/ARRIVALS

	Replacements	Recovered
Officers	1	1
NCOs / Other Ranks	331	142

OVER 1 YEAR ABSENT FROM DIVISION (NON-LEAVE)

TOTAL	287
Of That:	
12 to 18 Months	284
19 to 24 Months	3
Places allocated in Monthly Report	615

10.SS Panzer Division
Strength Report: 1st June 1944
Material Stocks

ARMOURED VEHICLES

	StuG	Pz III	Pz IV	Pz V	Other AFVs	Art (SP)
Authorised Strength	44	3	54	3	349	25
Ready for Action	34	3	32	-	287	19
Short term repair	1	-	1	-	10	3

MOTOR CYCLES

	Ketten	+Sidecars	Other
Authorised Strength	111	-	566
Ready for Action	6	88	369
Short term repair	-	21	52

CARS

	Cross country	Normal/Road
Authorised Strength	733	92
Ready for Action	668	70
Short term repair	20	37

TRUCKS

	Maultiere	Cross country	Normal/Road
Authorised Strength	71	982	888
Ready for Action	105	171	1124
Short term repair	6	27	98

TRACKED PRIME MOVERS

	1-5 Tons	8-18 Tons	RSO
Authorised Strength	147	85	-
Ready for Action	100	68	2
Short term repair	9	2	-

WEAPONS

	Heavy Anti-tank Guns	Artillery Guns	MG (MG 42)
Authorised Strength	31	29	1549 (1248)
Ready for Action	24	29	1411 (1256)

10.SS PANZER DIVISION
'Frundsberg'

1st June 1944

- Divisionstab (Divisional HQ)
  100% Manpower
  4 LMG

  Div. Kartenstelle (Mapping Section)
  100% Manpower

  Div. Begleitkompanie (Divisional Security Company)
  100% Manpower
  13 LMG. 4 HMG. 2 x 81mm Mortars. 4 x SdKfz 10/4 2cm Flakwagens

  Kriegsberichter (Divisional War Correspondence Unit)
  38% Manpower

  Feldgendarmerie kompanie (Military Police Company)
  58% Manpower
  3 LMG

- SS PANZER REGIMENT 10 (Tank Regiment)
  Regimentstab (Regimental HQ)
  95% Manpower
  20 LMG

  1. Panzer Abteilung (1st Tank Battalion)
  Not within the Division. At Mailly-le-Camp equipping with *Panthers*. 84% Manpower
  4 *Panthers*. 2 x SdKfz 7/1 Quad 2cm Flakwagens. 29 LMG. 38 HMG

  2. Panzer Abteilung (2nd Tank Battalion)
  95% Manpower
  39 Pz IV. 38 StuGs. 3 Pz III Command Tanks. 2 Light Armoured Halftracks. 1 Medium Armoured Halftracks. 3 x SdKfz 7/1 Quad 2cm Flakwagens. 32 LMG

- SS PANZERGRENADIER REGIMENT 21 (Armoured Infantry Regiment)
  Regimentstab (Regimental HQ)(Armoured)
  100% Manpower
  15 Medium Armoured Halftracks. 2 x 7.5cm Pak (Towed). 23 LMG. 12 Flamethrowers

  1. Bataillon (Armoured)
  83% Manpower
  98 Medium Armoured Halftracks (including 6 x SdKfz 251/2; 12 x 251/9). 163 LMG. 12 HMG. 6 x 81mm Mortars. 12 x 7.5cm KwK L/24 (Halftrack mounted). 2 x 7.5cm Inf. Guns (Towed). 3 x 7.5cm Pak (Towed). 6 Flamethrowers. 3 Panzerbüchse

  2. Bataillon (Motorised)
  75% Manpower
  41 LMG. 8 HMG. 11 x 81mm Mortars. 4 x 7.5cm Inf. Guns (Towed). 2 x 7.5cm Pak (Towed). 6 Flamethrowers. 6 Panzerbüchse

  3. Bataillon (Motorised)
  73% Manpower
  43 LMG. 8 HMG. 11 x 81mm Mortars. 4 x 7.5cm Inf. Guns (Towed). 2 x 7.5cm Pak (Towed). 3 Flamethrowers. 6 Panzerbüchse

  Flak Kompanie (Anti-aircraft Company)
  100% Manpower
  8 x SdKfz 10/4 2cm Flak (SP). 3 x 2cm Flak Guns (Towed). 4 LMG

  Infanteriegeschutz Kompanie (Infantry Gun Company)
  88% Manpower
  6 x 15cm Infantry Guns (Towed)

  Pionier Kompanie (Engineer Company)
  75% Manpower
  18 LMG. 2 HMG. 6 Flamethrowers. 6 Panzerbüchse

- SS PANZERGRENADIER REGIMENT 22 (Motorised Infantry Regiment)
  Regimentstab (Regimental HQ) (Armoured)
  100% Manpower
  1 Medium Armoured Halftrack. 7 LMG. 3 x 7.5cm Pak (Towed)

1. Bataillon (Motorised)
76% Manpower
44 LMG. 9 HMG. 11 x 81mm Mortars. 4 x 7.5cm Inf. Guns (Towed). 3 x 7.5cm Pak (Towed). 6 Flamethrowers. 6 Panzerbüchse

2. Bataillon (Motorised)
76% Manpower
42 LMG. 9 HMG. 12 x 81mm Mortars. 4 x 7.5cm Inf. Guns (Towed). 3 x 7.5cm Pak (Towed). 6 Flamethrowers. 6 Panzerbüchse

3. Bataillon (Motorised)
72% Manpower
44 LMG. 11 HMG. 12 x 81mm Mortars. 4 x 7.5cm Inf. Guns (Towed). 3 x 7.5cm Pak (Towed). 6 Flamethrowers. 9 Panzerbüchse

Flak Kompanie (Anti-aircraft Company)
100% Manpower
5 x SdKfz 10/4 2cm Flak (SP). 6 x 2cm Flak Guns (Towed). 4 LMG

Infanteriegeschutz Kompanie (Infantry Gun Company)
100% Manpower
5 x 15cm Infantry Guns (Towed). 3 LMG

Pionier Kompanie (Engineer Company)
56% Manpower
9 LMG. 1 x 81mm Mortars. 6 Flamethrowers

- SS AUFKLÄRUNGS ABTEILUNG 10
(Armoured Reconnaissance Battalion)
100% Manpower

Abteilungstab (HQ Company)
13 Light Armoured Halftracks. 1 Medium Armoured Halftrack. 20 LMG

1. (Armoured Car) Company
18 x '4 Wheeled' Armoured Cars (including SdKfz 221, 222, 223). 6 x '8 Wheeled' Armoured Cars (including SdKfz 231, 232). 23 LMG. 18 x 2cm KwK (Armoured Car mounted)

2. (Armoured Car) Company
25 Light Armoured Halftracks (including 16 x 250/9). 25 LMG. 16 x 2cm KwK (Armoured Car mounted)

3.(Armoured Reconnaissance) Company
33 Light Armoured Halftracks (including 3 x 250/7; 2 x 250/10). 40 LMG. 5 HMG. 3 x 81mm Mortars. 2 x 3.7cm Pak (Halftrack mounted)

4.(Armoured Reconnaissance) Company
33 Light Armoured Halftracks (including 3 x 250/7). 49 LMG. 6 HMG. 3 x 81mm Mortar. 2 x 2cm KwK (Halftrack mounted)

5.(Heavy) Company
23 Medium Armoured Halftracks. 35 LMG. 4 x 7.5cm KwK L/24 (Halftrack mounted). 2 x 7.5cm Infantry Guns (Towed). 3 x 7.5cm Pak (Towed. 1 x 3.7cm Pak (Halftrack mounted). 1 x 5cm Gun (Halftrack mounted). 6 Flamethrowers

Versorgungs Kompanie (Supply Company)
6 LMG

- SS PANZERJÄGER ABTEILUNG 10
(Anti-tank Battalion)
31% Manpower
No anti-tank guns. 4 LMG

- SS PANZER ARTILLERIE REGIMENT 10
(Armoured Artillery Regiment)
Regimentstab (Regimental HQ)
94% Manpower
6 LMG. 3 x SdKfz 7/1 Quad 2cm Flakwagons

1. Abteilung (Armoured Battalion)
99% Manpower
6 *Hummel*. 2 *Hummel* Munitions Carriers. 11 *Wespe*. 4 *Wespe* Munitions Carriers. 3 Pz III Observation Tanks. 4 Light Armoured Halftracks. 1 x 105cm LeFH 18 (Towed). 2 x 2cm Flak Guns. 40 LMG

2. Abteilung (Towed Battalion)
93% Manpower
12 x 105mm LeFH 18. 2 x 2cm Flak (Towed). 22 LMG

3. Abteilung (Towed Battalion)
97% Manpower
12 x 150mm SFH 18. 4 x 105mm Kanone. 2 x 2cm Flak (Towed). 30 LMG

- SS FLAKABTEILUNG 9 (Anti-aircraft Battalion)
  100% Manpower
  12 x 88mm Flak Guns (Towed). 9 x SdKfz 7/2 3.7cm Flakwagens. 8 x 2cm Flak Guns (Towed). 4 x 60cm Searchlights. 11 LMG

- SS PANZER PIONIER BATAILLON 10
  (Armoured Engineer Battalion)
  88% Manpower
  Stabs Kompanie (Company HQ)(Partially Armoured)
  4 Medium Armoured Halftracks. 13 LMG. 1 HMG.
  12 Flamethrowers

  1. Kompanie (Armoured)
  26 Medium Armoured Halftracks. 48 LMG.
  2 HMG. 2 x 81mm Mortars. 6 Flamethrowers.
  13 Panzerbüchse (1 Heavy, 12 Light)

  2. Kompanie (Motorised)
  17 LMG. 3 HMG. 2 x 81mm Mortars.
  6 Flamethrowers. 3 Panzerbüchse

  3. Kompanie (Motorised)
  17 LMG. 3 HMG. 2 x 81mm Mortars.
  4 Flamethrowers. 2 Panzerbüchse

  Brucken Kolonne (Light Bridging Column – Motorised)
  6 LMG

- SS PANZER NACHRICHTEN ABTEILUNG 10
  (Armoured Signals Battalion)
  100% Manpower
  7 Medium Armoured Halftracks. 58 LMG.
  4 Panzerbüchse

- SS FELDERS BATAILLON 10 (Replacement Battalion)
  96% Manpower
  121 LMG. 12 HMG. 6 x 81mm Mortars.
  2 Flamethrowers. 6 x 5.0cm Pak (Towed).
  3 x 7.5cm Inf. Gun (Towed). 65 Panzerbüchse

- SS NACHSCHUBTRUPPEN 10
  (Divisional Supply Battalion)
  56% Manpower
  7 Transportation Companies (237 Tonne Capacity).
  1 Supply Company.
  66 LMG

- SS INSTADSETZUNGS ABTEILUNG 10
  (Workshop Battalion)
  88% Manpower
  4 Workshop/Repair Companies. 1 Supply Company (55 Tonne Capacity).
  25 LMG

- SS WIRTSCHAFTS BATAILLON 10
  (Commissary Battalion)
  90% Manpower
  1 Bakery Company. 1 Butcher Company.
  1 Administration Company. 1 Field Post Office.
  13 LMG

- SS SANITÄTS ABTEILUNG 10 (Medical Battalion)
  81% Manpower
  3 Ambulance Columns. 2 Medical Companies.
  1 Field Hospitals
  13 LMG

10.SS Panzer Division
1. (Panther) Abteilung
Original German Strength Report: 1st June 1944

Geheim

I./SS-Panzer-Regiment 10
Ia Tgb.Nr. 302/44 geh.

Meldung vom 1. Juni 1944

Verband:
Unterstellungsverhältnis: Pz.Brigade 10

11

I. **Personelle Lage** am Stichtag der Meldung:

a) **Personal:**

	Soll	Fehl
Offiziere	36	7
Uffz.	358	159
Mannsch.	683	—
Hiwi.		
Insgesamt	1097	—

b) **Verluste und sonstige Abgänge** in der Berichtszeit vom 1.5. bis 1.6.

	tot	verw.	verm.	krank	sonst.
Offiziere	—	—	—	—	—
Uffz. und Mannsch.	—	—	—	—	—
Insgesamt					

c) **In der Berichtzeit eingetroffener Ersatz:**

	Ersatz	Genesene
Offiziere	—	—
Uffz. und Mannsch.	—	—

d) **über 1 Jahr nicht beurlaubt:**

insgesamt: — Köpfe — % d. Iststärke

davon:	12-18 Monate	19-24 Monate	über 24 Monate
	—	—	—

Platzkarten im Berichtsmonat zugewiesen:

2. **Materielle Lage:**

		Gepanzerte Fahrzeuge							Kraftfahrzeuge				
		Pi. Pz.	Berge Pz.	Bef. Pz.	V	VI	[illegible] Kw.		Kräder: Ketten	m. angetr. Bwg.	m. Krd	Pkw: gel.	O
Soll (Zahlen)		3	2	3	73	—	2	—	6	—	28	54	1
einsatzbereit	zahlenm.	—	—	—	3	—	—	—	—	—	17	14	4
	in % des Solls	—	—	—	3	—	—	—	—	—	55	35	300
in kurzfristiger Instandsetzung (bis 3 Wochen)	zahlenm.	—	—	—	1	—	—	—	—	1	5	4	
	in % des Solls	—	—	—	1	—	—	—	—	—	15	20	

		noch Kraftfahrzeuge							Waffen			
		Maultiere	Lkw: gel.	O	Tonnage	Ketten-Fahrzeuge: Zgkw.*)	Zgkw.**)	Anh.	Gew.	Pist. / M.Pi.	MG 34 (42)	Vierl. Flak.
Soll (Zahlen)		7	104	8	—	14	14	9	516	559 124	152 25	3
einsatzbereit	zahlenm.	1	2	10	35	5	1	7	488	685 151	29 38	2
	in % des Solls	10	0,3	110	10	30	1	80	92	124 130	20 152	70
in kurzfristiger Instandsetzung (bis 3 Wochen)	zahlenm.											
	in % des Solls											

*) Zgkw. mit 1—5 t, **) Zgkw. mit 8—18 t
( ) davon MG. 42

3. **Pferdefehlstellen:**

10.SS Panzer Division
1. (Panther) Abteilung
Strength Report: 1st June 1944

MANPOWER

	Authorised Strength	Shortages	Actual
TOTAL	1077	166	911

LOSSES

	Dead	Wounded	Missing	Hospital	Other Cases
Officers	-	-	-	-	-
Other Ranks	-	-	-	-	-

ARMOURED VEHICLES	Bef Pz	BergePz	Pz V	MSPW	Bef Pz III
Authorised Strength	3	2	73	5	-
Ready for Action	-	-	3	-	-
Short term repair	-	-	1	-	-

MOTOR CYCLES	Solo	+Sidecar	Ketten
Authorised Strength	28	-	6
Ready for Action	17	-	-
Short term repair	5	1	-

CARS	Cross country	Normal/Road
Authorised Strength	54	1
Ready for Action	14	4
Short term repair	4	

TRUCKS	Maultiere	Cross country	Normal/Road
Authorised Strength	7	104	1
Ready for Action	1	2	10
Short term repair	-	-	-

TRACKED PRIME MOVERS	1-5 Tons	8-18 Tons	Combat Trailers
Authorised Strength	14	14	9
Ready for Action	5	1	7
Short term repair	-	-	-

WEAPONS	Authorised Strength	Actual Strength
Flak Vierl	3	2
Pz V KwK	76	4
MG 34	152	29
MG 42	25	38
Rifles	516	488
Machine Pistols	124	151
Pistols	559	685

10.SS Panzer Division
1. (Panther) Abteilung
Original German Manpower and Vehicle Strength Report: 1st June 1944

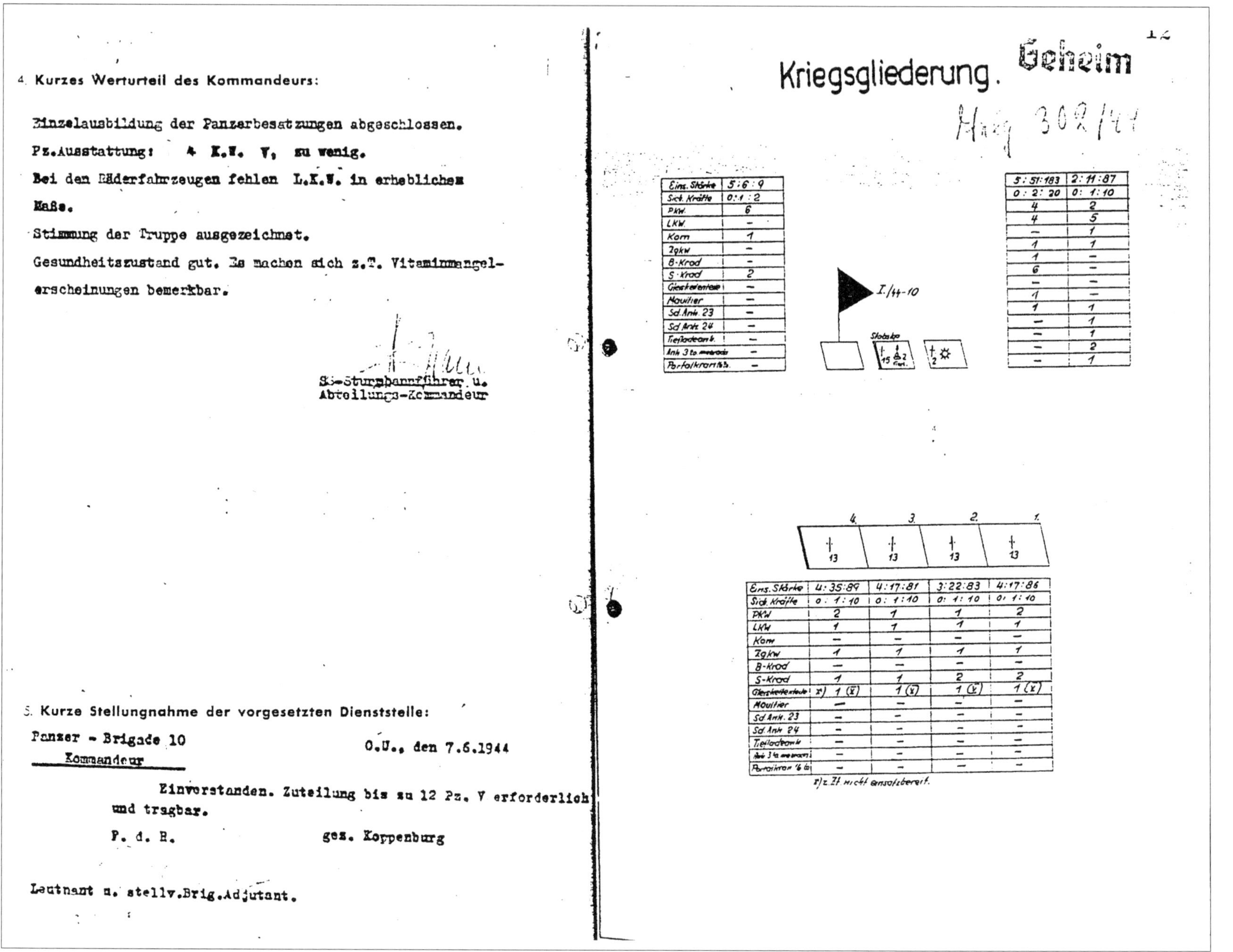

4. Kurzes Werturteil des Kommandeurs:

Einzelausbildung der Panzerbesatzungen abgeschlossen.

Pz.Ausstattung: 4 K.W. V, zu wenig.

Bei den Räderfahrzeugen fehlen L.K.W. in erheblichem Maße.

Stimmung der Truppe ausgezeichnet.

Gesundheitszustand gut. Es machen sich z.T. Vitaminmangelerscheinungen bemerkbar.

SS-Sturmbannführer u.
Abteilungs-Kommandeur

5. Kurze Stellungnahme der vorgesetzten Dienststelle:

Panzer - Brigade 10
Kommandeur

O.U., den 7.6.1944

Einverstanden. Zuteilung bis zu 12 Pz. V erforderlich und tragbar.

F. d. R. ges. Koppenburg

Leutnant u. stellv.Brig.Adjutant.

Kriegsgliederung. Geheim

Hptq 302/44

12

I./44-10

Stabskp

Eins. Stärke	5:6:9
Sich. Kräfte	0:1:2
PKW.	6
LKW.	–
Kom	1
Zgkw	–
B-Krad	–
S-Krad	2
Gleiskettenkrad	–
Maultier	–
Sd.Anh. 23	–
Sd.Anh. 24	–
Tiefladeanh.	–
Anh 3 to mehrachs	–
Portalkranfzg.	–

5:51:183	2:11:87
0:2:20	0:1:10
4	2
4	5
–	1
1	1
1	–
6	–
–	–
1	–
1	1
–	1
–	1
–	2
–	1

	4.	3.	2.	1.
	13	13	13	13
Eins. Stärke	4:35:89	4:17:81	3:22:83	4:17:86
Sich. Kräfte	0:1:10	0:1:10	0:1:10	0:1:10
PKW	2	1	1	2
LKW	1	1	1	1
Kom	–	–	–	–
Zgkw	1	1	1	1
B-Krad	–	–	–	–
S-Krad	1	1	2	2
Gleiskettenkrad	x) 1 (x)	1 (x)	1 (x)	1 (x)
Maultier	–	–	–	–
Sd.Anh. 23	–	–	–	–
Sd.Anh. 24	–	–	–	–
Tiefladeanh.	–	–	–	–
Anh 3 to mehrachs	–	–	–	–
Portalkran 16 to	–	–	–	–

x) z.Zt. nicht einsatzbereit.

10.SS Panzer Division
1. (Panther) Abteilung
Strength Report: 1st July 1944

MANPOWER	Authorised Strength	Shortages	Actual
TOTAL	984	-	1100

LOSSES	Dead	Wounded	Missing	Hospital	Other Cases
Officers	-	-	-	-	-
Other Ranks	1	-	-	-	-

ARMOURED VEHICLES	Bef Pz	BergePz	Pz V	MSPW	Bef Pz III
Authorised Strength	3	2	73	5	-
Ready for Action	-	-	2	-	1
Short term repair	-	-	2	-	-

MOTOR CYCLES	Solo	+Sidecar	Ketten
Authorised Strength	5	-	16
Ready for Action	19	1	-
Short term repair	1	-	-

CARS	Cross country	Normal/Road
Authorised Strength	38	-
Ready for Action	16	6
Short term repair	-	-

TRUCKS	Maultiere		Cross country	Normal/Road	Command
Authorised Strength	8	99	-	1	
Ready for Action	1	19	-	1	
Short term repair	-	-	-	-	

TRACKED PRIME MOVERS	1-5 Tons	8-18 Tons		Combat Trailers
Authorised Strength	9	10	7	
Ready for Action	5	1	7	
Short term repair	1	-	-	

WEAPONS	Authorised Strength	Actual Strength
Flak Vierl	3	2
Pz V KwK	76	4
MG 34	137	30
MG 42	15	38
Rifles	436	491
Machine Pistols	137	151
Pistols	418	677

10.SS Panzer Division
1. (Panther) Abteilung
Original German Manpower and Vehicle Strength Report: 1st July 1944

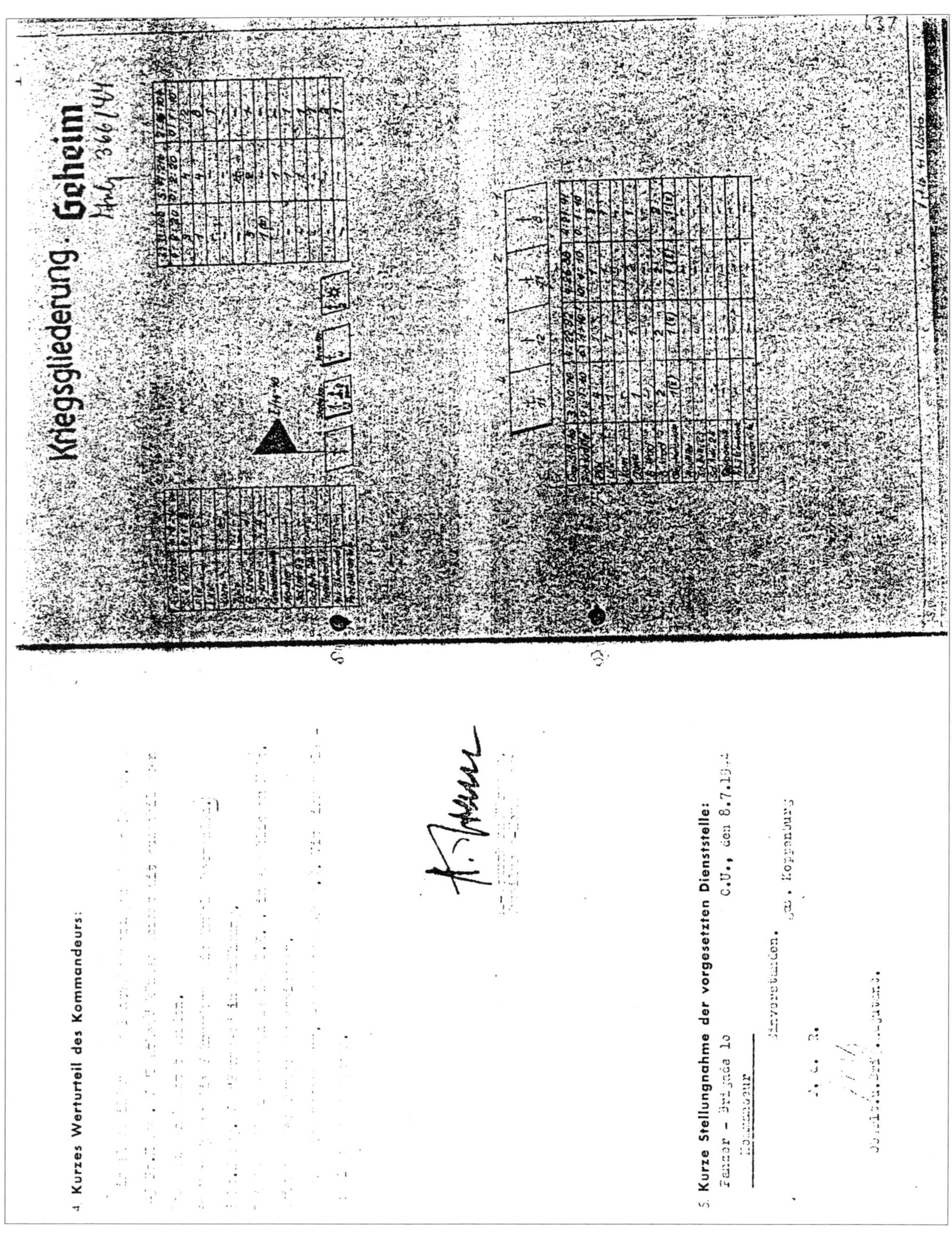
Kriegsgliederung. Geheim

4 Kurzes Werturteil des Kommandeurs:

5 Kurze Stellungnahme der vorgesetzten Dienststelle:

Panzer - Brigade 10

O.U., den 8.7.1944

10.SS Panzer Division
1. (Panther) Abteilung
Original German Strength Report: 1st August 1944

I./SS-Panzer-Regiment

Meldung vom 1. 8. 1944

Verband: Ia Tgb.Nr.429/44 geh.

Unterstellungsverhältnis: Panzer-Brigade 10

38

1. **Personelle Lage** am Stichtag der Meldung:

a) **Personal:**

	Soll	Fehl
Offiziere	34	5
Uffz.	353	143
Mannsch.	597	+ 259
Hiwi.	/	/
Insgesamt	984	+ 111

b) **Verluste und sonstige Abgänge** in der Berichtszeit vom 1.7.44 bis 1.8.44

	tot	verw.	verm.	krank	sonst.
Offiziere	/	/	/	/	/
Uffz. und Mannsch.	1	/	/	/	/
Insgesamt	1	/	/	/	/

c) **In der Berichtzeit eingetroffener Ersatz:**

	Ersatz	Genesene
Offiziere	/	/
Uffz. und Mannsch.	/	/

d) **über 1 Jahr nicht beurlaubt:**

insgesamt: / Köpfe / % d. Iststärke

davon:	12-18 Monate	19-24 Monate	über 24 Monate
	/	/	/

Platzkarten im Berichtsmonat zugewiesen: /

2. **Materielle Lage:**

		Gepanzerte Fahrzeuge							Kraftfahrzeuge				
									Kräder			Pkw	
		Pi.Pz. 251/7	Bef.Pz. V	Berge Pz.	V	gep. Kr.Pz.	Schtz. Pz. Pz. Sp. Art. Pz. B. (o. Pz. Fu Wg.)	Bef.Pz. III	Ketten	m. angetr. Bwg.	sonst.	gel.	O
Soll (Zahlen)		3	3	2	73	2	—	—	—	16	5	38	—
einsatzbereit	zahlenm.	—	—	—	7	—	—	1	—	1	5	15	—
	in % des Solls	—	—	—	9,5	—	—	—	—	6	100	42	—
in kurzfristiger Instandsetzung (bis 3 Wochen)	zahlenm.	—	—	—	3	—	—	—	—	—	—	—	—
	in % des Solls	—	—	—	4	—	—	—	—	—	—	—	—

		noch Kraftfahrzeuge							Waffen							
			Lkw			Ketten-Fahrzeuge										
		Maultiere	gel.	O	Tonnage	Zgkw. *)	Zgkw. **)	Anh.	Seit.Gew.	Gewehr	Kw.K.	Pz.Kw.V / Flak Vierl.	M.G.34	M.G.42	M.Pi.	Pist.
Soll (Zahlen)		8	97+2	1	400 t	9	3+7	7	289	434	76	3	156	15	137	419
einsatzbereit	zahlenm.	1	18+1	1	70 t	6	1	7	460	475	10	2	42	38	137	640
	in % des Solls	12	20	100	18	60	10	100	159	109	13	67	[illegible]	253	100	153
in kurzfristiger Instandsetzung (bis 3 Wochen)	zahlenm.	—	—	—	—	—	—	—	—	—	—	—	—	—	—	—
	in % des Solls	—	—	—	—	—	—	—	—	—	—	—	—	—	—	—

*) Zgkw. mit 1–5 t, davon MG
**) Zgkw. mit 8–18 t

3. **Pferdefehlstellen:**

Anl. zu Nr. 001007/44
Gen. Insp. d. Pz. Tr.

S. 416 Heidelberger, Gutenberg-Druckerei GmbH., - Paris 4-44

1 (Panther) Abteilung
SS Panzer Regiment 10
Strength Report: 1st August 1944

MANPOWER

	Authorised Strength	Shortages	Actual
TOTAL	984	-	1095

LOSSES

	Dead	Wounded	Missing	Hospital	Other Cases
Officers	-	-	-	-	-
Other Ranks	1	-	-	-	-

ARMOURED VEHICLES	Bef Pz V	BergePz	Pz V	MSPW	Bef Pz III
Authorised Strength	3	2	73	5	-
Ready for Action	-	-	7	-	1
Short term repair	-	-	3	-	-

MOTOR CYCLES	Solo	+ Sidecar	Ketten
Authorised Strength	5	-	16
Ready for Action	5	1	-
Short term repair	-	-	-

CARS	Cross country
Authorised Strength	38
Ready for Action	15
Short term repair	-

TRUCKS	Maultiere	Cross country	Normal/Road	Command
Authorised Strength	8	99	-	1
Ready for Action	1	19	-	1
Short term repair	-	-	-	-

TRACKED PRIME MOVERS	1-5 Tons	8-18 Tons	Combat Trailers
Authorised Strength	9	10	7
Ready for Action	6	1	7
Short term repair	-	-	-

WEAPONS	Authorised Strength	Actual Strength
Flak Vierl	3	2
Pz V KwK	76	10
MG 34	155	42
MG 42	15	38
Rifles	434	475
Machine Pistols	137	137
Pistols	419	640

10.SS Panzer Division

1. (Panther) Abteilung

Original German Manpower and Vehicle Strength Report: 1st August 1944

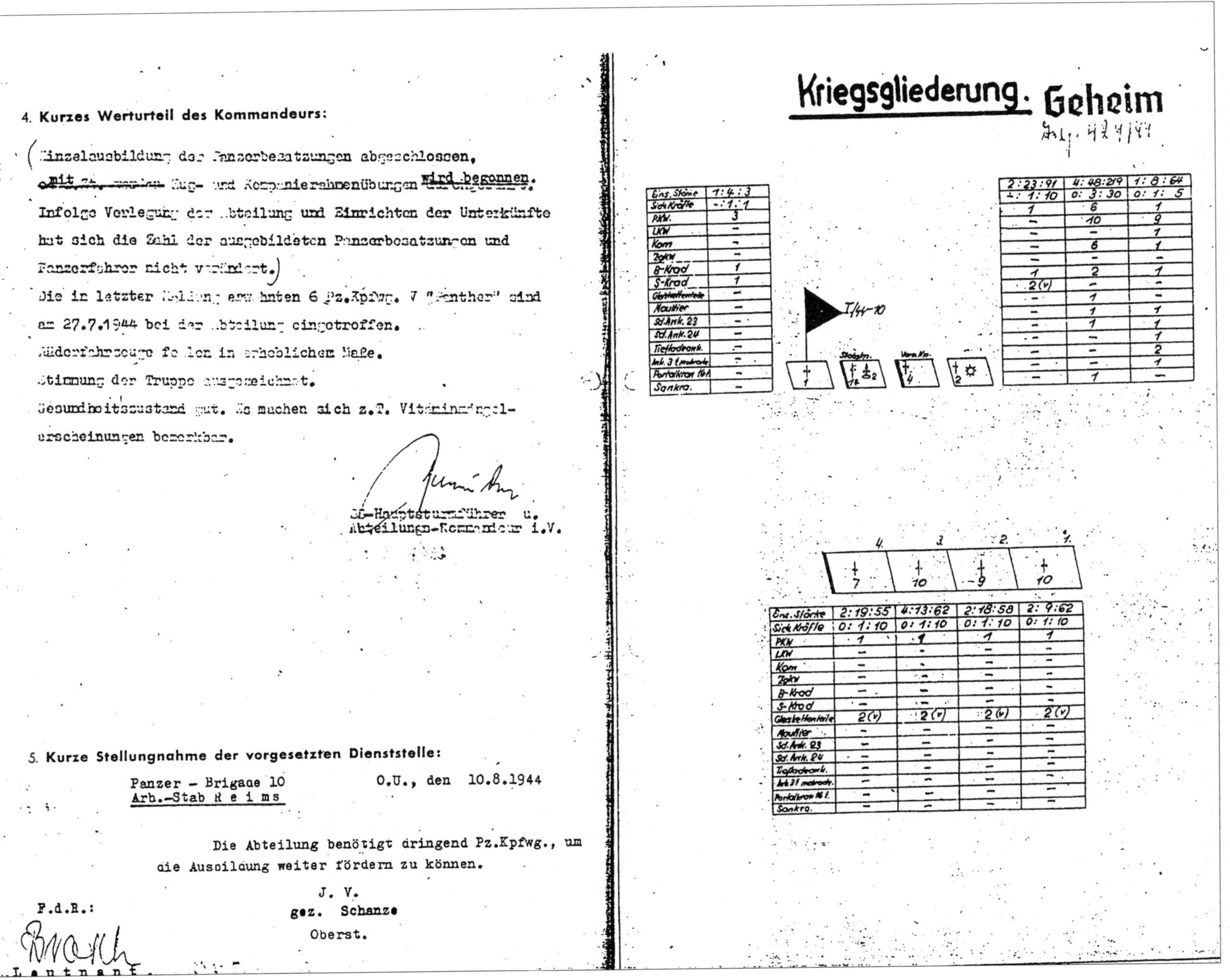

4. **Kurzes Werturteil des Kommandeurs:**

(Einzelausbildung der Panzerbesatzungen abgeschlossen, ~~mit Zt. wegen~~ Zug- und Kompanierahmenübungen **wird begonnen**. Infolge Verlegung der Abteilung und Einrichten der Unterkünfte hat sich die Zahl der ausgebildeten Panzerbesatzungen und Panzerfahrer nicht verändert.)

Die in letzter Meldung erwähnten 6 Pz.Kpfwg. V "Panther" sind am 27.7.1944 bei der Abteilung eingetroffen.

Räderfahrzeuge fehlen in erheblichem Maße.

Stimmung der Truppe ausgezeichnet.

Gesundheitszustand gut. Es machen sich z.T. Vitaminmangelerscheinungen bemerkbar.

SS-Hauptsturmführer u.
Abteilungs-Kommandeur i.V.

5. **Kurze Stellungnahme der vorgesetzten Dienststelle:**

Panzer - Brigade 10
Arb.-Stab R e i m s

O.U., den 10.8.1944

Die Abteilung benötigt dringend Pz.Kpfwg., um die Ausbildung weiter fördern zu können.

J. V.
gez. Schanze
Oberst.

F.d.R.:
Leutnant

Kriegsgliederung. Geheim

Anl. 4 2 4 / 44

I/44-10

Eins. Stärke	1:4:3	2:23:91	4:48:219	1:8:64
Sich. Kräfte	-:1:1	-:1:10	0:3:30	0:1:5
PKW.	3	1	6	1
LKW	–	–	10	9
Kom	–	–	–	1
Zgkw	–	–	6	1
B-Krad	1	–	–	–
S-Krad	1	1	2	1
Gleiskettenteile	–	2(v)	–	–
Maultier	–	–	1	–
Sd.Anh. 23	–	–	1	1
Sd.Anh. 24	–	–	1	1
Tiefladeanh.	–	–	–	1
Anh. 3 t mehrachs.	–	–	–	2
Portalkran 16 t	–	–	–	1
Sankra.	–	–	1	–

	4.	3	2.	1.
	7	10	9	10
Eins. Stärke	2:19:55	4:13:62	2:18:58	2:9:62
Sich. Kräfte	0:1:10	0:1:10	0:1:10	0:1:10
PKW	1	1	1	1
LKW	–	–	–	–
Kom	–	–	–	–
Zgkw	–	–	–	–
B-Krad	–	–	–	–
S-Krad	–	–	–	–
Gleiskettenteile	2(v)	2(v)	2(v)	2(v)
Maultier	–	–	–	–
Sd.Anh. 23	–	–	–	–
Sd.Anh. 24	–	–	–	–
Tiefladeanh.	–	–	–	–
Anh. 31 mehrachs.	–	–	–	–
Portalkran 16 t	–	–	–	–
Sankra.	–	–	–	–

12.SS PANZER DIVISION
'Hitler Jugend'

The 12.SS Panzer Division was formed in early 1943 as a Panzer-Grenadier unit. It converted to a Panzer Division in the autumn of that year.

In April 1944 the Division moved from its training grounds in Belgium to France where it was declared 'ready for action'.

12.SS Panzer Division was one of the first German armoured units to engage the Allies in Normandy.

On 1st June 1944 12.SS Panzer Division had the following units on strength:

Stab der Division
SS Panzer Regiment 12
SS Panzer Grenadier Regiment 25
SS Panzer Grenadier Regiment 26
SS Panzer Aufklärungs Abteilung12
SS Panzerjäger Abteilung 12
SS Panzer Artillerie Regiment 12
SS Werfer Abteilung 12
SS Flak Abteilung 12
SS Panzer Pionier Bataillon 12
SS Panzer Nachrichten Abteilung 12
SS Felders Bataillon 12
SS Divisionsnachschubtruppen 12
SS Panzer Instandsetzungs Abteilung 12
SS Wirtschafts Bataillon 12
SS Sanitäts Abteilung 12
SS Feldgendarmerie Kompanie 12

- SS Panzer Regiment 12

By 1/6/44 I. Abteilung had received only 61% of its authorised number of tanks. More *Panthers* arrived during the week before D Day, and when the unit went into action it was at full strength.

Tanks received by I. Abteilung	
Delivered by 1/6/44	50 Pz V
Delivered between 1/6/44-7/6/44	29 Pz V
TOTAL	79 Pz V*

(Including 6 Command Tanks)

Tank received by II. Abteilung*	
Delivered by 1/6/44	98 Pz IV

II. Abteilung was organised with 5 Companies of 17 tanks each, instead of the normal 4 Companies of 22 tanks. The extra (9th) Company was later disbanded and its remaining tanks integrated into the other companies.

Also received in the same period	
2 cm (38(t)) Flakpanzer	12
Quad 2cm Flak Guns (vierl)	3
Quad 2cm Flakpanzer IV*	3
2cm Flak Guns (Towed)	6

* *Wirbelwind (Panzer workshop conversions)*

- SS Panzerjäger Abteilung 12

On 1st June 1944 SS Panzerjäger Abt. 12 was still in the process of forming, having only 10 Jagdpanzer IV's and 3 Marders on strength.

On 3rd August the Abteilung possessed a further 11 vehicles, bringing its total to 24.

SS Panzer Regiment 12
Tank Strengths 4th July 1944 – 5th August 1944

Between 4/7/44 and 5/8/44, SS Panzer Regiment 12 had the following Panzers ready for action:

4/7/44	Pz V	Pz IV
	24	37
5/7/44	Pz V	Pz IV
	18	9
7/7/44 Pz V	Pz V	Pz IV
	28	32
9/7/44 Pz V	Pz V	Pz IV
	18	10
11/7/44	Pz V	Pz IV
	14	17
16/7/44	Pz V	Pz IV
	18	21
25/7/44	Pz V	Pz IV
	21	37
30/7/44	Pz V	Pz IV
	22	39
2/8/44	Pz V	Pz IV
	39	-

Battle Group 'Wünsche'*

	Pz IV	Pz V	Pz VI
	17	66	19**

5/8/44 Pz V	Pz V	Pz IV
	9	37

12/8/44	Pz V	Pz IV	Pz VI	Jagdpz IV
	7	17	11	27
20/8/44	Pz V	Pz IV	Pz VI	Jagdpz IV
	?	6	?	3

22/8/44 10 Panzers of all types

Replacements

In July SS Panzer Regt 12 received 8 new Panzer V's.

In late July, the Regiment's 3. and 4. Companies returned to Sennenlager and received 34 new Panzer V's. 3. Company returned to France immediately, but due to transport delays, 4. Company did not return to action until late August.

In early September 4. Company's strength was reported as 14 Pz V's.

** Obersturmbannführer Wünsche was the commander of SS Panzer Regiment 12*

*** The Pz VI (Tigers) belonged to Schwere SS Panzer Abteilung 101 which was also attached to Battle Group Wünsche.*

12.SS Panzer Division
Original German Strength Report
1st June 1944

Unterlagen 31   29

Meldung vom 1./6. 1944

Verband: 12.SS-Pz. Div. "H.J."
Unterstellungsverhältnis: ....

1. Personelle Lage am Stichtag der Meldung:

a) Personal:

	Soll	Fehl
Offiziere	664	144
Uffz.	4 575	2 192
Mannsch.	15 277	+2 360
Hiwi	(1 103)	(887)
Insgesamt	20 516	+ 24

b) Verluste und sonstige Abgänge in der Berichtszeit vom .... bis ....

	tot	verw.	verm.	krank	sonst.
Offiziere	1	-	-	-	13
Uffz. und Mannsch.	20	11	-	25	2042
Insgesamt	21	11	-	25	2055

c) in der Berichtszeit eingetroffener Ersatz:

	Ersatz	Genesene
Offiziere	26	-
Uffz. und Mannsch.	125 + 216 Hiwi 341	-

d) über 1 Jahr nicht beurlaubt:

insgesamt: 181 Köpfe 0,9 % d. Iststärke

davon:	12 - 18 Monate	19 - 24 Monate	über 24 Monate
	170	8	3

Platzkarten im Berichtsmonat zugewiesen: ....

2. Materielle Lage:

		Gepanzerte Fahrzeuge							Kraftfahrzeuge				
		Stu. Gesch.	III	IV	V	VI	Schtz. Pz. Pz. Sp. Art. Pz. B. (o Pz. Fu. Wg)	Pak Sf.	Kräder Ketten	Kräder m. angetr. Bwg.	Kräder sonst.	Pkw gel.	Pkw O
Soll (Zahlen)		-	4	101	81	-	390	45	132		671	908	99
einsatzbereit	zahlenm.	-	2	91	48	-	306	12	2	(22)	670 +(692)	474	265
	in % des Solls	-	50	90	59,2	-	78,4	26,6	1,5		99,8 (103,1)	52,2	267
in kurzfristiger Instandsetzung (bis 3 Wochen)	zahlenm.	-	-	7	2	-	27	1	-	-	128	31	153
	in % des Solls	-	-	6,9	2,3	-	6,9	2,2	-	-	19	3,5	154,5

		noch Kraftfahrzeuge							Waffen			
		Maultiere	Lkw gel.	Lkw O	Lkw Tonnage	Ketten-Fahrzeuge Zgkw. *)	Ketten-Fahrzeuge Zgkw. **)	RSO	s Pak	Art.-Gesch.	MG. ( )	sonstige Waffen
Soll (Zahlen)		50	1245	969	935	201	112	-	24	47	1730 (1308)	27 1.I.G 38 2cmFl
einsatzbereit	zahlenm.	-	232	1320+)	604	39	63	-	28	50	1539 (1243)	20 42
	in % des Solls	-	18,6	136	64,5	19,4	56,2	-	116	106	89 (94)	74% 110%
in kurzfristiger Instandsetzung (bis 3 Wochen)	zahlenm.	-	8	274	-	2	2	-	-	2	90	2 2cmFl
	in % des Solls	-	0,6	28,2	-	0,9	1,7	-	-	4,2	5,2	5,2%

SS K.K.St. 1 (Nr 79c)

*) Zgkw. mit 1-5t, **) Zgkw. mit 8-18t
( ) davon MG. 42

3. Pferdefehlstellen:

+) davon 160 Lieferwagen m. je 420 kg Nutzlast und 128 le. Lkw mit je 800 - 1000 kg Nutzlast.

12.SS Panzer Division
Original German Report highlighting Vehicle Shortages
1st June 1944

4. Kurzes Werturteil des Kommandeurs:

1. Ausbildungsstand:

Die Division außer SS-Pz. Jäger-Abt.12 und SS-Nebelwerfer-Abt.12 befindet sich in der Verbandsausbildung.

2. Besondere Schwierigkeiten:

a) Fehl von 3 Pz. Bef.-Wagen V,
b) Fehl an Bergepanzern,
c) Fehl der sollmäßigen Kfz.-Ausstattung der Panther-Abt.,
d) Der I.(Sf.)/SS-Pz. Art.Rgt.12 fehlen noch 2 Art. Beob.-Panzer (III)
e) Mangel an Mun.-Trägern für I.(Sf.)/SS-Pz. Art.Rgt.12,
f) Mangel an 1 t - Zugmaschinen zum Umbau der 2 cm Flak (mot-Z) in 2 cm Flak (Sf.),
g) Fehl von 12 Sd.-Kfz. 222 und 6 Sd.-Kfz. 233 bei SS-Pz.Aufkl.Abt.
h) Fehl von 11 SPW bei SS-Pz. Nachr.-Abt. 12,
i) Fehl sämtlicher Zugmittel für SS-Werfer-Abt. 12,
k) Fehl der Befehlspanzer für SS-Pz. Jäger-Abt. 12.

3. Einsatzbereitschaft:

Die Division ist für Angriffsaufgaben einsatzbereit.

SS-Brigadeführer und
Generalmajor der Waffen-SS

Anmerkung zur "Personellen Lage":

58 Unterführer und Mannschaften sind seit 1.5., bzw. 15.5. zu den Junkerschulen kommandiert. Ihre Versetzung wurde bisher nicht verfügt.

5. Kurze Stellungnahme der vorgesetzten Dienststelle:

Division ist mit Ausnahme der Werferabteilung und der Panzer-Jäger-Abteilung im Westen für jede Aufgabe voll einsatzbereit.

Für das Generalkommando
Der Chef des Generalstabes

12.SS Panzer Division
Original German Weapons Stocks Report
1st June 1944

I. Deutsche Waffen

(In der Kriegsgliederung nicht eingezeichnet)

12 351	Karabiner 98 k
200	Karabiner 98 k ZF. 41
200	Gewehre 41
6 544	Pistolen
1 700	M.Pi. 38/40
69	Granatbüchsen 39
459	Gew.Gr. Gerät

II. Beutewaffen

4	7,62 cm J.K.H. 290 (r)

12.SS Panzer Division
Original German Theoretical Organisation Chart
1st June 1944

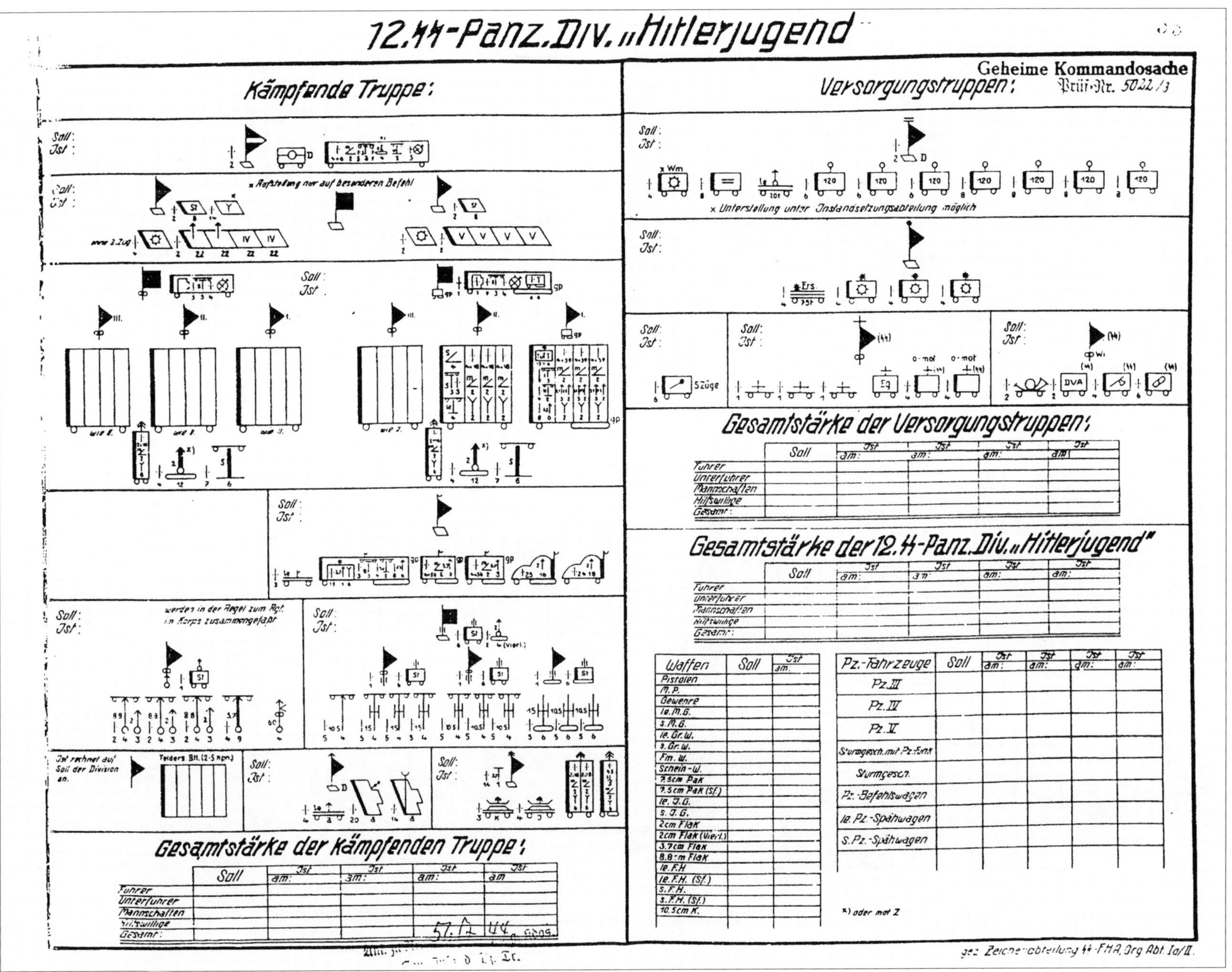

Gesamtstärke der Versorgungstruppen:

	Soll	Ist am:	Ist am:	Ist am:	Ist am:
Führer					
Unterführer					
Mannschaften					
Hilfswillige					
Gesamt:					

Gesamtstärke der 12. SS-Panz.Div. „Hitlerjugend"

	Soll	Ist am:	Ist am:	Ist am:	Ist am:
Führer					
Unterführer					
Mannschaften					
Hilfswillige					
Gesamt:					

Waffen	Soll	Ist am:
Pistolen		
M.P.		
Gewehre		
le.M.G.		
s.M.G.		
le.Gr.W.		
s.Gr.W.		
Fm.W.		
Schein-W.		
7.5cm Pak		
7.5cm Pak (Sf.)		
le.J.G.		
s.J.G.		
2cm Flak		
2cm Flak (Vierl.)		
3.7cm Flak		
8.8cm Flak		
le.F.H.		
le.F.H. (Sf.)		
s.F.H.		
s.F.H. (Sf.)		
10.5cm K.		

Pz.-Fahrzeuge	Soll	Ist am:	Ist am:	Ist am:	Ist am:
Pz.III					
Pz.IV					
Pz.V					
Sturmgesch. mit Pz.-Funk					
Sturmgesch.					
Pz.-Befehlswagen					
le.Pz.-Spähwagen					
s.Pz.-Spähwagen					

Gesamtstärke der kämpfenden Truppe:

	Soll	Ist am:	Ist am:	Ist am:	Ist am:
Führer					
Unterführer					
Mannschaften					
Hilfswillige					
Gesamt:					

12.SS Panzer Division
Original German Actual Organisation Chart
1st June 1944

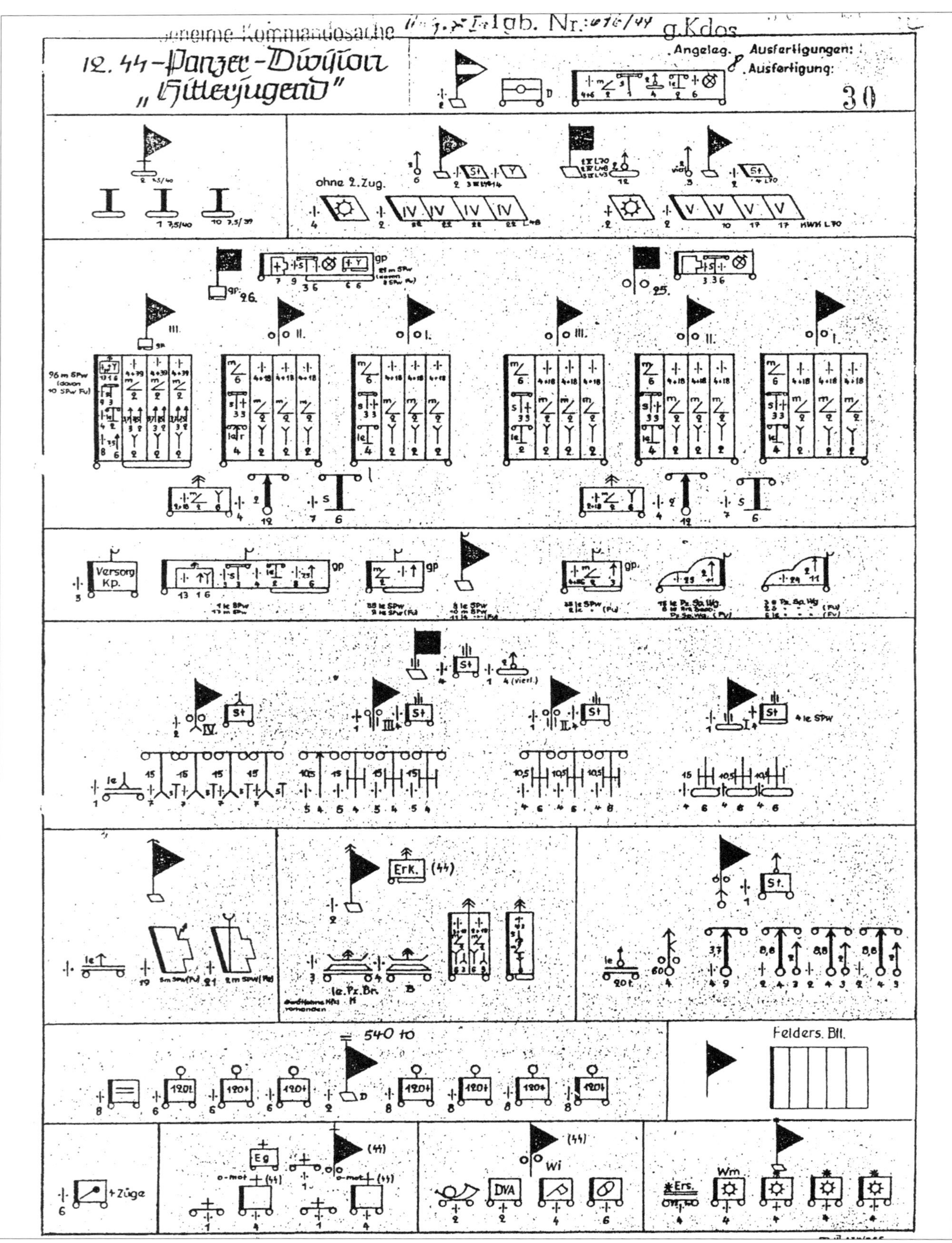

12.SS Panzer Division
Strength Report: 1st June 1944

MANPOWER

	Authorised Strength	Shortages	Actual
Officers	664	144	520
NCOs	4,575	2,192	2,383
Other Ranks	15,277	2,360+	17,637
Hiwis	(1,103)	(887)	(216)
TOTAL	20,516	24+	20,540

LOSSES FOR PREVIOUS FOUR WEEKS

	Dead	Wounded	Missing	Hospital	Other Cases
Officers	1	-	-	-	13
NCOs / Other Ranks	20	11	-	25	2042
TOTAL	21	11	-	25	2055

REPLACEMENTS/ARRIVALS

	Replacements	Recovered
Officers	26	-
NCOs / Other Ranks	125 + 216 Hiwis	-

OVER 1 YEAR ABSENT FROM DIVISION (NON-LEAVE)

TOTAL	181
Of That:	
12 to 18 Months	170
19 to 24 Months	8
Over 24 Months	3

12.SS Panzer Division
Strength Report: 1st June 1944
Material Stocks

ARMOURED VEHICLES

	Pz III	Pz IV	Pz V	Other AFVs	Jagd IV
Authorised Strength	4	101	81	390	45
Ready for Action	2	91	48	306	12
Short term repair	-	7	2	27	1

MOTOR CYCLES

	Ketten	+Sidecars	Other
Authorised Strength	132	-	671
Ready for Action	2	22	670
Short term repair	-	-	128

CARS

	Cross country	Normal/Road
Authorised Strength	908	99
Ready for Action	474	265
Short term repair	31	153

TRUCKS

	Maultiere	Cross country	Normal/Road
Authorised Strength	50	1245	969
Ready for Action	-	232	1320*
Short term repair	-	8	274

**Including 160 Supply Wagons with 420kg payload and 120 Light Trucks with 800-1000 Kg Payload*

TRACKED PRIME MOVERS

	1-5 Tons	8-18 Tons
Authorised Strength	201	112
Ready for Action	39	63
Short term repair	2	2

WEAPONS

	Heavy Anti-tank Guns	Artillery Guns	MG (MG 42)	LeFH Inf Gun	2cm Flak
Authorised Strength	24	47	1730(1308)	27	38
Ready for Action	28	50	1539 (1243)	20	42
Short Term Repair		2	90		2

12.SS PANZER DIVISION
'Hitler Jugend'

1st June 1944

Divisional manpower strength at slightly over 100%.

- Divisionstab (Divisional HQ)
  2 LMG

  Div. Kartenstelle (Mapping Section)

  Div. Begleitkompanie (Divisional Security Company)
  12 LMG. 4 HMG. 2 x 81mm Mortars. 1 x 7.5cm Pak (Towed). 2 x 7.5cm Inf. Guns (Towed).
  4 x SdKfz 7/1 Quad 2cm Flakwagens

- SS PANZER REGIMENT 12 (Tank Regiment)
  Regimentstab (Regimental HQ)
  2 *Panthers.* 2 x Pz IV (L/48). 3 x Pz IV (L/43).
  12 x (2cm) Flakpanzer 38(t)

  1. Panzer Abteilung (1st Tank Battalion)
  48 *Panthers.* 3 x Quad 2cm Flak Guns (Towed).
  6 LMG

  2. Panzer Abteilung (2nd Tank Battalion)
  91 Pz IV (L/48). 6 x Quad 2cm Flak Guns (Towed)
  8 LMG

  Pionier Kompanie (Engineer Company)
  14 LMG

- SS PANZERJÄGER ABTEILUNG 12
  (Anti-tank Battalion)
  10 x Jagdpanzer IV (L/48). 3 x Marder III (38(t) – Pak 40)

- SS PANZERGRENADIER REGIMENT 25
  (Motorised Infantry Regiment)
  Regimentstab (Regimental HQ)(Armoured)
  3 x 7.5cm Pak (Towed). 9 LMG

  1. Bataillon (Motorised)
  57 LMG. 12 HMG. 12 x 81mm Mortars. 4 x 7.5cm Inf. Guns. 3 x 7.5cm Pak (Towed).
  6 Flamethrowers

  2. Bataillon (Motorised)
  57 LMG. 12 HMG. 12 x 81mm Mortars. 4 x 7.5cm Inf. Guns (Towed). 3 x 7.5cm Pak (Towed).
  6 Flamethrowers

  3. Bataillon (Motorised)
  57 LMG. 12 HMG. 12 x 81mm Mortars. 2 x 7.5cm Inf. Guns (Towed). 3 x 7.5cm Pak (Towed).
  6 Flamethrowers

  Flak Kompanie (Anti-aircraft Company)
  12 x 2cm Flak Guns (Towed). 4 LMG

  Infanteriegeschutz Kompanie (Infantry Gun Company)
  6 x 15cm Infantry Guns (Towed). 7 LMG

  Pionier Kompanie (Engineer Company)
  18 LMG. 2 HMG. 2 x 81mm Mortars.
  6 Flamethrowers

- SS PANZERGRENADIER REGIMENT 26
  (Armoured Infantry Regiment)
  Regimentstab (Regimental HQ)(Armoured)
  21 Medium Armoured Halftracks (including 8 x SdKfz 251/3). 28 LMG. 3 x 7.5cm Pak (Towed). 6 Flamethrowers

  1. Bataillon (Motorised)
  57 LMG. 12 HMG. 12 x 81mm Mortars. 4 x 7.5cm Inf. Guns. 3 x 7.5cm Pak (Towed).
  6 Flamethrowers

  2. Bataillon (Motorised)
  57 LMG. 12 HMG. 12 x 81mm Mortars. 4 x 7.5cm Inf. Guns (Towed). 3 x 7.5cm Pak (Towed).
  6 Flamethrowers

3. Bataillon (Armoured)
96 Medium Armoured Halftracks (including 10 x SdKfz 251/3; 12 x SdKfz 251/9; 10 x SdKfz 251/10; 6 x SdKfz 251/2). 151 LMG. 12 HMG. 6 x 81mm Mortars. 12 7.5cm KwK L/24 (Halftrack mounted). 2 x 7.5cm Inf. Guns (Towed). 3 x 7.5cm Pak (Towed).
10 x 3.7cm Pak (Halftrack mounted).
12 Flamethrowers

Flak Kompanie (Anti-aircraft Company)
12 x 2cm Flak Guns (Towed). 4 LMG

Infanteriegeschutz Kompanie (Infantry Gun Company)
6 x 15cm Infantry Guns (Towed). 7 LMG

Pionier Kompanie (Engineer Company)
18 LMG. 2 HMG. 2 x 81mm Mortars.
6 Flamethrowers

- SS PANZER AUFKLÄRUNGS ABTEILUNG 12
(Armoured Reconnaissance Battalion)
Abteilungstab (HQ Company)
14 Light Armoured Halftracks (including 11 x SdKfz 250/3). 10 Medium Armoured Halftracks

1. Kompanie (Armoured Car Company)
6 x SdKfz 223 (4 Wheeled) Armoured Cars. 5 x 8 Wheeled Armoured Cars (including 2 x SdKfz 232; 3 x SdKfz 231). This unit also included about 90 Motorcycles. 24 LMG. 11 x 2cm KwK (Armoured Car mounted)

2. Kompanie (Armoured Car Company)
23 Light Armoured Halftracks (including 15 x SdKfz 250/9; 8 x SdKfz 250/4). 25 LMG. 11 x 2cm KwK (Armoured Car mounted)

3. Kompanie (Armoured Reconnaissance Company)
37 Light Armoured Halftracks (including SdKfz 250/3). 56 LMG. 4 HMG 2 x 81mmMortars

4. Kompanie (Armoured Reconnaissance Company)
37 Light Armoured Halftracks (including 2 x SdKfz 250/3). 56 LMG. 4 HMG. 2 x 81mm Mortars

5. Kompanie (Heavy Company)
1 Light Armoured Halftrack. 17 Medium Armoured Halftracks (including 6 x SdKfz 251/9). 28 LMG.
6 x 7.5cm KwK L/24. (Halftrack mounted).
2 x 7.5cm Inf. Guns (Towed). 3 x 7.5cm Pak (Towed). 6 Flamthrowers

Versorgungs Kompanie (Supply Company)
3 LMG

- SS PANZER ARTILLERIE REGIMENT 12
(Armoured Artillery Regiment)
Regimentstab (Regimental HQ)
5 LMG. 4 x SdKfz 7/1 Quad 2cm Flakwagons

1. Abteilung (Armoured Battalion)
6 *Hummel*. 12 *Wespe*. 4 Light Armoured Halftracks. 17 LMG

2. Abteilung (Towed Battalion)
18 x 105mm LeFH 18. 17 LMG

3. Abteilung (Towed Battalion)
12 x 150mm SFH 18. 4 x 105mm Kanone. 25 LMG

4. Abteilung (Werfer Battalion)
No Nebelwerfer. 31 LMG

- SS FLAKABTEILUNG 12 (Anti-aircraft Battalion)
12 x 88mm Flak Guns (Towed). 9 x 3.7cm Flak Guns (Towed). 9 x 2cm Flak Guns (Towed).
4 x 60cm Searchlights. 11 LMG

- SS PANZER PIONIER BATAILLON 12
(Armoured Engineer Battalion)
Stabs Kompanie (Company HQ)(Partially Armoured)
2 LMG

1. Kompanie (Armoured)
Medium Armoured Halftracks. 43 LMG. 2 x 81mm Mortars. 6 Flamethrowers. 3 Panzerbüchse

2. Kompanie (Motorised)
18 LMG. 2 HMG. 2 x 81mm Mortars.
6 Flamethrowers. 3 Panzerbüchse

3. Kompanie (Motorised)
18 LMG. 2 HMG. 2 x 81mm Mortars.
6 Flamethrowers. 3 Panzerbüchse

Brucken Kolonne (Bridging Column – Motorised)
4 LMG

Brucken Kolonne (Light Bridging Column – Motorised)
3 LMG

- SS PANZER NACHRICHTEN ABTEILUNG 12
  (Armoured Signals Battalion)
  7 Medium Armoured Halftracks (including 5 x SdKfz 251/3; 2 x SdKfz 251/11). 40 LMG

- SS NACHSCHUBTRUPPEN 12
  (Divisional Supply Battalion)
  7 Transportation Companies (540 Tonne Capacity).
  1 Supply Company.
  64 LMG

- SS INSTADSETZUNGS ABTEILUNG 12
  (Workshop Battalion)
  4 Workshop/Repair Companies. 1 Supply Company
  20 LMG

- SS WIRTSCHAFTS BATAILLON 12
  (Commissary Battalion)
  1 Bakery Company. 1 Butcher Company.
  1 Administration Company. 1 Field Post Office.
  14 LMG

- SS SANITÄTS ABTEILUNG 12 (Medical Battalion)
  3 Ambulance Columns. 2 Medical Compaies.
  1 Field Hospitals
  11 LMG

- SS FELDGENDARMERIE KOMPANIE 12
  (Military Police Company)
  4 Platoons
  6 LMG

12.SS Panzer Division
Original German Strength Report
27th June 1944

Geheime Kommandosache

Meldung vom 27. Juni 1944

Verband: 12.SS-Pz.Div."H.J."
Unterstellungsverhältnis:

1. **Personelle Lage** am Stichtag der Meldung:

a) Personal:

	Soll	Fehl
Offiziere	647	164
Uffz.	4 185	1 857
Mannsch.	14 258	+ 1 736
lavon Hiwi	(1 029)	(823)
Insgesamt	19 090	285

b) Verluste und sonstige Abgänge in der Berichtszeit vom .... bis ....

	tot	verw.	verm.	krank	sonst.
Offiziere	33	55	16	12	4
Uffz. und Mannsch.	845	2061	882	112	54
Insgesamt	878	2116	898	124	58

c) in der Berichtszeit eingetroffener Ersatz:

	Ersatz	Genesene
Offiziere	16	-32
Uffz. und Mannsch.	83	-

d) über 1 Jahr nicht beurlaubt:

insgesamt: 663 Köpfe 3,5 % d. Iststärke

davon:	12 - 18 Monate	19 - 24 Monate	über 24 Monate
	630	27	6

Platzkarten im Berichtsmonat zugewiesen ....

2. **Materielle Lage:**

	Gepanzerte Fahrzeuge							Kraftfahrzeuge				
	Stu. Gesch.	III	IV	V	VI	Schtz. Pz. Pz. Sp. Art. Pz. B. (o. Pz. Fu. Wg)	Pak Sf.	Kräder: Ketten	Kräder: m. angetr. Bwg.	Kräder: sonst.	Pkw: gel.	Pkw: O
Soll (Zahlen)	-	6	103	81	-	524	31	357	150	163	900	85
einsatzbereit zahlenm.	-	-	32	24	-	298	2	2	20	418	379	188
einsatzbereit in % des Solls	-	-	31	29,6	-	56,8	6,4	0,5	13,3	256,4	42,1	221,1
in kurzfristiger Instandsetzung (bis 3 Wochen) zahlenm.	-	-	22	16	-	21	10	-	-	133	82	80
in kurzfristiger Instandsetzung (bis 3 Wochen) in % des Solls	-	-	21,3	19,7	-	4	32,2	-	-	81,5	9,1	94,1

	noch Kraftfahrzeuge							Waffen			
	Lkw: Maultiere	Lkw: gel.	Lkw: O	Lkw: Tonnage	Ketten-Fahrzeuge: Zgkw. *)	Ketten-Fahrzeuge: Zgkw. **)	RSO	s Pak	Art.-Gesch.	M.G. ()	sonstige Waffen
Soll (Zahlen)	140	959	932	729	126	105	-	25	59	(1395)12[illegible]	S.I. 53
einsatzbereit zahlenm.	-	121	1216	329	28	54	-	19	33	(11[illegible])[illegible]	35
einsatzbereit in % des Solls	-	12,6	130,4	45	22,2	51,4	-	76	56	81	66
in kurzfristiger Instandsetzung (bis 3 Wochen) zahlenm.	-	34	142		4	4	-	1	3	[illegible]	-
in kurzfristiger Instandsetzung (bis 3 Wochen) in % des Solls	-	3,6	15,2		3,1	3,8	-	4	5,1	6,[illegible]	-

SS K.K.St. 1 (Nr 79c)

*) Zgkw. mit 1-5t, **) Zgkw. mit 8-13t
() davon MG. 42

~~Pferdefehlstellen:~~
+) davon 149 Lieferwagen mit 420 kg Nutzlast und 128 Lkw mit 800 bis 1000 kg Nutzlast.

Anl. zu Nr. 01451/44 geh.
Gen. Insp. d. Pz.Tr.

12.SS Panzer Division
Original German Theoretical Organisation Chart
27th June 1944

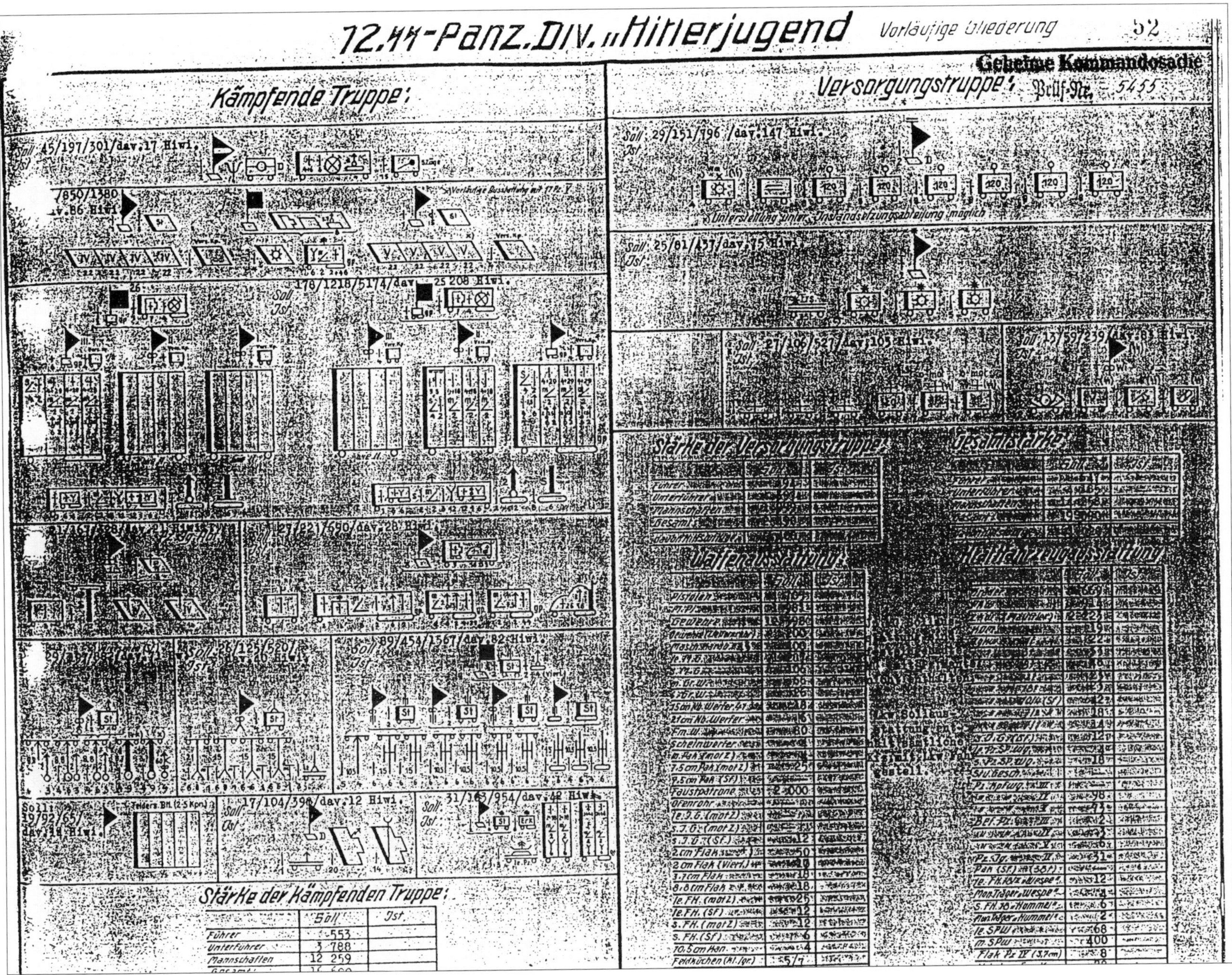

12.SS-Panz.Div. „Hitlerjugend" Vorläufige Gliederung 52

Geheime Kommandosache

Prüf-Nr. 5455

Kämpfende Truppe:

Versorgungstruppe:

Soll: 45/197/301/dav. 17 Hiwi.

Soll: 29/151/196 /dav. 147 Hiwi.

Unterstellung unter Instandsetzungsabteilung möglich

Soll: 25/91/431/dav. 75 Hiwi.

178/1218/5174/dav. 25 208 Hiwi.

Soll: 27/106/527/dav. 105 Hiwi.

Soll: 17/104/398/dav. 12 Hiwi.

Soll: 31/163/954/dav. 42 Hiwi.

Soll: 89/454/1567/dav. 82 Hiwi.

Stärke der Versorgungstruppe:

Gesamtstärke:

Waffenausstattung:

	Soll	Ist
Pistolen	[illegible]	[illegible]
M.Pi.	[illegible]	[illegible]
Gewehre	[illegible]	[illegible]
Gewehr (Zielfernrohr)	[illegible]	[illegible]
Masch.Karab.	[illegible]	[illegible]
le.M.G.	[illegible]	[illegible]
s.M.G.	[illegible]	[illegible]
m.Gr.W.	[illegible]	[illegible]
s.Gr.W.	[illegible]	[illegible]
15 cm Nb.Werfer 41	18	[illegible]
21 cm Nb.Werfer	[illegible]	[illegible]
Fm.W.	80	[illegible]
Scheinwerfer	[illegible]	[illegible]
m.Pak (mot Z)	[illegible]	[illegible]
7.5 cm Pak (mot Z)	25	[illegible]
7.5 cm Pak (Sf)	[illegible]	[illegible]
Faustpatrone	2 000	[illegible]
Ofenrohr	[illegible]	[illegible]
le.I.G. (mot Z)	[illegible]	[illegible]
s.I.G. (mot Z)	[illegible]	[illegible]
s.I.G. (Sf)	12	[illegible]
2 cm Flak	50	[illegible]
2 cm Flak (Vierl.)	[illegible]	[illegible]
3.7 cm Flak	18	[illegible]
8.8 cm Flak	18	[illegible]
le.F.H. (mot Z)	25	[illegible]
le.F.H. (Sf)	12	[illegible]
s.F.H. (mot Z)	12	[illegible]
s.F.H. (Sf)	6	[illegible]
10.5 cm Kan.	4	[illegible]
Feldküchen (kl./gr.)	5/7	[illegible]

Kraftfahrzeugausstattung:

	Soll	Ist
Stu.Gesch.	[illegible]	[illegible]
Pz.Kpfwg. III	[illegible]	[illegible]
[illegible] IV	98	[illegible]
[illegible] V	[illegible]	[illegible]
Bef.Pz. III	2	[illegible]
[illegible] IV	[illegible]	[illegible]
[illegible] V	6	[illegible]
Pz.Jg. IV	31	[illegible]
Pak (Sf) (38 t)	[illegible]	[illegible]
le.F.H. 18/2 „Wespe"	12	[illegible]
Mun.Träger „Wespe"	4	[illegible]
s.F.H. 18 „Hummel"	6	[illegible]
Mun.Träger „Hummel"	2	[illegible]
le.SPW	68	[illegible]
m.SPW	400	[illegible]
Flak Pz IV (3,7 cm)	8	[illegible]

Stärke der Kämpfenden Truppe:

	Soll	Ist
Führer	553	
Unterführer	3 788	
Mannschaften	12 259	
Gesamt	[illegible]	

12.SS Panzer Division
Original German Actual Organisation Chart
27th June 1944

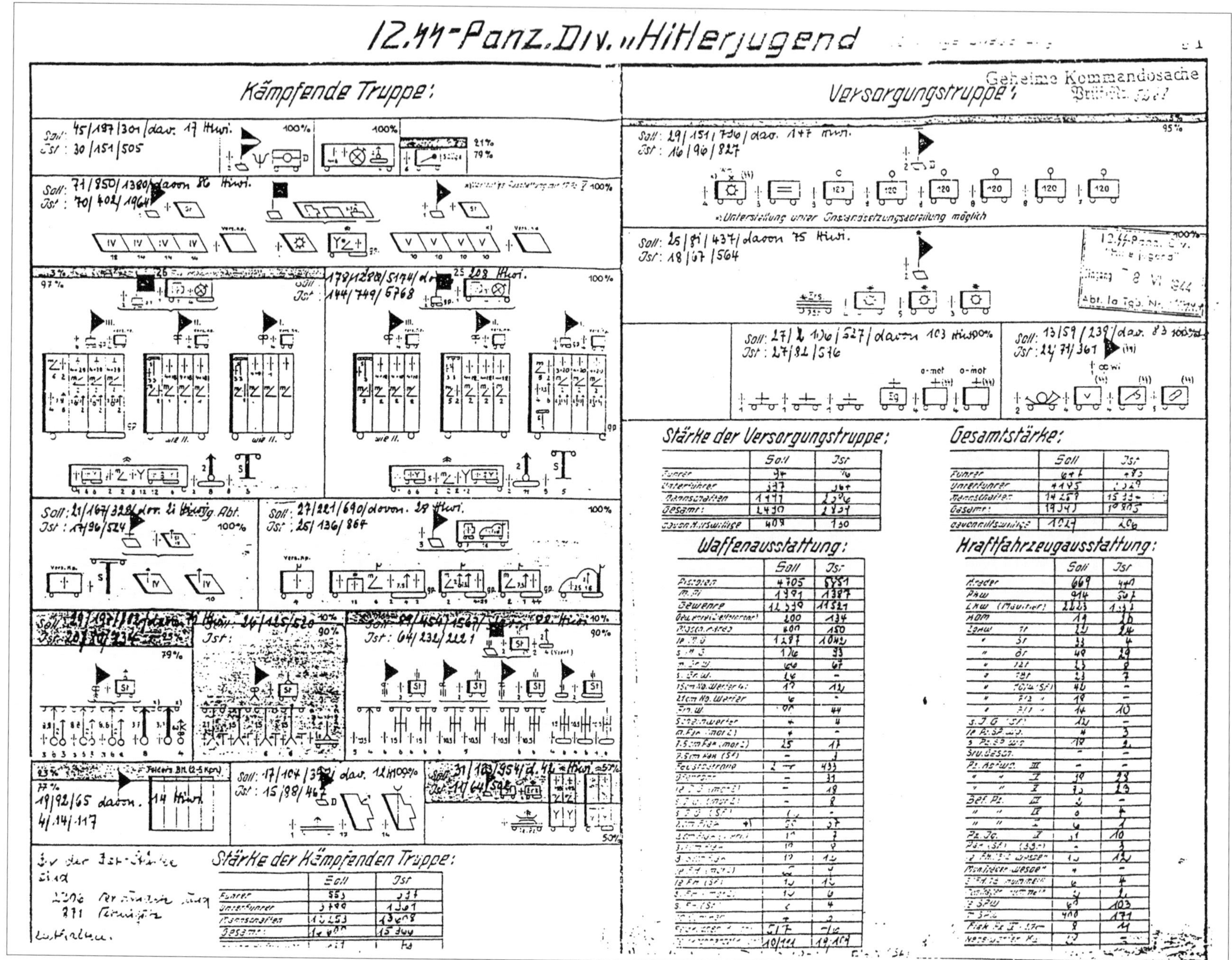

12.SS Panzer Division
Strength Report: 27th J une 1944
Under Command of I.SS Panzer Korps

MANPOWER

	Authorised Strength	Shortages	Actual
Officers	647	164	483
NCOs	4185	1857	2328
Other Ranks	14,258	1736+	15,994
Hiwis	(1029)	(823)	(206)
TOTAL	19,090	285	18,805

LOSSES BETWEEN 6/6/44 – 27/6/44

	Dead	Wounded	Missing	Hospital	Other Cases
Officers	33	55	16	12	4
NCOs / Other Ranks	845	2061	882	112	54
TOTAL	878	2116	898	124	58

REPLACEMENTS/ARRIVALS

	Replacements	Recovered
Officers	16	-
NCOs / Other Ranks	83	-

OVER 1 YEAR ABSENT FROM DIVISION (NON-LEAVE)

TOTAL	663
Of That:	
12 to 18 Months	630
19 to 24 Months	27
Over 24 Months	6

12.SS Panzer Division
Strength Report: 27th June 1944
Material Stocks

ARMOURED VEHICLES

	Pz III	Pz IV	Pz V	Other AFVs	Jagd IV
Authorised Strength	6	103	81	524	31
Ready for Action	-	32	24	298	2
Short term repair	-	22	16	21	10

MOTOR CYCLES

	Ketten	+Sidecars	Other
Authorised Strength	357	150	163
Ready for Action	2	20	418
Short term repair	-	-	133

CARS

	Cross country	Normal/Road
Authorised Strength	900	85
Ready for Action	379	188
Short term repair	82	80

TRUCKS

	Maultiere	Cross country	Normal/Road
Authorised Strength	140	959	932
Ready for Action	-	121	1216*
Short term repair	-	34	142

**Including 149 Supply Wagons with 420kg payload and 128 Light Trucks with 800-1000 Kg Payload*

TRACKED PRIME MOVERS

	1-5 Tons	8-18 Tons
Authorised Strength	126	105
Ready for Action	28	54
Short term repair	4	4

WEAPONS

	Heavy Anti-tank Guns	Artillery Guns	MG	Heavy Inf. Gun
Authorised Strength	25	59	1393	12
Ready for Action	19	54	1155	8
Short Term Repair	1	3	85	-

12.SS PANZER DIVISION
'Hitler Jugend'

27th June 1944

- Divisionstab (Divisional HQ)
  100% Manpower
  2 LMG

  Div. Kartenstelle (Mapping Section)
  100% Manpower

  Div. Begleitkompanie (Divisional Security Company)
  100% Manpower
  6 LMG. 4 HMG. 4 x SdKfz 7/1 Quad 2cm Flakwagens

  Feldgendarmerie Kompanie (Military Police Company)
  79% Manpower
  5 x Zug (Platoons). 6 LMG

- SS PANZER REGIMENT 12 (Tank Regiment)
  Regimentstab (Regimental HQ)
  100% Manpower
  11 x (2cm) Flakpanzer 38(t)

  1. Panzer Abteilung (1st Tank Battalion)
  100% Manpower
  40 *Panthers* (24 ready for action). 1 LMG

  2. Panzer Abteilung (2nd Tank Battalion)
  100% Manpower
  54 Pz IV (32 ready for action). 1 LMG

- SS PANZERGRENADIER REGIMENT 25
  (Armoured Infantry Regiment)
  100% Manpower
  Regimentstab (Regimental HQ)(Armoured)
  100% Manpower
  7 LMG

  1. Bataillon (Partially Armoured)
  100% Manpower
  Medium Armoured Halftracks. 76 LMG. 11 HMG. 11 x 81mm Mortars. 4 x 7.5cm Infantry Guns. 1 x 7.5cm Pak (Towed). 6 x 7.5cm KwK L/24 (Halftrack mounted)

  2. Bataillon (Motorised)
  100% Manpower
  45 LMG. 12 HMG. 11 x 81mm Mortars. 3 x 7.5cm Pak (Towed)

  3. Bataillon (Motorised)
  100% Manpower
  40 LMG. 12 HMG. 11 x 81mm Mortars. 3 x 7.5cm Pak (Towed)

  Flak Kompanie (Anti-aircraft Company)
  100% Manpower
  11 x 2cm Flak Guns (Towed). 2 LMG

  Infanteriegeschutz Kompanie (Infantry Gun Company)
  100% Manpower
  5 x 15cm Infantry Guns (Towed). 8 LMG

  Pionier Kompanie (Engineer Company)(Armoured)
  100% Manpower
  9 LMG. 2 HMG. 2 x 81mm Mortars.
  18 Flamethrowers

- SS PANZERGRENADIER REGIMENT 26
  (Armoured Infantry Regiment)
  97% Manpower
  Regimentstab (Regimental HQ)(Armoured)
  Medium Armoured Halftracks. 14 LMG

  1. Bataillon (Motorised)
  19 LMG. 4 HMG. 3 x 7.5cm Pak (Towed)

  2. Bataillon (Motorised)
  63 LMG. 12 HMG. 3 x 81mm Mortars. 3 x 7.5cm Pak (Towed)

  3. Bataillon (Armoured)
  Medium Armoured Halftracks (including 11 x SdKfz 251/9; 12 x SdKfz 251/2). 103 LMG. 12 HMG. 12 x 81mm Mortars. 11 x 7.5cm KwK L/24 (Halftrack mounted)

Flak Kompanie (Anti-aircraft Company)
8 x 2cm Flak Guns (Towed). 2 LMG

Infanteriegeschutz Kompanie (Infantry Gun Company)
3 x 15cm Infantry Guns (Towed). 8 LMG

Pionier Kompanie (Engineer Company)(Armoured)
Medium Armoured Halftracks. 27 LMG. 2 HMG.
2 x 81mm Mortars. 24 Flamethrowers

- SS PANZER AUFKLÄRUNGS ABTEILUNG 12
(Armoured Reconnaissance Battalion)
100% Manpower
Abteilungstab (HQ Company)
3 x SdKfz 223 (4 Wheeled) Armoured Cars. 2 x 8 Wheeled Armoured Cars (SdKfz 232 or SdKfz 231). 26 LMG

1. (Armoured Car) Company
25 Light Armoured Halftracks (including 16 x SdKfz 250/9; 9 x SdKfz 250/4). 25 LMG. 16 x 2cm KwK (Armoured Car mounted)

2. (Armoured Reconnaissance) Company
Light Armoured Halftracks (including 2 x SdKfz 250/7; 1 x SdKfz 250/8). 44 LMG. 2 x 81mm Mortars. 1 x 7.5cm KwK 37 L/24 (Halftrack mounted)

3.(Armoured Reconnaissance) Company
Light Armoured Halftracks (including SdKfz 250/7). 29 LMG. 4 HMG 2 x 81mm Mortars

4. (Heavy) Company
Medium Armoured Halftracks (including 4 x SdKfz 251/9; 6 x SdKfz 251/2). 17 LMG. 4 x 7.5cm KwK L/24. (Halftrack mounted). 6 x 81mm Mortars

Versorgungs Kompanie (Supply Company)
4 LMG

- SS PANZERJÄGER ABTEILUNG 12
(Anti-tank Battalion)
100% Manpower
10 x Jagdpanzer IV (L/48). 3 x Marder III (38(t) – Pak 40)

- SS PANZER ARTILLERIE REGIMENT 12
(Armoured Artillery Regiment)
90% Manpower

Regimentstab (Regimental HQ)
4 LMG. 4 x SdKfz 7/1 Quad 2cm Flakwagens

1. Abteilung (Armoured Battalion)
6 *Hummel* (4 ready for action). 12 *Wespe* (all ready for action). 14 LMG

2. Abteilung (Towed Battalion)
6 x 105mm LeFH 18. 8 LMG

3. Abteilung (Towed Battalion)
No Guns. 13 LMG

4. Abteilung (Towed Battalion)
12 x 150mm SFKH 18. 4 x 105mm Kanone. 19 LMG

- SS WERFER ABTEILUNG 12
(Rocket Projector Battalion)
90% Manpower
12 x 15cm Nebelwerfer

- SS FLAKABTEILUNG 12 (Anti-aircraft Battalion)
79% Manpower
18 x 88mm Flak Guns (Towed). 8 x 3.7cm Flak Guns (Towed). 8 x 2cm Flak Guns (Towed).
4 x 60cm Searchlights. 9 LMG

- SS PANZER PIONIER BATAILLON 12
(Armoured Engineer Battalion)
50% Manpower
Stabs Kompanie (Company HQ)(Partially Armoured)
Medium Armoured Halftracks. 8 LMG

1. Kompanie (Armoured)
Medium Armoured Halftracks. No heavy weapons

2. Kompanie (Armoured)
Medium Armoured Halftracks. No heavy weapons

3. Kompanie (Motorised)
13 LMG

4. Kompanie (Motorised)
18 LMG

Brucken Kolonne (Light Bridging Column – Motorised)

- SS PANZER NACHRICHTEN ABTEILUNG 12
  (Armoured Signals Battalion)(Partially Armoured)
  100% Manpower
  Medium Armoured Halftracks. 32 LMG

- SS FELDERS BATAILLON 12
  (Replacement Battalion)
  77% Manpower

- SS NACHSCHUBTRUPPEN 12
  (Divisional Supply Battalion)
  95% Manpower
  6 Transportation Companies. 1 Supply Company.
  1 Workshop Company
  62 LMG

- SS INSTADSETZUNGS ABTEILUNG 12
  (Workshop Battalion)
  100% Manpower
  3 Workshop/Repair Companies. 1 Supply Company
  14 LMG

- SS WIRTSCHAFTS BATAILLON 12
  (Commissary Battalion)
  100% Manpower
  1 Bakery Company. 1 Butcher Company.
  1 Administration Company. 1 Field Post Office.
  16 LMG

- SS SANITÄTS ABTEILUNG 12 (Medical Battalion)
  3 Ambulance Columns. 2 Medical Companies.
  1 Field Hospital
  11 LMG

12.SS Panzer Division
Strength Report: 27th June 1944

DIVISIONAL UNIT MANPOWER STRENGTHS

	Authorised Strength			Actual Strength		
	Officers	NCOs	Other Ranks	Officers	NCOs	Other Ranks
Division Stab	45	197	301	30	151	505
Panzer Regiment	71	850	1380	70	402	1964
Panzer Gren. Regt. 25 } Panzer Gren. Regt. 26 }	178	1218	5174	144	749	5768
Panzer Aufkl. Abt.	27	221	690	25	136	864
Panzerjäger Abt.	21	167	328	17	96	524
Panzer Art. Regt.	89	454	1567 }	64	232	2221
Werfer Abt.	26	125	520 }			
Flak Abt.	29	197	882	20	80	734
Pionier Bn.	31	163	954	11	64	592
Nachrichten Abt.	17	104	398	15	88	467
Felders Bn.	19	92	65	4	14	117
Div. Nachschub.	29	151	796	16	96	827
Instand. Abt.	25	81	437	18	67	564
Wirtschafts Bn.	13	59	239	22	71	361
Sanitäts Abt.	27	106	527	27	82	576
TOTAL	647	4,185	14,258	483	2,328	15,994
COMBINED TOTALS		19,090			18,805*	

**This figure includes 2,306 wounded, 871 missing and 206 'Hiwis' (Russian Helpers)*

12.SS Panzer Division
Original German Strength Report
3rd August 1944

4. Kurzes Werturteil des Kommandeurs:

Besondere Schwierigkeiten:

a) Infolge der hohen Ausfälle an Führern und eines hohen Prozentsatzes der wenigen ursprünglich vorhandenen Unterführer bei den Panzergrenadier-Regimentern ergeben sich hier außergewöhnliche Führungsschwierigkeiten.

b) Durch Mangel an Volkswagen und Krädern ist die Führung im Bewegungskrieg außerordentlich erschwert.

c) Mangel an Panzerersatzteilen, insbesondere Seitenvorgelegen.

d) Mangel an Tonnage bei den Versorgungstruppen.

Werturteil:

Der Kampfwert der Grenadier-Regimenter ist infolge der hohen Verluste, insbesondere an Führern und Unterführern, außerordentlich gesunken.

Die Division ist für Angriffsaufgaben einsatzbereit.

SS-Standartenführer und
Divisions-Kommandeur

5. Kurze Stellungnahme der vorgesetzten Dienststelle:

Anl. 3 / Ia 1182/44 — 38

Geheime Kommandosache

19

Meldung vom ... 1944, 12.SS-Panz.-Div. "Hitlerjugend"

42

1. Personelle Lage am Stichtag der Meldung:

a) Personal:

	Soll	Fehl
Offiziere	647	187
Uffz	4 185	1 969
Mannsch.	14 258	+ 591
Hiwi	(1 029)	(833)
Insgesamt	19 090	1 565

b) Verluste und sonstige Abgänge in der Berichtszeit vom ... bis ...

	tot	verw.	verm.	krank	sonst.
Offiziere	16	10	15	4	4
Uffz. und Mannsch.	438	677	574	139	182
Insgesamt	454	687	589	143	186

c) In der Berichtszeit eingetr. Ersatz:

	Ersatz	Genesene
Offiziere	5	5
Uffz. und Mannsch.	202	74

d) Über 1 Jahr nicht beurlaubt:

insgesamt: 2462	höchste 14	Monate
davon: 12 – 18 Monate	19 – 24 Monate	über 24 Monate
2425	30	7

2. Materielle Lage:

		Gepanzerte Fahrzeuge							Kraftfahrzeuge				
									Kräder			PKW	
		Stu-Gesch.	III	IV	V	VI	Schtz.Pz.Wg.	Pak Sfl.	Ketten	m. angetr. Bwg.	sonst.	gel.	o
Soll (Zahlen)		–	4	101	81	–	542	31	338	150	181	821	93
einsatzbereit	Zahlenm.	–	–	39	22	–	256	8	2	22	289	344	155
	in % des Solls	–	–	38,6	27,1	–	47,2	25,8	0,5	14,6	159,6	41,9	164
in kurzfristiger Instands. bis 3 Wochen	Zahlenm.	–	–	15	15	–	31	16	–	5	184	85	141
	in % d. Solls	–	–	14,8	18,5	–	5,7	51,6	–	3,3	101,6	10,3	151

		noch Kraftfahrzeuge							Waffen			
		LKW				Ketten-Fahrzeuge						
		Maultiere	gel.	o	Tonnage	Zgkw.		RSO	s. Pak	Art. Gesch.	MG. ( )	sonst. Waffen
Soll (Zahlen)		122	1164	956	7200	*) 126	**) 129	–	25	59	(1399) [illegible]	[illegible]
einsatzbereit	Zahlenm.	–	123	962	3905	16	46	–	16	34	820 (733)	[illegible]
	in % des Solls	–	10,5	100	54,2	12,6	35,6	–	64	57,6	59	8
einsatzbereit	Zahlenm.	–	68	312		5	8	–	2	11	86	–
	in % des Solls	–	5,8	32,6		3,9	6,2	–	8	18,6	6,3	–

*) Zgkw. mit 1-5 t / **) 8-18 t
( ) davon MG 42

Anl. zu Nr. 00940 / 44 geh.
Gen. Insp. d. Pz. Tr.

12.SS Panzer Division
Original German Organisation Chart
3rd August 1944

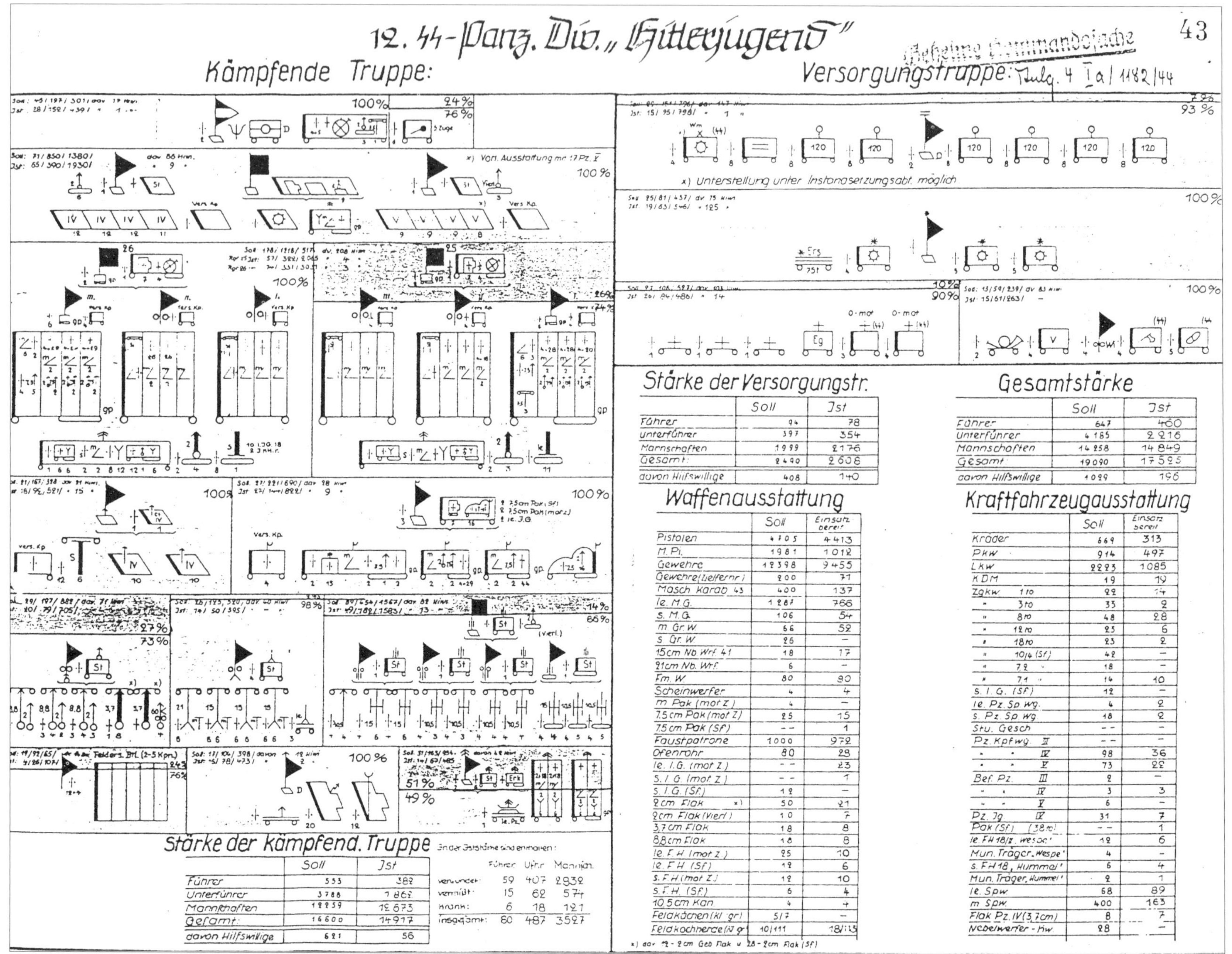

12. SS-Panz. Div. „Hitlerjugend"

Kämpfende Truppe:

Versorgungstruppe:

x) Von Ausstattung mit 17 Pz. V

x) Unterstellung unter Instandsetzungsabt. möglich

Stärke der kämpfend. Truppe

	Soll	Ist
Führer	553	382
Unterführer	3788	1862
Mannschaften	12259	12673
Gesamt:	16600	14917
davon Hilfswillige	621	56

In der Iststärke sind enthalten:

	Führer	Uffz.	Mannsch.
verwundet:	59	407	2832
vermißt:	15	62	574
krank:	6	18	121
insgesamt:	80	487	3527

Stärke der Versorgungstr.

	Soll	Ist
Führer	94	78
Unterführer	397	354
Mannschaften	1999	2176
Gesamt:	2490	2608
davon Hilfswillige	408	140

Gesamtstärke

	Soll	Ist
Führer	647	400
Unterführer	4185	2216
Mannschaften	14258	14849
Gesamt	19090	17525
davon Hilfswillige	1029	196

Waffenausstattung

	Soll	Einsatzbereit
Pistolen	4705	4413
M.Pi.	1981	1012
Gewehre	12398	9455
Gewehre (Zielfernr.)	200	71
Masch. Karab. 43	400	137
le. M.G.	1287	766
s. M.G.	106	54
m. Gr.W.	66	52
s. Gr.W.	26	–
15cm Nb. Wrf. 41	18	17
21cm Nb. Wrf.	6	–
Fm. W.	80	90
Scheinwerfer	4	4
m. Pak (mot Z.)	4	–
7,5 cm Pak (mot Z)	25	15
7,5 cm Pak (Sf)	--	1
Faustpatrone	1000	972
Ofenrohr	80	29
le. I.G. (mot Z.)	--	23
s. I.G. (mot Z.)	--	1
s. I.G. (Sf.)	12	–
2cm Flak x)	50	21
2cm Flak (Vierl.)	10	7
3,7cm Flak	18	8
8,8cm Flak	18	8
le. F.H. (mot Z.)	25	10
le. F.H. (Sf)	12	6
s. F.H. (mot Z.)	12	10
s. F.H. (Sf.)	6	4
10,5cm Kan.	4	4
Feldküchen (kl. gr.)	5/7	–
Feldkochherde (kl. gr.)	10/111	18/113

x) dav. 12 - 2cm Geb Flak u. 28 - 2cm Flak (Sf)

Kraftfahrzeugausstattung

	Soll	Einsatzbereit
Kräder	669	313
Pkw	914	497
Lkw	2223	1085
KDM	19	19
Zgkw. 1 to	22	14
" 3 to	33	2
" 8 to	48	28
" 12 to	23	6
" 18 to	23	2
" 10/4 (Sf.)	42	–
" 7,2	18	–
" 7,1	14	10
s. I.G. (Sf)	12	–
le. Pz. Sp. Wg.	4	2
s. Pz. Sp. Wg.	18	2
Stu. Gesch.	--	–
Pz. Kpfwg. III	--	–
" " IV	98	36
" " V	73	22
Bef. Pz. III	2	–
" " IV	3	3
" " V	6	–
Pz. Jg. IV	31	7
Pak (Sf) (38 t)	--	1
le. FH 18/II „Wespe"	12	6
Mun. Träger „Wespe"	4	–
s. FH 18 „Hummel"	6	4
Mun. Träger „Hummel"	2	1
le. Spw.	68	89
m. Spw.	400	163
Flak Pz. IV (3,7cm)	8	7
Nebelwerfer - Kw.	28	–

12.SS Panzer Division
Strength Report: 3rd August 1944
Under Command of I.SS Panzer Korps

MANPOWER

	Authorised Strength	Shortages	Actual
Officers	647	187	460
NCOs	4,185	1,969	2,216
Other Ranks	14,258	591+	14,849
Hiwis	(1,029)	(833)	(196)
TOTAL	19,090	1565	17,525

LOSSES BETWEEN 27/6/44 – 3/8/44

	Dead	Wounded	Missing	Hospital	Other Cases
Officers	16	10	15	4	4
NCOs / Other Ranks	438	677	574	139	182
TOTAL	454	687	589	143	186

REPLACEMENTS/ARRIVALS

	Replacements	Recovered
Officers	5	5
NCOs / Other Ranks	202	74

OVER 1 YEAR ABSENT FROM DIVISION (NON-LEAVE)

TOTAL	2462
Of That:	
12 to 18 Months	2425
19 to 24 Months	30
Over 24 Months	7

12.SS Panzer Division
Strength Report: 3rd August 1944
Material Stocks

ARMOURED VEHICLES

	Pz III	Pz IV	Pz V	Other AFVs	Jagd IV
Authorised Strength	4	101	81	542	31
Ready for Action	-	39	22	256	8
Short term repair	-	15	15	31	16

MOTOR CYCLES

	Ketten	+Sidecars	Other
Authorised Strength	338	150	181
Ready for Action	2	22	289
Short term repair	-	5	184

CARS

	Cross country	Normal/Road
Authorised Strength	821	93
Ready for Action	344	153
Short term repair	85	141

TRUCKS

	Maultiere	Cross country	Normal/Road
Authorised Strength	122	1164	956
Ready for Action	-	123	962
Short term repair	-	68	312

TRACKED PRIME MOVERS

	1-5 Tons	8-18 Tons
Authorised Strength	126	129
Ready for Action	16	46
Short term repair	5	8

WEAPONS

	Heavy Anti-tank Guns	Artillery Guns	MG (MG 42)
Authorised Strength	25	59	(1393)
Ready for Action	16	34	820 (733)
Short Term Repair	2	11	86

12.SS PANZER DIVISION
'Hitler Jugend'

3rd August 1944

- Divisionstab (Divisional HQ)
100% Manpower
2 LMG

Div. Kartenstelle (Mapping Section)
100% Manpower

Div. Begleitkompanie (Divisional Security Company)
100% Manpower
5 LMG. 4 HMG. 3 x SdKfz 7/1 Quad 2cm Flakwagens. 1 x 7.5cm Pak (Towed)

- SS PANZER REGIMENT 12 (Tank Regiment)
Regimentstab (Regimental HQ)
100% Manpower
9 x (2cm) Flakpanzer 38(t)

1. Panzer Abteilung (1st Tank Battalion)
100% Manpower
35 *Panthers* (22 ready for action). 3 x SdKfz 7/1 Quad 2cm Flakwagens. 1 LMG

2. Panzer Abteilung (2nd Tank Battalion)
100% Manpower
47 Pz IV (39 ready for action). 6 x 2cm Flak Guns (Towed). 1 LMG

- SS PANZERGRENADIER REGIMENT 25
(Armoured Infantry Regiment)
74% Manpower
Regimentstab (Regimental HQ)(Armoured)
Medium Armoured Halftracks. 14 LMG

1. Bataillon (Partially Armoured)
Medium Armoured Halftracks. 88 LMG. 12 HMG. 12 x 81mm Mortars. 3 x 7.5cm Pak (Towed)

2. Bataillon (Motorised)
16 LMG. 4 HMG. 2 x 81mm Mortars

3. Bataillon (Motorised)
No heavy weapons

Flak Kompanie (Anti-aircraft Company)
3 x 2cm Flak Guns (Towed). 2 LMG

Infanteriegeschutz Kompanie (Infantry Gun Company)
11 x 7.5cm Infantry Guns (Towed)

Pionier Kompanie (Engineer Company)(Armoured)
No heavy weapons

- SS PANZERGRENADIER REGIMENT 26
(Armoured Infantry Regiment)
Regimentstab (Regimental HQ)(Armoured)
100% Manpower
Medium Armoured Halftracks. 14 LMG

1. Bataillon (Motorised)
100% Manpower
No heavy weapons

2. Bataillon (Motorised)
100% Manpower
52 LMG. 3 x 81mm Mortars

3. Bataillon (Armoured)
100% Manpower
Medium Armoured Halftracks (including 11 x SdKfz 251/9; 11 x SdKfz 251/2). 103 LMG. 12 HMG. 11 x 81mm Mortars. 11 x 7.5cm KwK L/24 (Halftrack mounted)

Flak Kompanie (Anti-aircraft Company)
100% Manpower
4 x 2cm Flak Guns (Towed). 2 LMG

Infanteriegeschutz Kompanie (Infantry Gun Company)
100% Manpower
1 x 15cm Infantry Guns (Towed). 10 x 7.5cn Inf. Guns (Towed). 2 x 7.62cm (Russian) 'JKH' Guns (Towed)

Pionier Kompanie (Engineer Company)(Armoured)
100% Manpower
Medium Armoured Halftracks. 27 LMG. 2 HMG.
2 x 81mm Mortars. 24 Flamethrowers. 1 x 2cm Flak Gun (Halftrack mounted)

- SS PANZER AUFKLÄRUNGS ABTEILUNG 12
(Armoured Reconnaissance Battalion)
100% Manpower
Abteilungstab (HQ Company)
2 x SdKfz 223 (4 Wheeled) Armoured Cars. 2 x 8 Wheeled Armoured Cars (SdKfz 232 or SdKfz 231). 26 LMG. 2 x 7.5cm Pak (SP). 2 x 7.5cm Pak (Towed). 2 x 7.5cm Infantry Guns (Towed)

1. Kompanie (Armoured Car Company)
25 Light Armoured Halftracks (including 16 x SdKfz 250/9; 9 x SdKfz 250/4). 25 LMG. 16 x 2cm KwK (Armoured Car mounted)

2. Kompanie (Armoured Reconnaissance Company)
Light Armoured Halftracks (including 2 x SdKfz 250/7; 1 x 250/8). 44 LMG. 2 x 81mm Mortars.
1 x 7.5cm KwK 37 L/24 (Halftrack mounted)

3. Kompanie (Armoured Reconnaissance Company)
Light Armoured Halftracks (including 2 x SdKfz 250/7; 2 x SdKfz 250/8)). 29 LMG. 4 HMG.
2 x 81mm Mortars. 2 x 7.5cm KwK 37 L/24 (Halftrack mounted)

4. Kompanie (Heavy Company)
Medium Armoured Halftracks (including 1 x SdKfz 251/9). 19 LMG. 1 x 7.5cm KwK L/24. (Halftrack mounted)

Versorgungs Kompanie (Supply Company)
4 LMG

- SS PANZERJÄGER ABTEILUNG 12
(Anti-tank Battalion)
100% Manpower
Stabs Kompanie (HQ Company)
1 x Jagdpanzer V (L/48). 1 LMG

1. Kompanie (Armoured)
10 x Jagdpanzer IV (L/48)

2. Kompanie (Armoured)
10 x Jagdpanzer IV (L/48)

3. Kompanie
6 x 7.5cm Pak (Towed). 12 LMG
(Only 7 Jagdpanzer IV ready for action)

- SS PANZER ARTILLERIE REGIMENT 12
(Armoured Artillery Regiment)
86% Manpower

1. Abteilung (Armoured Battalion)
4 *Hummel*. 1 *Hummel* Munitions Carrier.
8 *Wespe* (6 ready for action). 13 LMG

2. Abteilung (Towed Battalion)
8 x 105mm LeFH 18. 9 LMG

3. Abteilung (Towed Battalion)
6 x 105mm LeFH 18. 9 LMG

4. Abteilung (Towed Battalion)
12 x 150mm SFKH 18. 4 x 105mm Kanone.
13 LMG

- SS WERFER ABTEILUNG 12
(Rocket Projector Battalion)
98% Manpower
18 x 15cm Nebelwerfer. 31 LMG. (17 ready for action)

- SS FLAKABTEILUNG 12 (Anti-aircraft Battalion)
73% Manpower
8 x 88mm Flak Guns (Towed). 8 x 3.7cm Flak Guns (Towed). 5 x 2cm Flak Guns (Towed).
4 x 60cm Searchlights. 7 LMG

- SS PANZER PIONIER BATAILLON 12
(Armoured Engineer Battalion)
49% Manpower
Stabs Kompanie (Company HQ)(Partially Armoured)
Medium Armoured Halftracks. 8 LMG

1. Kompanie (Armoured)
Medium Armoured Halftracks (including 2 x SdKfz 251/2). 2 x 81mm Mortars (Halftrack mounted).
6 Flamethrowers

2. Kompanie (Armoured)
Medium Armoured Halftracks (including 2 x SdKfz 251/2). 2 x 81mm Mortars. 6 Flamethrowers

3. Kompanie (Motorised)
18 LMG. 2 HMG. 2 x 81mm Mortars.
6 Flamethrowers

4. Kompanie (Motorised)
18 LMG. 2 HMG. 2 x 81mm Mortars.
6 Flamethrowers

Brucken Kolonne (Light Bridging Column – Motorised)
1 LMG

- SS PANZER NACHRICHTEN ABTEILUNG 12
(Armoured Signals Battalion)(Partially Armoured)
100% Manpower
Medium Armoured Halftracks. 32 LMG

- SS FELDERS BATAILLON 12
(Replacement Battalion)
76% Manpower
12 LMG. 4 HMG

- SS NACHSCHUBTRUPPEN 12
(Divisional Supply Battalion)
93% Manpower
6 Transportation Companies. 1 Supply Company.
1 Workshop Company
62 LMG

- SS INSTADSETZUNGS ABTEILUNG 12
(Workshop Battalion)
100% Manpower
3 Workshop/Repair Companies. 1 Supply Company
14 LMG

- SS WIRTSCHAFTS BATAILLON 12
(Commissary Battalion)
100% Manpower
1 Bakery Company. 1 Butcher Company.
1 Administration Company. 1 Field Post Office.
19 LMG

- SS SANITÄTS ABTEILUNG 12 (Medical Battalion)
90% Manpower
3 Ambulance Columns. 2 Medical Compaies.
1 Field Hospital
10 LMG

12.SS Panzer Division
Strength Report: 3rd August 1944

DIVISIONAL UNIT MANPOWER STRENGTHS

	Authorised Strength			Actual Strength		
	Officers	NCOs	Other Ranks	Officers	NCOs	Other Ranks
Division Stab	45	197	301	28	152	439
Panzer Regiment	71	850	1380	65	390	1930
Panzer Gren. Regt. 25	89	609	2587	57	322	2065
Panzer Gren. Regt. 26	89	609	2587	74	331	3031
Panzer Aufkl. Abt.	27	221	690	27	144	822
Panzerjäger Abt.	21	167	328	18	92	521
Panzer Art. Regt.	89	454	1567	49	182	1583
Werfer Abt.	26	125	520	14	50	595
Flak Abt.	29	197	882	20	79	705
Pionier Bn.	31	163	954	14	67	485
Nachrichten Abt.	17	104	398	15	78	473
Felders Bn.	19	92	65	4	26	107
Div. Nachschub.	29	151	796	15	95	798
Instand. Abt.	25	81	437	19	63	546
Wirtschafts Bn.	13	59	239	15	61	263
Sanitäts Abt.	27	106	527	26	84	486
TOTAL	647	4,185	14,258	460	2,216	14,849
COMBINED TOTALS		19,090			17,525*	

** The above figure includes:*
3,298 wounded
651 missing
145 sick
196 Hiwis

17.SS PANZER GRENADIER DIVISION
'Götz von Berlichingen'

The 17.SS Panzer Division was formed in France in late 1943. It spent the next seven months training and equipping in western France where it was still stationed when the Allied invasion began.

'Götz von Berlichingen' was in action within a week of the Normandy landings. It fought mainly alongside the 2.SS Panzer Division in the western sector ofthe invasion front.

On 1st June 1944 17.SS Panzer Grenadier Division had the following units on strength:

Stab der Division
SS Panzer Grenadier Regiment 37
SS Panzer Grenadier Regiment 38
SS Panzer Aufklärungs Abteilung17
SS Panzer Abteilung 17
SS Artillerie Regiment 17
SS Flak Abteilung 17
SS Panzer Pionier Bataillon 17
SS Panzer Nachrichten Abteilung 17
SS Felders Bataillon 17
SS Divisionsnachschubtruppen 17
SS Panzer Instandsetzungs Abteilung 17
SS Wirtschafts Bataillon 17
SS Sanitäts Abteilung 17
SS Feldgendarmerie Kompanie 17
SS Feldpost AMT 17

- SS Panzer Abteilung 17

SS Panzer Abteilung 17 theoretically comprised an HQ of 3 Bef. Pz III (Command Tanks) and 3 Companies of 14 StuGs each. On 1st June 1944 the unit had its full complement of 42 StuGs (37 ready for action), but no Bef. Pz IIIs.

StuG Deliveries	
Delivered in February 1944	5
Delivered in March 1944	20
Delivered in April 1944	17
TOTAL	42

Also received were 3 x 2cm Quad Flak Guns (Towed)

- SS Panzerjäger Abteilung 17

On 1st June 1944, SS Panzerjäger Abteilung 17 had 12 Marder III (38(t)). By 18th June 1944 the unit had received a full complement of 31 Jagdpanzer IVs.

17.SS Panzer Grenadier Division
Original German Strength Report
1st June 1944

17.SS-Pz.Gren.Div."G.v.B."
Ia Tgb.Nr.372/44 g.Kdos

Meldung vom 1.Juni 1944

Verband: I./SS-Pz.Korps
Unterstellungsverhältnis:

1. Personelle Lage am Stichtag der Meldung

a) Personal:

	Soll	Fehl
Offiziere	584	233
Uffz.	3566	1541
Mannsch.	14204	+ 741
Hiwi	(959)	—
Insgesamt	18354	1033

b) Verluste und sonstige Abgänge in der Berichtszeit vom ______ bis ______

	tot	verw.	verm.	krank	sonst.
Offiziere	—	—	—	1	2
Uffz. und Mannsch.	8	—	—	63	83
Insgesamt	8	—	—	64	85

c) In der Berichtszeit eingetroffener Ersatz:

	Ersatz	Genesene
Offiziere	14	
Uffz. und Mannsch.	40	

d) über 1 Jahr nicht beurlaubt.

insgesamt:	— Köpfe — % d. Ist.stärke		
Jahre	12-18 Monate	19-24 Monate	über 24 Monate
	—	—	—

Platzkarten im Berichtsmonat zugewiesen ______

2. Materielle Lage:

		Gepanzerte Fahrzeuge: Stu. Gesch.	III	IV	V	VI	Schtz.Pz. Pz.Sp. Artl.Pz.B. (o.Pz.Funkwg.)	Flak SF	Kraftfahrzeuge – Kräder: Ketten	Kräder: m. angetr. Bwg.	Kräder: sonst.	Pkw: gel.	Pkw: o
Soll (Zahlen)		42	3	—	—	—	35	26	42	274	369	1043	83
einsatzbereit	zahlenm.	37	—	—	—	—	26	11	—	61	389	763	459
	in % des Solls	88	—	—	—	—	74	43	—	22	108	73	553
in kurzfristiger Instandsetzung (bis 3 Wochen)	zahlenm.	5	—	—	—	—	—	—	—	6	34	47	9
	in % des Solls	9	—	—	—	—	—	—	—	2	1	5	18

		noch Kraftfahrzeuge: Maultiere	Lkw: gel.	Lkw: o	Tonnage	Ketten-Fahrzeuge: Zgkw. *)	Zgkw. **)	RSO	Waffen: s. Pak	Art.-Gesch.	MG ( )	sonstige Waffen
Soll (Zahlen)		31	874	812	+)	171	50	2	27	41	1154	225+
einsatzbereit	zahlenm.	18	50	121		5	6	2	8++) 22	40	1050 (950)	232
	in % des Solls	58	6	15		3	12	100	81	98	91	103
in kurzfristiger Instandsetzg. (bis 3 Wochen)	zahlenm.	2	7	22		—	—	—	1++)	1	24 (8)	13
	in % des Solls	65	1	3		—	—	—	12++)	2	0,5	5,5

*) Zgkw. mit 1-5t **) Zgkw. mit 8-18t
( ) davon MG 42

3. Pferdefehlstellen:

Soll: —
Ist: —

+) Erst nach Eintreffen von Kolonnenraum möglich.

++) Pz.Jäg.Kp.(Sf.) im Soll nicht vorhanden.

+++) Erläut gen s. Rückse

17.SS Panzer Grenadier Division
Original GermanTheoretical Organisation Chart
1st June 1944

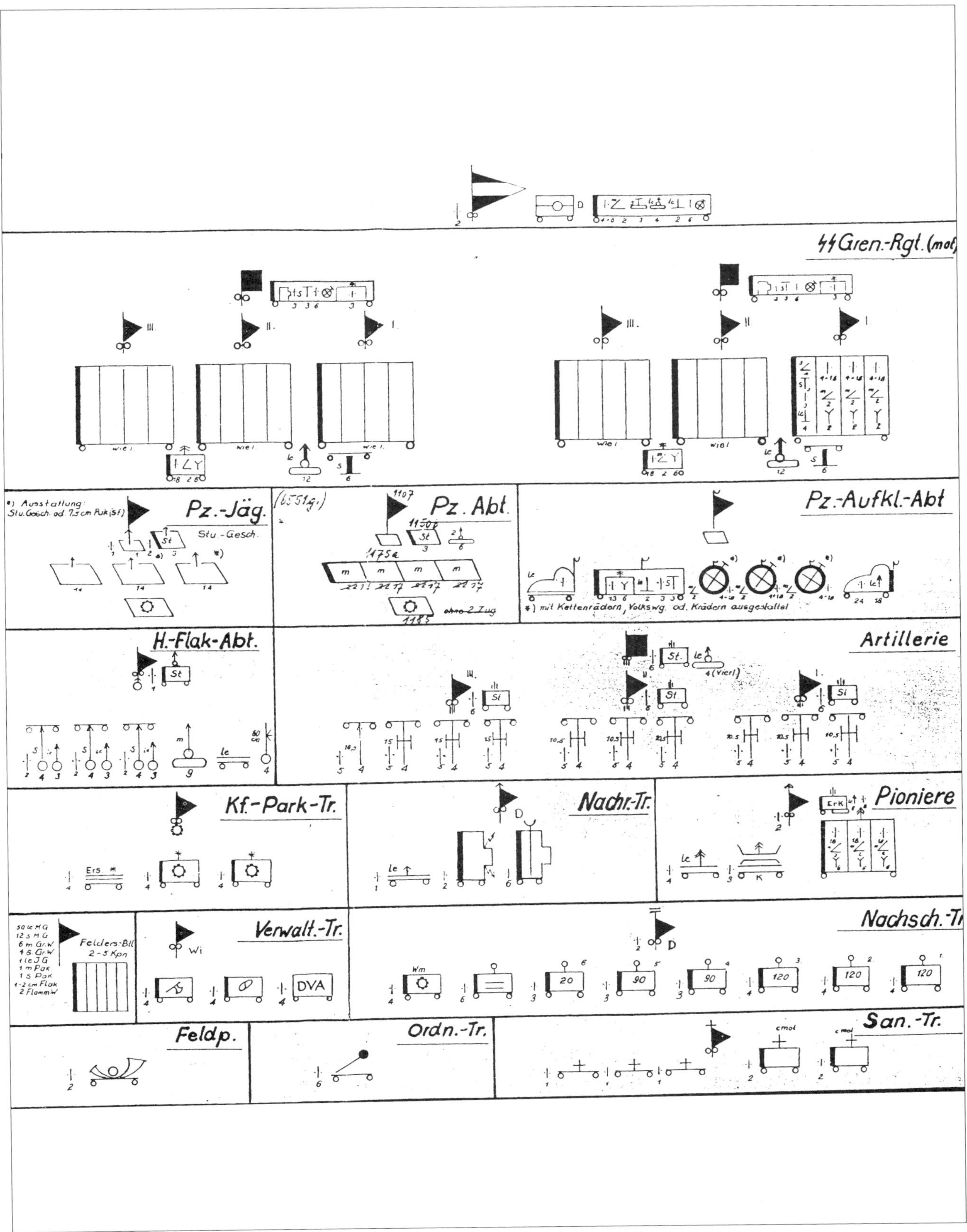

17.SS Panzer Grenadier Division
Original German Actual Organisation Chart (a)
1st June 1944

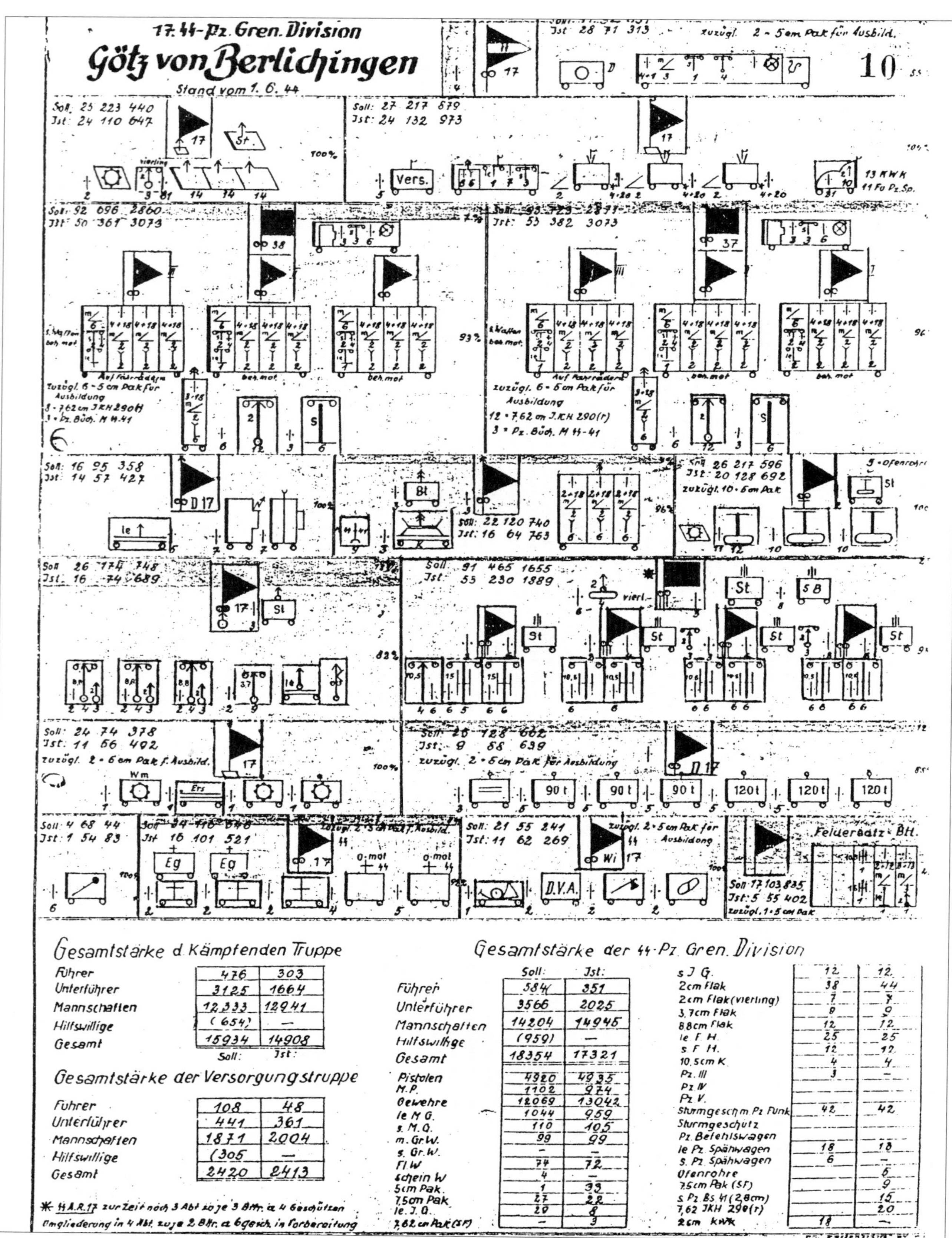

17. ℌ-Pz. Gren. Division

Götz von Berlichingen

Stand vom 1. 6. 44

Gesamtstärke d. Kämpfenden Truppe

	Soll:	Ist:
Führer	476	303
Unterführer	3125	1664
Mannschaften	12333	12941
Hilfswillige	(654)	—
Gesamt	15934	14908

Gesamtstärke der Versorgungstruppe

	Soll:	Ist:
Führer	108	48
Unterführer	441	361
Mannschaften	1871	2004
Hilfswillige	(305	—
Gesamt	2420	2413

✱ ℌ A.R.17 zur Zeit noch 3 Abt zu je 3 Bttr. a 4 Geschützen Umgliederung in 4 Abt. zu je 2 Bttr. a 6 gesch. in Vorbereitung

Gesamtstärke der ℌ-Pz. Gren. Division

	Soll:	Ist:
Führer	584	351
Unterführer	3566	2025
Mannschaften	14204	14945
Hilfswillige	(959)	—
Gesamt	18354	17321
Pistolen	4920	4935
M.P.	1102	974
Gewehre	12069	13042
le M.G.	1044	959
s. M.G.	110	105
m. Gr.W.	99	99
s. Gr.W.	–	–
Fl W	74	72
schein W	4	–
5cm Pak.	1	39
7,5cm Pak	27	22
le. J.G.	29	8
7,62 cm Pak (SF)	–	3

	Soll:	Ist:
s J G.	12	12
2cm Flak	38	44
2cm Flak (vierling)	7	7
3,7cm Flak	8	9
8,8cm Flak	12	12
le F H.	25	25
s. F H.	12	12
10,5cm K.	4	4
Pz. III	3	–
Pz IV		
Pz V.		
Sturmgesch m. Pz Funk	42	42
Sturmgeschutz		
Pz. Befehlswagen		
le Pz. Spähwagen	18	18
s. Pz. Spähwagen	6	–
Ofenrohre		6
7,5cm Pak (SF)		9
s. Pz. Bs. 41 (2,8cm)		15
7,62 JKH 290 (r)		20
2cm KwK	18	–

17.SS Panzer Grenadier Division
Original German Actual Organisation Chart (b)
1st June 1944

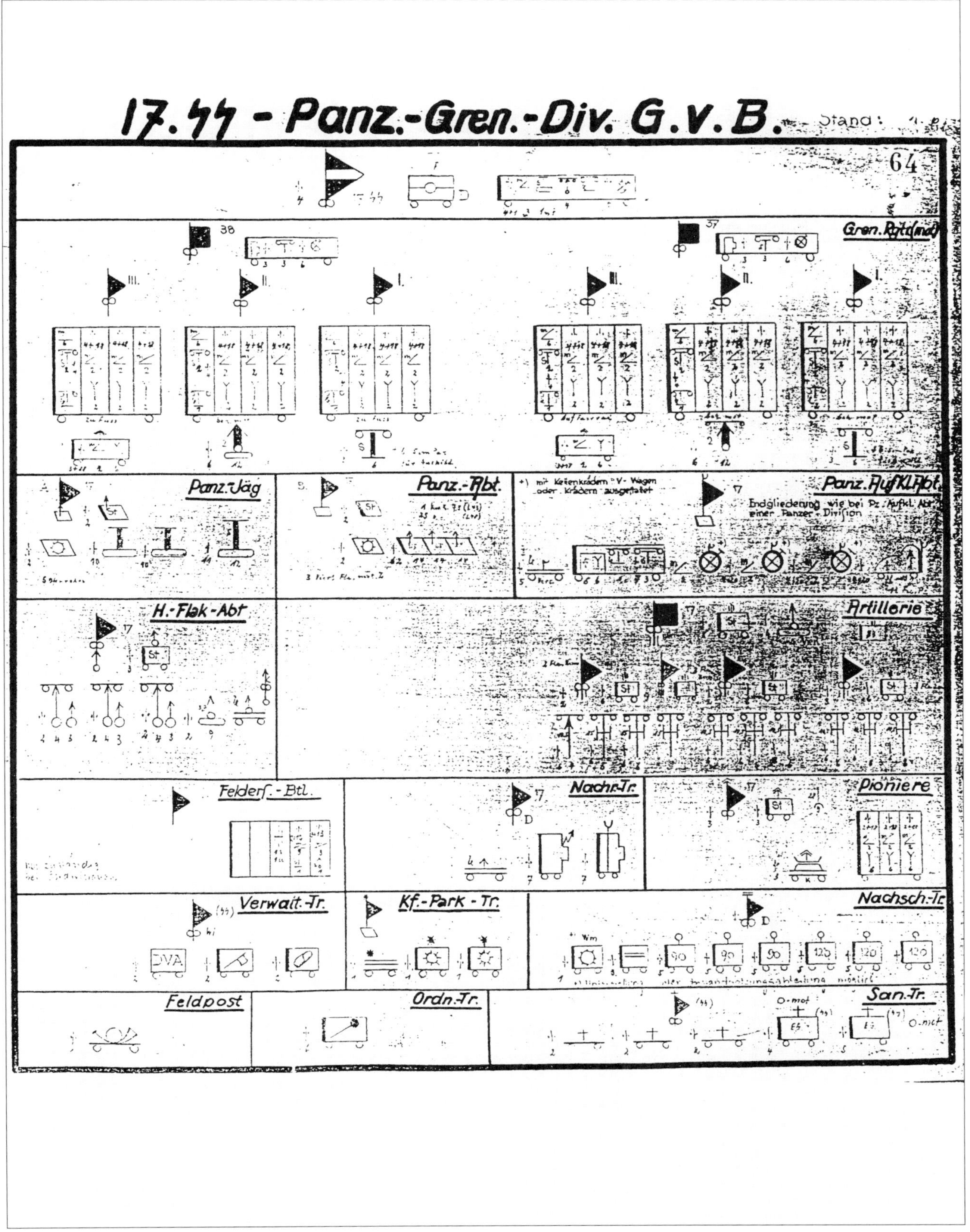

17.SS Panzer Grenadier Division
Original German Proposed Battle Group (Kampfgruppe) Organisation
1st June 1944

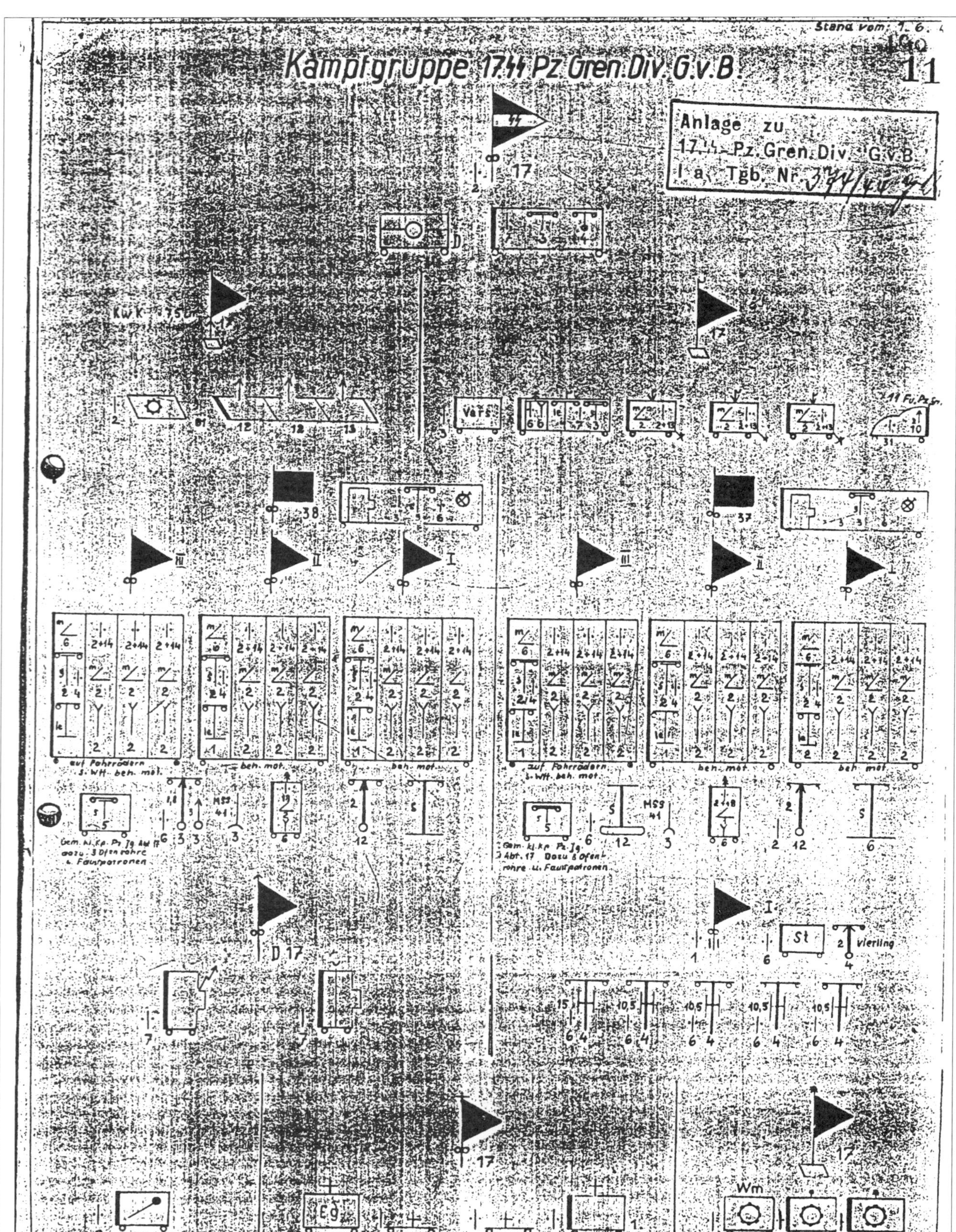

17.SS Panzer Grenadier Division
Original German Manpower Strength Report
1st June 1944

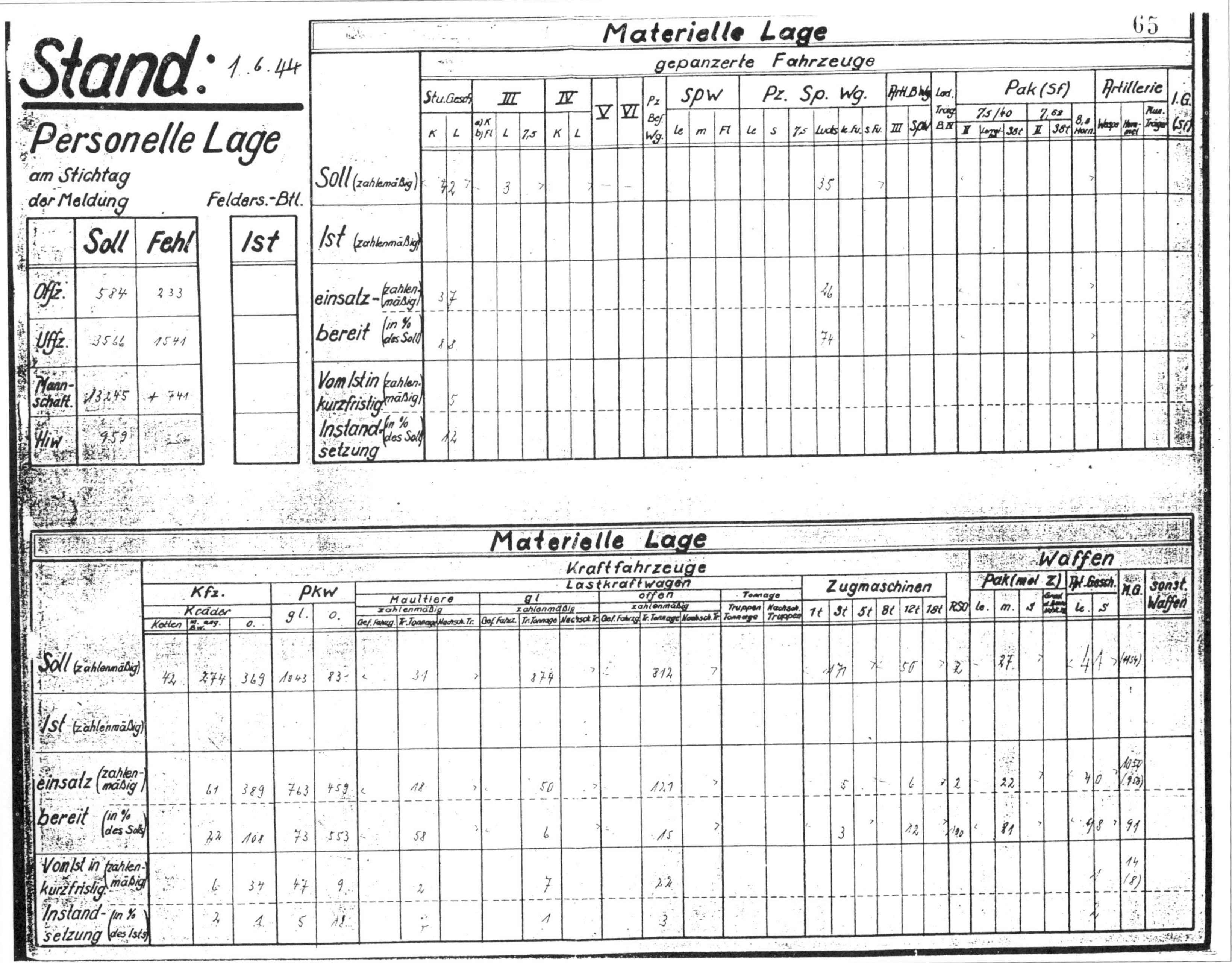

65

Stand: 1.6.44

Personelle Lage am Stichtag der Meldung

	Soll	Fehl
Offz.	584	233
Uffz.	3566	1541
Mannschaft.	13245	+ 741
Hiw	959	[illegible]

Felders.-Btl. Ist

Materielle Lage – gepanzerte Fahrzeuge

	Stu.Gesch. K	Stu.Gesch. L	III a) K b) Fl	III L	III 7,5	IV K	IV L	V	VI	Pz Bef. Wg.	SPW le	SPW m	SPW Fl	Pz. Sp. Wg. le	Pz. Sp. Wg. s	Pz. Sp. Wg. 7,5	Pz. Sp. Wg. Luchs	Pz. Sp. Wg. k.Fu.	Pz. Sp. Wg. s.Fu.	Art.B.Wg. III	Art.B.Wg. SPW	Lad. Träg. B.IV	Pak (Sf) 7,5/40 II	Pak (Sf) 7,5/40 Lorr.	Pak (Sf) 7,5/40 38t	Pak (Sf) 7,62 II	Pak (Sf) 7,62 38t	Pak (Sf) 8,8 Horn.	Artillerie Wespe	Artillerie Hummel	Artillerie Mun. Träger	I.G. (Sf)
Soll (zahlenmäßig)	42			3				–	–								35															
Ist (zahlenmäßig)																																
einsatzbereit (zahlenmäßig)	37																26															
einsatzbereit (in % des Soll)	88																74															
Vom Ist in kurzfristiger Instandsetzung (zahlenmäßig)	5																															
Vom Ist in kurzfristiger Instandsetzung (in % des Soll)	12																															

Materielle Lage – Kraftfahrzeuge / Waffen

	Kfz. Kräder Ketten	Kfz. Kräder m. angetr. Bw.	Kfz. Kräder o.	Pkw gl.	Pkw o.	Lastkraftwagen Maultiere Gel. Fahrzg.	Maultiere Tr. Tonnage	Maultiere Nachsch. Tr.	gl Gel. Fahrz.	gl Tr. Tonnage	gl Nachsch. Tr.	offen Gel. Fahrzg.	offen Tr. Tonnage	offen Nachsch. Tr.	Tonnage Truppen Tonnage	Tonnage Nachsch. Truppen	Zugmaschinen 1t	3t	5t	8t	12t	18t	RSO	Pak (mot Z) le.	Pak m.	Pak s	Grad. [illegible]	Inf. Gesch. le.	Inf. Gesch. s	M.G.	Sonst. Waffen
Soll (zahlenmäßig)	42	274	369	1843	83		31			874			812					171			50		2		27			41		(1154)	
Ist (zahlenmäßig)																															
einsatzbereit (zahlenmäßig)		61	389	763	459		18			50			121					5			6		2		22			40		1050 (958)	
einsatzbereit (in % des Soll)		22	108	73	553		58			6			15					3			12		100		81			98		91	
Vom Ist in kurzfristiger Instandsetzung (zahlenmäßig)		6	34	47	9		2			7			22																1	14 (8)	
Vom Ist in kurzfristiger Instandsetzung (in % des Ist)		2	1	5	11		7			1			3																2		

17.SS Panzer Grenadier Division
Original German Weapons Stocks Report
1st June 1944

4.) **Kurzer Werturteil des Kommandeurs:**

(Division mit 2/3 der Mannschaften in der 25.Ausbildungswoche, mit 1/3 in der 22. Ausbildungswoche. Division steht in der Verbandsausbildung.)

Bewegliche Kampfgruppe siehe Anlage.

Haltung der Truppe sehr gut.

gez. O s t e n d o r f f .

F.d.R.:

SS-Sturmbannführer und Ia

+++) Erläuterungen:

Soll:	Ist:	
99	99	8 cm Gr.Werfer
-	5	Ofenrohre
1	33	5 cm Pak
-	3	7,62 cm Pak
29	8	le.JG. 18
12	12	s.JG. 33
18	13	2 cm KwK
38	44	2 cm Flak 38
7	7	2 cm Flak-Vierling
9	9	3,7 cm Flak
12	12	8,8 cm Flak
225	245	

5.) **Kurzer Stellungnahme der vorgesetzten Dienststelle.**

Die Kampfgruppe der Division ist infolge Kfz.-Mangel (besonders Mangel an Zugmitteln für schw. Waffen) für Angriffsaufgaben nur bedingt einsatzbereit, Kolonnenraum bei den Nachschubtruppen fehlt völlig.
Bei der Division wird mit Nachdruck an der Ausbildung und Erhöhung der Einsatzbereitschaft gearbeitet.

Für das Generalkommando
Der Chef des Generalstabes

17.SS Panzer Division
Strength Report: 1st June 1944
Under Command of I.SS Panzer Korps

MANPOWER

	Authorised Strength	Shortages	Actual
Officers	584	233	351
NCOs	3,566	1,541	2,025
Other Ranks	14,204	741+	14,945
Hiwis	959	-	-
TOTAL	18,354	1,033	17,321

LOSSES FOR PREVIOUS 4 WEEKS

	Dead	Wounded	Missing	Hospital	Other Cases
Officers	-	-	-	1	2
NCOs / Other Ranks	8	-	-	63	83
TOTAL	8	-	-	64	85

REPLACEMENTS/ARRIVALS

	Replacements	Recovered
Officers	14	-
NCOs / Other Ranks	40	-

OVER 1 YEAR ABSENT FROM DIVISION (NON-LEAVE)

TOTAL	NONE
Of That:	
12 to 18 Months	-
19 to 24 Months	-
Over 24 Months	-

17.SS Panzer Grenadier Division
Strength Report: 1st June 1944
Material Stocks

ARMOURED VEHICLES

	Pz III	StuG	Other AFVs
Authorised Strength	3	42	35
Ready for Action	-	37	26
Short term repair	-	5	-

MOTOR CYCLES

	Ketten	+Sidecars	Other
Authorised Strength	42	274	369
Ready for Action	-	61	389
Short term repair	-	6	34

CARS

	Cross country	Normal/Road
Authorised Strength	1043	83
Ready for Action	763	459
Short term repair	47	9

TRUCKS

	Maultiere	Cross country	Normal/Road
Authorised Strength	31	874	812
Ready for Action	18	50	121
Short term repair	2	7	22

TRACKED PRIME MOVERS

	1-5 Tons	8-18 Tons	RSO
Authorised Strength	171	50	2
Ready for Action	5	6	2
Short term repair	-	-	-

WEAPONS

	Heavy Anti-tank Guns	Artillery Guns	MG (MG 42)
Authorised Strength	27	41	1154
Ready for Action	22	40	1050 (950)
Short Term Repair	-	1	14 (8)

17.SS PANZER GRENADIER DIVISION
'Gotz von Berlichingen'

1st June 1944

- Divisionstab (Divisional HQ)
  85% Manpower
  4 LMG

  Div. Kartenstelle (Mapping Section)
  85% Manpower

  Div. Begleitkompanie (Divisional Security Company)
  85% Manpower
  1 LMG. 4 HMG. 3 x 81mm Mortars. 1 x 7.5cm Pak (Towed). 4 x 2cm Flak Guns (Towed). 2 x 5cm Pak (Towed)

- SS PANZER AUFKLÄRUNGS ABTEILUNG 17
  (Armoured Reconnaissance Battalion)
  100% Manpower

  1. Kompanie (Armoured Car Company)
  13 x '4 Wheeled' Armoured Cars (including 2 x SdKfz 222; 11 x SdKfz 223). 31 LMG. 13 x 2cm KwK (Armoured Car mounted)

  2. Kompanie (Motorised Reconnaissance Company)
  20 LMG. 4 HMG. 2 x 81mm Mortars

  3. Kompanie (Motorised Reconnaissance Company)
  20 LMG. 4 HMG. 2 x 81mm Mortars

  4. Kompanie (Motorised Reconnaissance Company)
  20 LMG. 4 HMG. 2 x 81mm Mortars

  5.Kompanie (Heavy Motorised Company)
  13 LMG. 3 x 7.5cm Pak (Towed). 1 x 2cm Flak Gun (Towed). 6 Flamethrowers

- SS PANZER ABTEILUNG 17 (Assault Gun Battalion)
  100% Manpower
  42 Assault Guns. 83 LMG. 3 x 2cm Flak Guns (Towed)

- SS PANZERGRENADIER REGIMENT 37
  (Motorised Infantry Regiment)
  96% Manpower

  Regimentstab (Regimental HQ)
  9 LMG. 3 x 7.5cm Pak (Towed)

  1. Bataillon (Motorised)
  58 LMG. 12 HMG. 12 x 81mm Mortars. 2 x 7.5cm Infantry Guns (Towed). 2 x 7.5cm Pak (Towed). 6 Flamethrowers

  2. Bataillon (Motorised)
  58 LMG. 12 HMG. 12 x 81mm Mortars. 1 x 7.5cm Infantry Gun. 2 x 7.5cm Pak (Towed). 6 Flamethrowers

  3. Bataillon (Infantry Bicycle Mounted; Heavy Weapons Towed)
  58 LMG. 12 HMG. 12 x 81mm Mortars. 1 x 7.5cm Infantry Gun (Towed). 2 x 7.5cm Pak (Towed). 6 Flamethrowers

  Flak Kompanie (Anti-aircraft Company)
  12 x 2cm Flak Guns (Towed). 6 LMG

  Infanteriegeschutz Kompanie (Infantry Gun Company)
  6 x 15cm Infantry Guns (Towed). 3 LMG

  Pionier Kompanie (Engineer Company)
  18 LMG. 3 HMG. 2 x 81mm Mortars. 6 Flamethrowers

  The Regiment's weapons stocks also included:
  6 x 5cm Pak Towed). 12 x 7.62cm Guns (captured Russian – Towed). 3 Panzerbüsche

- SS PANZERGRENADIER REGIMENT 38
  (Motorised Infantry Regiment)
  93% Manpower
  Regimentstab (Regimental HQ)
  9 LMG. 3 x 7.5cm Pak (Towed)

  1. Bataillon (Motorised)
  58 LMG. 12 HMG. 12 x 81mm Mortars. 1 x 7.5cm Infantry Gun (Towed). 2 x 7.5cm Pak (Towed). 6 Flamethrowers

2. Bataillon (Motorised)
58 LMG. 12 HMG. 12 x 81mm Mortars. 1 x 7.5cm Infantry Gun (Towed). 2 x 7.5cm Pak (Towed). 6 Flamethrowers

3. Bataillon (Infantry Bicycle Mounted; Heavy Weapons Towed)
58 LMG. 12 HMG. 12 x 81mm Mortars. 1 x 7.5cm Infantry Gun (Towed). 2 x 7.5cm Pak (Towed). 6 Flamethrowers

Flak Kompanie (Anti-aircraft Company)
100% Manpower
12 x 2cm Flak Guns (Towed). 6 LMG

Infanteriegeschutz Kompanie (Infantry Gun Company)
6 x 15cm Infantry Guns (Towed). 3 LMG

Pionier Kompanie (Engineer Company)
18 LMG. 3 HMG. 2 x 81mm Mortars. 6 Flamethrowers

The Regiments weapons stocks also included
6 x 5cm Pak (Towed). 8 x 7.62cm Guns (captured Russian) (Towed). 3 Panzerbüchse

- SS PANZERJÄGER ABTEILUNG 17
(Anti-tank Battalion)
100% Manpower
9 Marder III 38(t) (7.5cm Pak). 3 Marder III 38(t) (7.62cm Pak – captured Russian). 10 x 5cm Pak (Towed). 33 LMG. 5 'Ofenrohre' 8.8cm Hand-held Anti-tank Weapon

- SS PANZER PIONIER BATAILLON 17
(Engineer Battalion)
96% Manpower
Stabs Kompanie (Company HQ)
6 LMG

1. Kompanie (Motorised)
18 LMG. 2 HMG. 2 x 81mm Mortars. 6 Flamethrowers

2. Kompanie (Motorised)
18 LMG. 2 HMG. 2 x 81mm Mortars. 6 Flamethrowers

3. Kompanie (Motorised)
18 LMG. 2 HMG. 2 x 81mm Mortars. 6 Flamethrowers

Brucken Kolonne (Bridging Column – Motorised)
3 LMG. 9 Panzerbüchse

- SS PANZER NACHRICHTEN ABTEILUNG 17
(Signals Battalion)
100% Manpower
19 LMG

- SS ARTILLERIE REGIMENT 17
(Motorised Artillery Regiment)
98% Manpower
Regimentstab (Regimental HQ)
19 LMG. 4 x SdKfz 7/1 Quad 2cm Flakwagens

1. Abteilung (Towed Battalion)
12 x 105mm LeFH 18. 21 LMG. 3 x 2cm Flak Guns (Towed)

2. Abteilung (Towed Battalion)
12 x 105mm LeFH 18. 26 LMG. 3 x 2cm Flak Guns (Towed)

3. Abteilung (Towed Battalion)
No heavy weapons. 18 LMG

4. Abteilung (Towed Battalion)
11 x SFH 18. 26 LMG. 4 x 105mm Kanone. 27 LMG

- SS FLAKABTEILUNG 17(Anti-aircraft Battalion)
82% Manpower
12 x 88mm Flak Guns (Towed). 9 x 3.7cm Flak Guns (Towed). 9 x 2cm Flak Guns (Towed). 11 LMG

- SS NACHSCHUBTRUPPEN 17
(Divisional Supply Battalion)
88% Manpower
6 Transportation Companies. 1 Supply Company.
28 LMG. 2 x 5cm Pak (Towed)

- SS INSTADSETZUNGS ABTEILUNG 17
(Workshop Battalion)
100% Manpower
3 Workshop/Repair Companies. 1 Supply Company
4 LMG. 2 x 5cm Pak (Towed)

- SS FELDERS BATAILLON 17
(Replacement Battalion)
48% Manpower
25 LMG. 5 HMG. 6 x 81mm Mortars. 1 x 7.5cm
Infantry Gun (Towed). 1 x 2cm Flak Gun (Towed).
1 x 5cm Pak Towed. 1 x 105mm LeFH 18 (Towed).
1 x 150mm SFH 18 (Towed)

- SS WIRTSCHAFTS BATAILLON 17
(Commissary Battalion)
100% Manpower
1 Bakery Company. 1 Butcher Company.
1 Administration Company. 1 Field Post Office.
7 LMG. 2 x 5cm Pak (Towed)

- SS SANITÄTS ABTEILUNG 17 (Medical Battalion)
92% Manpower
3 Ambulance Columns. 2 Medical Compaies.
2 Field Hospitals
15 LMG. 2 x 5cm Pak (Towed)

- SS FELDGENDARMERIE KOMPANIE 17
(Military Police Company)
100% Manpower
6 LMG

17.SS Panzer Grenadier Division
Strength Report: 1st June 1944

DIVISIONAL UNIT MANPOWER STRENGTHS

	Authorised Strength			Actual Strength		
	Officers	NCOs	Other Ranks	Officers	NCOs	Other Ranks
Division Stab	41	92	351	28	71	313
Panzer Aufkl. Abt.	27	217	879	24	132	973
Sturmgeschütz Abt.	25	223	440	24	110	647
Panzer Gren. Regt. 37	93	723	2871	53	382	3073
Panzer Gren. Regt. 38	92	696	2860	50	361	3073
Panzerjäger Abt.	26	217	596	20	128	692
Panzer Art. Regt.	91	465	1655	53	230	1889
Flak Abt.	26	174	748	16	74	689
Pionier Bn.	22	120	740	16	64	763
Nachrichten Abt.	16	95	358	14	57	427
Felders Bn.	17	103	835	5	55	402
Div. Nachschub.	25	128	662	9	88	639
Instand. Abt.	24	74	378	11	56	492
Wirtschafts Bn.	21	55	241	11	62	269
Sanitäts Abt.	34	116	546	16	101	521
Feldgendarm. Komp.	4	68	44	1	54	83
TOTAL	584	3566	14204	351	2025	14945
COMBINED TOTALS		18,354			17,321	

17.SS Panzer Grenadier Division
Strength Report: 15th June 1944

MANPOWER	Authorised Strength	Shortages	Actual
Officers	584	245	339
NCOs	3,566	1,611	1,955
Other Ranks	14,204	361+	14,565
Hiwis	977	780	197
TOTAL	18,354	1,495	16,859

LOSSES BETWEEN 1/6/44 – 15/6/44

	Dead	Wounded	Missing	Hospital	Other Cases
Officers	1	14	2	-	2
NCOs / Other Ranks	78	302	59	7	12
TOTAL	79	316	61	7	14

ARMOURED VEHICLES

	Pz III	StuG	Other AFVs	(SF)Pak
Authorised Strength	3	42	35	26
Ready for Action	-	24	26	11
Short term repair	-	13	-	-

MOTOR CYCLES

	Ketten	+Sidecars	Other
Authorised Strength	42	274	369
Ready for Action	-	61	389
Short term repair	-	6	34

CARS

	Cross country	Normal/Road
Authorised Strength	1043	83
Ready for Action	764	459
Short term repair	47	9

TRUCKS

	Maultiere	Cross country	Normal/Road
Authorised Strength	31	875	812
Ready for Action	18	50	121
Short term repair	2	7	22

TRACKED PRIME MOVERS

	1-5 Tons	8-18 Tons	RSO
Authorised Strength	171	50	2
Ready for Action	5	6	2
Short term repair	-	-	

17.SS Panzer Grenadier Division
Strength Report: 15th June 1944
Weapons Stocks

WEAPONS

	Heavy Anti-tank Guns	Artillery Guns	MG	(MG 42)
Authorised Strength	27	41	1154	
Ready for Action	20+7 (SP)	39	1008	(906)
Short Term Repair	2+2 (SP)	2	24	(18)

COMPLETE WEAPONS STOCKS

Type	Authorised Number	Actual Number
Seitengewehr	12069	12695
Karabiner 98K	11469	11948
Gewehr 98/40	-	368
Pistole	4920	4870
MP 38/40	1102	937
Gr. B. 39	78	-
Gew. Gr. Gerät	404	78
Karabiner 98mm Zielf.	200	195
Geweher 41	400	395
Ie MG	1044	930
S MG	110	102
8cm Gr. W. 34	99	93
FM. W. 41	74	72
Leuchtpistole	600	410
Panzerschreck	-	5
Pz Bü M SS 41	-	15
5cm Pak 38	1	31
7.5cm Pak 40	27	22
7.5cm Pak 40 (SF)	-	9
7.62cm Pak 37 (SF)	-	3
Le I.G. 18	29	8
S.I.G. 33	12	12
2cm Flak 38	38	44
2cm Flak-Vierling	7	7
3.7cm Flak 37	9	9
8.8cm Flak 37	12	12
Le FH 18(M)	25	25
S FH 18	12	12
S 10cm K.18	4	4
2cm Kw. 30/38	18	13
7.5cm Stu.K. 40L48	76	38
7.62cm J.K.H. (290)R	-	20
Brüuck. Kol. K (Mot)	1	1
Backanhänger	5	4

17.SS Panzer Grenadier Division
Strength Report: 7th July 1944
Vehicle Stocks

	Motorcycles	Cross country Cars	Road Cars	Cross country Trucks
Authorised Strength	675	1093	86	1105
Actual Strength	382	516	1144	676
Shortages	293	577	1058+	429

	Road Trucks	Tracked Prime Movers	Armoured Cars	Armoured Halftracks & SP flak
Authorised Strength	915	273	25	25
Actual Strength	539	204	7	15
Shortages	379	69	18	10

	Other Armoured Vehicles (StuG, *Jagdpanther,* etc)
Authorised Strength	90
Actual Strength	45
Shortages	

DIVISIONAL UNIT VEHICLE STRENGTHS

	Motor Cycles	Field Cars	Trucks	Prime Movers	Armoured Cars	Armoured Halftracks	Other AFVs
Division Stab	45	52	34	-	1	4	-
Panzer Aufk. Abt.	10	6	81	9	6	-	-
Sturmgeschütz Abt.	11	15	73	16	-	8	22
Panzer Gren. Regt. 37	82	129	277	53	-	-	-
Panzer Gren. Regt. 38	70	677	122	60	-	-	-
Panzerjäger Abt.	16	54	53	25	-	1	23
Panzer Art. Regt.	14	100	162	4	-	-	-
Flak Abt.	5	20	84	17	-	-	-
Pionier Bn.	32	7	88	19	-	-	-
Nachrichten Abt.	4	29	27	-	-	2	-
Div. Nachschub.	51	80	46	-	-	-	-
Instand. Abt.	10	24	67	1	-	-	-
Wirtschafts Bn.	2	15	39	-	-	-	-
Sanitäts Abt.	16	197	60	-	-	-	-
Feldgendarm. Komp.	14	27	2	-	-	-	-
TOTAL	382	1432	1215	204	7	15	45

17.SS PANZER GRENADIER DIVISION
'Gotz von Berlichingen'

17.SS Panzer Grenadier Division
Strength Report: 23rd July 1944

Divisional Strength 23rd July 1944

2 weak combat battalions. 5 'worn out' combat battalions. 10 x 7.5cm Pak. 10 Assault Guns. 5 light Artillery Batteries. Division 30% motorised.

After 23rd July, Strength documents relating to the 17.SS Division are very scarce. However it seems clear that by early August the Division was a mere shadow of its former self, possessing virtually no heavy armour or heavy weapons.

Following its withdrawal back to Germany it was rebuilt and re-equipped prior to its use in 'Operation Nordwind' in January 1945.

1.SS Panzer Korps
Original German Strength Report (HQ only)
1st June 1944

19

Meldung vom 1. 6. 1944

Verband: Gen. Kdo. I SS-Pz. Kps mit Kps. Truppen
Unterstellungsverhältnis: [illegible]

1. Personelle Lage am Stichtag der Meldung:

a) Personal:

	Soll	Fehl
Offiziere	179	59
Uffz.	851	273
Mannsch.	2972	1138
Hiwi	257	140
Insgesamt	4002	194

b) Verluste und sonstige Abgänge in der Berichtszeit vom 15.5 bis 31.5.44

	tot	verw.	verm.	krank	sonst.
Offiziere	–	–	–	1	3
Uffz. und Mannsch.	2	–	2	29	24
Insgesamt	2	–	2	30	27

c) in der Berichtszeit eingetroffener Ersatz:

	Ersatz	Genesene
Offiziere	–	–
Uffz. und Mannsch.	17	8

d) über 1 Jahr nicht beurlaubt:

insgesamt: 120 Köpfe 3 % d. Iststärke

davon:	12 - 18 Monate	19 - 24 Monate	über 24 Monate
	99	14	2

Platzkarten im Berichtsmonat zugewiesen: –

2. Materielle Lage:

		Gepanzerte Fahrzeuge: Stu. Gesch.	III	IV	V (Bergepz)	VI	Schtz. Pz. Pz. Sp. Art. Pz. B. (o. Pz. Fu. Wg)	Pz. Fu.	Kraftfahrzeuge: Kräder: Ketten	Kräder: m. angetr. Bwg.	Kräder: sonst.	Pkw: gel.	Pkw: o
Soll (Zahlen)						45	11	2	11	94	170	175	60
einsatzbereit	zahlenm.				1	37	10	2		30	91	135	71
	in % des Solls					82	90.1	100		40	53%	154	118
in kurzfristiger Instandsetzung (bis 3 Wochen)	zahlenm.					8				1	25%	18	11
	in % des Solls					17				1.1	12%	10	18

		noch Kraftfahrzeuge: Lkw: Maultiere	Lkw: gel.	Lkw: o	Lkw: Tonnage	Ketten-Fahrzeuge: Zgkw. *)	Zgkw. **)	RSO	Waffen: s Pak	Art.-Gesch.	MG. ()	sonstige Waffen
Soll (Zahlen)		4	281	270	1436.5	7	58	1	3	22	(94) 228	
einsatzbereit	zahlenm.	19	93	385	1080	8	40		3	22	(113) 273	
	in % des Solls	475	33	142.5	75	114	98.4		100	100		
in kurzfristiger Instandsetzung (bis 3 Wochen)	zahlenm.	2	4	28	87		3					
	in % des Solls	50	1.4	1.05	6.1		5.1					

SS K.K.St. 1 (Nr 19c)

*) Zgkw. mit 1-5t, **) Zgkw. mit 8-18t
() davon MG. 42

3. Pferdefehlstellen:

Anl. zu Nr. 0065/44 geh.
Gen. Insp. d. Pz. Tr.

1.SS Panzer Korps
Original German Organisation Chart (HQ only)
1st June 1944

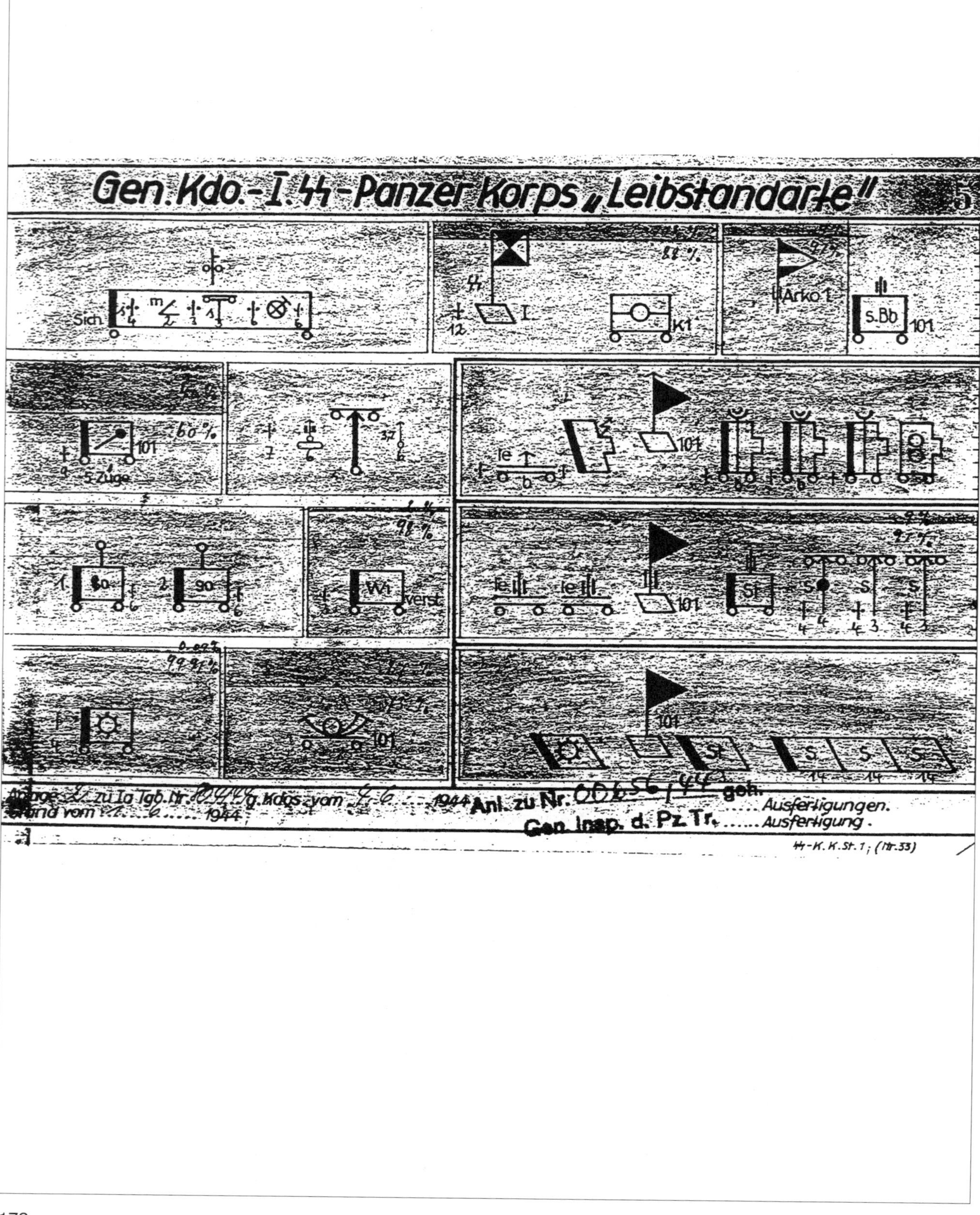

1.SS PANZER KORPS (HQ only)

Strength Report: 1st June 1944
Under Command of Panzer Group West

MANPOWER

	Authorised Strength	Shortages	Actual
Officers	179	59	120
NCOs	851	273	578
Other Ranks	2,972	138+	3,110
Hiwis	257	140	117
TOTAL	4,002	194	3,808

LOSSES BETWEEN 15/5/44 – 31/5/44

	Dead	Wounded	Missing	Hospital	Other Cases
Officers	-	-	-	1	3
NCOs / Other Ranks	2	-	2	29	24
TOTAL	2	-	2	30	27

REPLACEMENTS/ARRIVALS

	Replacements	Recovered
Officers	-	-
NCOs / Other Ranks	17	8

OVER 1 YEAR ABSENT FROM HQ (NON-LEAVE)

TOTAL	120
Of That:	
12 to 18 Months	99
19 to 24 Months	19
Over 24 Months	2

1.SS Panzer Korps (HQ only)
Strength Report: 1st June 1944
Material Stocks

ARMOURED VEHICLES

	Berg Pz V	Pz VI	Other AFVs	Armoured Radio Vehicles
Authorised Strength	-	45	11	2
Ready for Action	1	37	10	4
Short term repair	-	8	-	-

MOTOR CYCLES

	Ketten	+Sidecars	Other
Authorised Strength	11	89	196
Ready for Action	-	36	69
Short term repair	-	1	25

CARS

	Cross country	Normal/Road
Authorised Strength	175	60
Ready for Action	235	71
Short term repair	18	11

TRUCKS

	Maultiere	Cross country	Normal/Road
Authorised Strength	4	281	270
Ready for Action	19	93	385
Short term repair	2	4	28

TRACKED PRIME MOVERS

	1-5 Tons	8-18 Tons	RSO
Authorised Strength	7	58	1
Ready for Action	8	40	-
Short term repair	-	3	-

WEAPONS

	Heavy Anti-tank Guns	Artillery Guns	MG	(MG 42)
Authorised Strength	3	22	228	(64)
Ready for Action	3	22	273	
Short Term Repair	-	-		(137)

1.SS Panzer Korps
Original German Strength Report (HQ only)
1st July 1944

Meldung vom 1.7. 1944

Verband: Gen.Kdo.I.SS-Pz.Kps. 6
Unterstellungsverhältnis: mit Kps.-Truppen

[illegible] 935/44 [illegible] 6.7.44

1. Personelle Lage am Stichtag der Meldung:

a) Personal:

	Soll	Fehl
Offiziere	175	52
Uffz.	823	247
Mannsch.	2854	+ 259
davon Hiwi	231	135
Insgesamt	3852	40

b) Verluste und sonstige Abgänge in der Berichtszeit vom 15.6. bis 1.7.44

	tot	verw.	verm.	krank	sonst.
Offiziere	2	4	-	1	-
Uffz. und Mannsch.	33	78	7	19	13
Insgesamt	35	82	7	20	13

c) in der Berichtszeit eingetroffener Ersatz:

	Ersatz	Genesene
Offiziere	4	-
Uffz. und Mannsch.	45	12

d) über 1 Jahr nicht beurlaubt:

insgesamt: 180 Köpfe ______ % d. Iststärke

davon:	12 - 18 Monate	19 - 24 Monate	über 24 Monate
	156	21	3

Platzkarten im Berichtsmonat zugewiesen: —

2. Materielle Lage:

		Gepanzerte Fahrzeuge							Kraftfahrzeuge				
									Kräder			Pkw	
		Stu. Gesch.	III	IV	V Berge	VI	Schtz. Pz. Pz. Sp. Art. Pz. B. (o. Pz. Fu. Wg.)	Pak Sf.	Ketten	m. angetr. Bwg.	sonst.	gel.	O
Soll (Zahlen)						45	13	-	11	89	194	183	61
einsatzbereit	zahlenm.					11	13	-	1	29	60	241	70
	in % des Solls					24,4	100	-	9	32,5	30,9	131,6	114,7
in kurzfristiger Instandsetzung (bis 3 Wochen)	zahlenm.				1	19	1	-	-	6	24	26	15
	in % des Solls					42,2	7,6	-	-	6,7	12,3	14,2	24,3

		noch Kraftfahrzeuge							Waffen			
			Lkw			Ketten-Fahrzeuge						
		Maultiere	gel.	O	Tonnage	Zgkw. *)	Zgkw. **)	RSO	s Pak	Art.-Gesch.	MG. ( )	sonstige Waffen
Soll (Zahlen)		4	282	271	1446,5	8	57	1	3	22	228 (64)	-
einsatzbereit	zahlenm.	20	117	472	1060,5	7	39	-	2	23	238 (32)	-
	in % des Solls	500	41,4	174,1	73,3	87,5	68,4	-	66,6	104,5	104,3	-
in kurzfristiger Instandsetzung (bis 3 Wochen)	zahlenm.	-	15	32	141	1	4	-	1	2	(1)	-
	in % des Solls	-	5,3	11,8	9,5	12,5	7	-	33,3	9	0,4	-

SS K.K.St. 1 (Nr 79 c)

*) Zgkw. mit 1-5t, **) Zgkw. mit 8-18t
( ) davon MG. 42

3. Pferdefehlstellen:

Anl. zu Nr. [illegible] / 44 geh.
Gen. Insp. d. Pz. Tr.

1.SS Panzer Korps
Original German Organisation Chart (HQ only)
1st July 1944

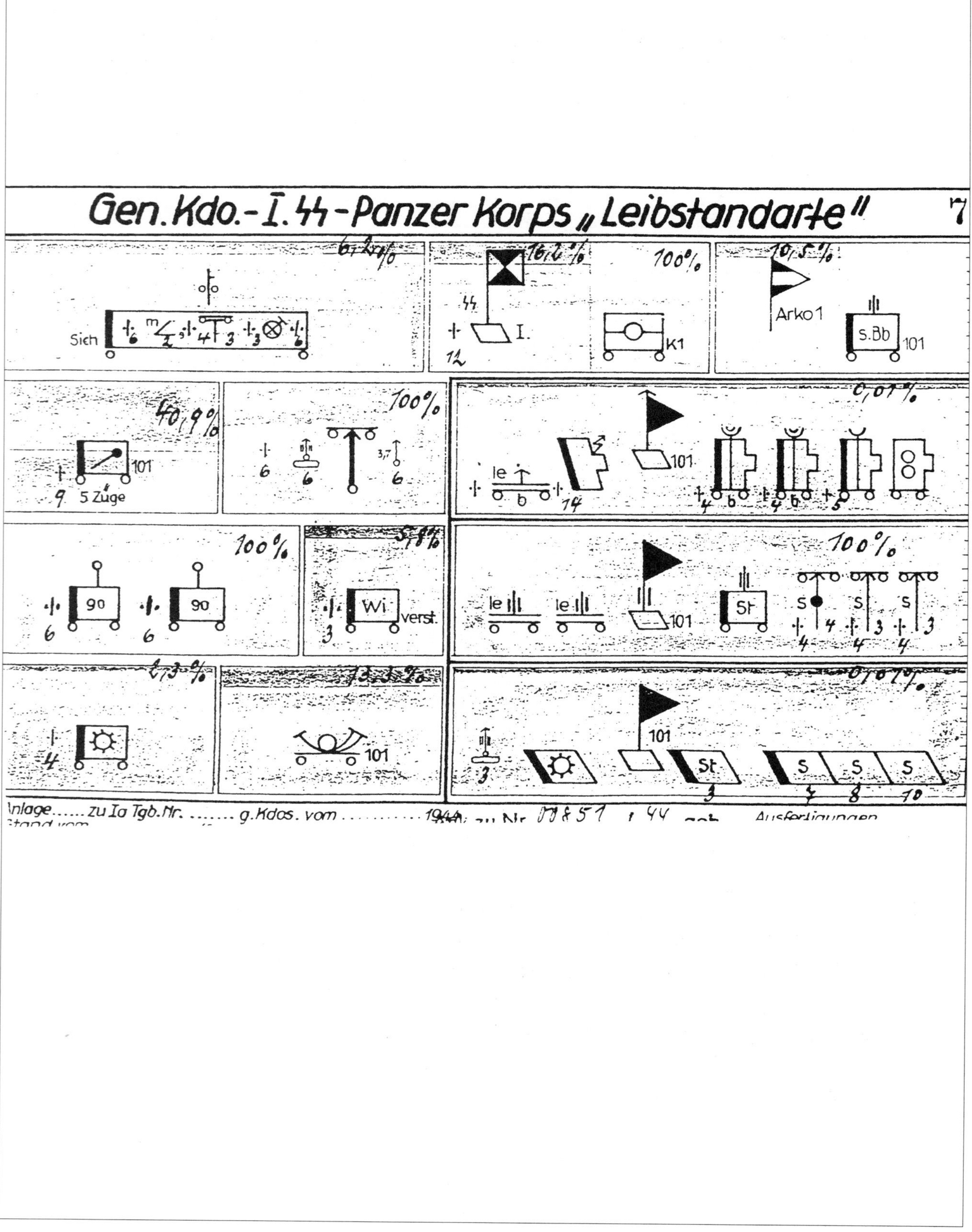

1.SS Panzer Korps (HQ only)
Strength Report: 1st July 1944
Under Command of Panzer Group West

MANPOWER

	Authorised Strength	Shortages	Actual
Officers	175	52	123
NCOs	823	247	576
Other Ranks	2,854	259+	3,113
Hiwis	231	135	96
TOTAL	3,852	40	3,812

LOSSES BETWEEN 15/6/44 – 1/7/44

	Dead	Wounded	Missing	Hospital	Other Cases
Officers	2	4	-	1	-
NCOs / Other Ranks	33	78	7	19	13
TOTAL	35	82	7	20	13

REPLACEMENTS/ARRIVALS

	Replacements	Recovered
Officers	4	-
NCOs / Other Ranks	45	12

OVER 1 YEAR ABSENT FROM DIVISION (NON-LEAVE)

TOTAL	180
Of That:	
12 to 18 Months	156
19 to 24 Months	21
Over 24 Months	3

1.SS Panzer Korps (HQ only)
Strength Report: 1st July 1944
Material Stocks

ARMOURED VEHICLES

	Berg Pz V	Pz VI	Other AFVs
Authorised Strength	-	45	13
Ready for Action	-	11	13
Short term repair	1	19	1

MOTOR CYCLES

	Ketten	+Sidecars	Other
Authorised Strength	11	89	194
Ready for Action	1	29	60
Short term repair	-	6	24

CARS

	Cross country	Normal/Road
Authorised Strength	183	61
Ready for Action	241	70
Short term repair	26	15

TRUCKS

	Maultiere	Cross country	Normal/Road
Authorised Strength	4	282	271
Ready for Action	20	117	472
Short term repair	-	15	32

TRACKED PRIME MOVERS

	1-5 Tons	8-18 Tons	RSO
Authorised Strength	8	57	1
Ready for Action	7	39	-
Short term repair	1	4	-

WEAPONS

	Heavy Anti-tank Guns	Artillery Guns	MG	(MG 42)
Authorised Strength	3	22	228	(64)
Ready for Action	2	23	238	(92)
Short Term Repair	1	2		(1)

1.SS Panzer Korps
Original German Strength Report (HQ only)
1st August 1944

Geheime Kommandosache

~~Meldung vom~~ 1.8.44 ~~1943~~

Verband: Gen.Kdo.I.SS-Pz.Kps. mit Korps-Truppen 9

Unterstellungsverhältnis: Pz.Gr.West

Anlg. 1 / Ia 1182/44

1. Personelle Lage am Stichtag der Meldung:

a) Personal:

	Soll	Fehl
Offiziere	179	61
Uffz.	843	261
Mannsch.	3015	96
davon Hiwi	262	200
Insgesamt	4037	418

b) Verluste und sonstige Abgänge in der Berichtszeit vom 15.7. bis 1.8.44

	tot	verw.	verm.	krank	sonst.
Offiziere	1	1	-	-	7
Uffz. und Mannsch.	23	56	2	25	64
Insgesamt	24	57	2	25	71

c) in der Berichtszeit eingetroffener Ersatz:

	Ersatz	Genesene
Offiziere	1	-
Uffz. und Mannsch.	12	8

d) über 1 Jahr nicht beurlaubt:

insgesamt: 320 Köpfe ______ % d. Iststärke

davon:	12 - 18 Monate	19 - 24 Monate	über 24 Monate
	284	31	5

Platzkarten im Berichtsmonat zugewiesen. ....

2. Materielle Lage:

		Gepanzerte Fahrzeuge							Kraftfahrzeuge				
		Stu. Gesch.	III	IV	V (Berg.)	VI	Schtz. Pz. Pz. Sp. Art. Pz. B. (o. Pz. Fu. Wg.)	Pak Sf.	Kräder Ketten	Kräder m. angeh. Bwg.	Kräder sonst.	Pkw gel.	Pkw O
Soll (Zahlen)		-	-	-	-	45	13	-	8	89	194	180	61
einsatzbereit	zahlenm.	-	-	-	1	20	14	-	3	33	61	238	65
	in % des Solls	-	-	-	-	44,4	107	-	37,5	37,1	31,4	132,2	106,6
in kurzfristiger Instandsetzung (bis 3 Wochen)	zahlenm.	-	-	-	-	5	-	-	-	3	31	19	9
	in % des Solls	-	-	-	-	11,1	-	-	-	3,4	16	10,6	14,8

		noch Kraftfahrzeuge							Waffen			
		Lkw Maultiere	Lkw gel.	Lkw O	Lkw Tonnage	Ketten-Fahrzeuge Zgkw. *)	Ketten-Fahrzeuge Zgkw. **)	Ketten-Fahrzeuge RSO	s Pak	Art.-Gesch.	MG. ( )	sonstige Waffen
Soll (Zahlen)		4	281	279	1452	8	54	1	3	10	(86) 228	
einsatzbereit	zahlenm.	18	106	392	1154	7	45	-	3	7	(141) 236	
	in % des Solls	450	37,7	140,5	79,5	87,5	83,3	-	100	70	(164) 103,5	
in kurzfristiger Instandsetzung (bis 3 Wochen)	zahlenm.	-	10	35	116	-	3	-	-	2	(1)	
	in % des Solls	-	3,6	12,5	8	-	5,6	-	-	20	1,2	

SS K.K.St. 1 (Nr 79c)

*) Zgkw. mit 1-5t, **) Zgkw. mit 8-18t

( ) davon MG. 42

3. Pferdefehlstellen:

....

Anl. zu Nr. 00940 / 44 geh.

Gen. Insp. d. Pz. Tr.

1.SS Panzer Korps
Original German Organisation Chart (HQ only)
1st June 1944

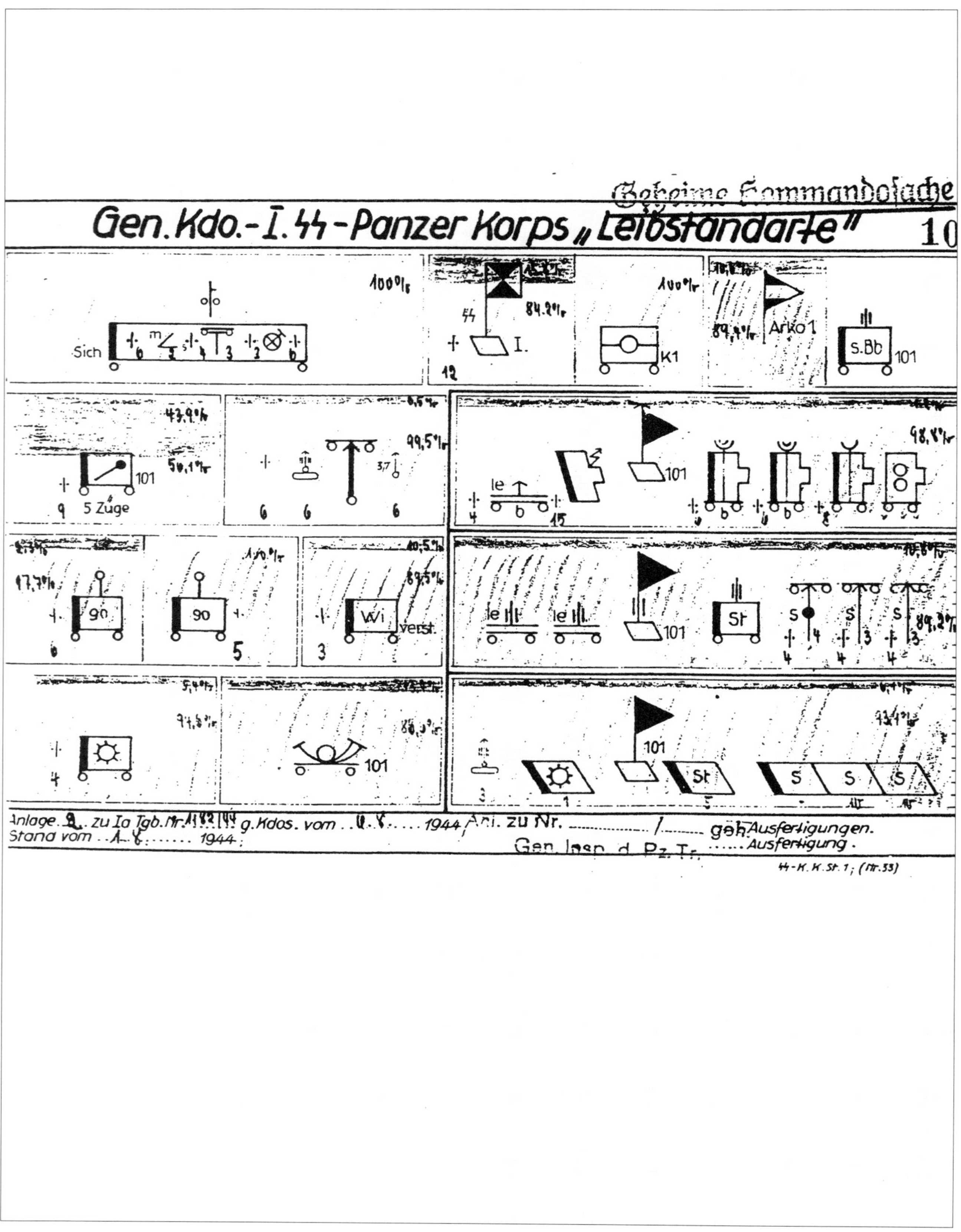

1.SS Panzer Korps (HQ only)
Strength Report: 1st August 1944
Under Command of Panzer Group West

MANPOWER

	Authorised Strength	Shortages	Actual
Officers	179	61	118
NCOs	843	261	582
Other Ranks	3,015	96	2,919
Hiwis	262	200	62
TOTAL	4,037	418	3,619

LOSSES BETWEEN 15/7/44 – 1/8/44

	Dead	Wounded	Missing	Hospital	Other Cases
Officers	1	1	-	-	7
NCOs / Other Ranks	23	56	2	25	64
TOTAL	24	57	2	25	71

REPLACEMENTS/ARRIVALS

	Replacements	Recovered
Officers	1	-
NCOs / Other Ranks	12	8

OVER 1 YEAR ABSENT FROM DIVISION (NON-LEAVE)

TOTAL	320
Of That:	
12 to 18 Months	284
19 to 24 Months	31
Over 24 Months	5

1.SS Panzer Korps (HQ only)
Strength Report: 1st August 1944
Material Stocks

ARMOURED VEHICLES

	Berg Pz V	Pz VI	Other AFVs
Authorised Strength	-	45	13
Ready for Action	1	20	14
Short term repair	-	5	-

MOTOR CYCLES

	Ketten	+Sidecars	Other
Authorised Strength	8	89	194
Ready for Action	3	33	61
Short term repair	-	3	31

CARS

	Cross country	Normal/Road
Authorised Strength	180	61
Ready for Action	238	65
Short term repair	19	9

TRUCKS

	Maultiere	Cross country	Normal/Road
Authorised Strength	4	281	279
Ready for Action	18	106	392
Short term repair	-	10	35

TRACKED PRIME MOVERS

	1-5 Tons	8-18 Tons	RSO
Authorised Strength	8	54	1
Ready for Action	7	45	-
Short term repair	-	3	-

WEAPONS

	Heavy Anti-tank Guns	Artillery Guns	MG	(MG 42)
Authorised Strength	3	10	228	(86)
Ready for Action	3	7	236	(141)
Short Term Repair	-	2		(1)

Schwere SS Panzer Abteilung 101
(SS Tiger Tank Battalion 101)
I.SS Panzer Korps

Between 4/7/44 and 31/7/44, SS Panz. Abt. 101 had the following *Tiger Is* on strength

4/7/44
Pz VI 25
Berge Pz V 1
In repair
Pz VI 5

5/7/44
Pz VI 25
In repair
Pz VI 5

7/7/44
Pz VI 25
Berge Pz V 1
In repair
Pz VI 5

8/7/44
Pz VI 20
Bef Pz VI 1
In repair
Pz VI 7
Berge Pz V 1

11/7/44
Pz VI 13
In repair
Pz VI 15
Berge Pz V 1

13/7/44
Pz VI 14
In repair
Pz VI 13
Berge Pz V 1
Bef PzVI 1

16/7/44
Pz VI 17
Bef Pz VI 3
Berge Pz V 1
In repair
Pz VI 8

26/7/44
Pz VI 13
Bef Pz VI 1

In repair
Pz VI 11

28/7/44
Pz VI 20
Berge Pz V 1
In repair
Pz VI 4

30/7/44
Pz VI 18
Bef Pz VI 3
In repair
Pz VI 4

31/7/44
Pz VI 18
Bef Pz VI 2

2/8/44
Pz VI 19

Total losses from 6/6/44 to 5/7/44: 15 *Tigers*.
I Company received a further 14 *Tiger IIs*, but these were all lost during the retreat through France

Schwere SS Panzer Abteilung 102
(SS Tiger Tank Battalion 102)
Original German Strength Report: 1st June 1944

Geheim! 457/44 pf. 6

Meldung vom 1. Juni 1944

Verband: s.SS-Panzer Abteilung 102
Unterstellungsverhältnis:

1. **Personelle Lage** am Stichtag der Meldung:

a) **Personal:**

	Soll	Fehl
Offiziere	32	5
Uffz.	268	14
Mannsch.	736	24
Hiwi.	(54)	(78)
Insgesamt	44!	

b) **Verluste und sonstige Abgänge** in der Berichtszeit vom bis

	tot	verw.	verm.	krank	sonst.
Offiziere	–	–	–	–	–
Uffz. und Mannsch.	–	–	–	–	–
Insgesamt					

c) **in der Berichtzeit eingetroffener Ersatz:**

	Ersatz	Genesene
Offiziere	1	–
Uffz. und Mannsch.	24	–

d) **über 1 Jahr nicht beurlaubt:**

insgesamt: 1 Köpfe 0,9 % d. Iststärke

davon:	12-18 Monate	19-24 Monate	über 24 Monate
	8	1	–

Platzkarten im Berichtsmonat zugewiesen: –

2. **Materielle Lage:**

		Gepanzerte Fahrzeuge							Kraftfahrzeuge				
									Kräder			Pkw	
		Stu. Gesch.	III	IV	V	VI	Schtz. Pz. Pz. Sp. Art. Pz. B. (o. Pz. Fu. Wg.)	Pak SF	Ketten	m. angetr. Bwg.	sonst.	gel.	O
Soll (Zahlen)		–	–	–	–	45	11	–	5	7	20	11	37
einsatzbereit	zahlenm.	–	–	–	–	28	10	–	–	–	16	16	31
	in % des Solls	–	–	–	–	62,2	90,9	–	–	–	80	98%	
in kurzfristiger Instandsetzung (bis 3 Wochen)	zahlenm.	–	–	–	–	1	1	–	–	–	4	–	–
	in % des Solls	–	–	–	–	2,2	9,1	–	–	–	20	–	–

		noch Kraftfahrzeuge							Waffen			
			Lkw			Ketten-Fahrzeuge						
		Maultiere	gel.	O	Tonnage	Zgkw. *)	Zgkw. **)		s Pak	Art.-Gesch.	MG. ( )	sonstige Waffen
Soll (Zahlen)		6	103	16	496	7	23	–	–	45	129 (37)	3
einsatzbereit	zahlenm.	20	13	80	384,5	2	10	–	–	30	93 (37)	3
	in % des Solls		90,4		77,5	28,5	43,4	–	–	67	73	100
in kurzfristiger Instandsetzung (bis 3 Wochen)	zahlenm.	–	–	8	31,5	–	–	–	–	–	–	–
	in % des Solls	–	–	6,4	6,4	–	–	–	–	–	–	–

*) Zgkw. mit 1–5 t, **) Zgkw. mit 8–18 t
( ) davon MG. 42

3. **Pferdefehlstellen:**

Anl. zu Nr. 00734/44 geh.
Gen. Insp. d. Pz. Tr.

Schwere SS Panzer Abteilung 102
(SS Tiger Battalion 102)
Strength Report: 1st June 1944
Under Command of II.SS Panzer Korps

MANPOWER

	Authorised Strength	Shortages	Actual
Officers	32	5	27
NCOs	268	14	254
Other Ranks	736	24	712
Hiwis	(84)	(78)	6
TOTAL	1,036	43	993

LOSSES

	Dead	Wounded	Missing	Hospital	Other Cases
Officers	-	-	-	-	-
NCOs / Other Ranks	-	-	-	-	-
TOTAL	-	-	-	-	-

REPLACEMENTS/ARRIVALS

	Replacements	Recovered
Officers	1	-
NCOs / Other Ranks	24	-

OVER 1 YEAR ABSENT FROM DIVISION (NON-LEAVE)

TOTAL	9
Of That:	
12 to 18 Months	8
19 to 24 Months	1

Schwere SS Panzer Abteilung 102
(SS Tiger Battalion 102)
Strength Report: 1st June 1944
Material Stocks

ARMOURED VEHICLES*

	Pz VI	Other AFVs
Authorised Strength	45	11
Ready for Action	28	10
Short term repair	1	1

MOTOR CYCLES

	Ketten	+Sidecars	Other
Authorised Strength	5	7	20
Ready for Action	-	-	16
Short term repair	-	-	4

CARS

	Cross country	Normal/Road
Authorised Strength	11	37
Ready for Action	16	31
Short term repair	-	-

TRUCKS

	Maultiere	Cross country	Normal/Road
Authorised Strength	6	103	16
Ready for Action	20	13	80
Short term repair	-	-	8

TRACKED PRIME MOVERS

	1-5 Tons	8-18 Tons	
Authorised Strength	7	23	
Ready for Action	2	10	
Short term repair	-	-	-

WEAPONS

	8.8cm (Pz VI)	MG	(MG 42)	SdKfz 7/1 (Quad 2cm Flak)
Authorised Strength	45	129	(37)	3
Ready for Action	30	93	(37)	3
Short Term Repair	-	-	-	-

**The Battalion received its last 15 Tigers by 3rd June 1944, bringing it up to full strength*

Schwere SS Panzer Abteilung 102
(SS Tiger Tank Battalion 102)
II.SS Panzer Korps

Between 4/7/44 and 31/7/44, SS Panz. Abt. 102 had the following *Tiger Is* on strength

8/7/44

Pz VI 25

In Transit

Pz VI 10

Bef Pz VI 2

Berge Pz V 5

In repair

Pz VI 8

11/7/44

Pz VI 14

In Transit

Pz VI 11

Bef Pz VI 2

Berge Pz V 5

In repair

Pz VI 13

TOTAL LOSSES

Pz VI 4

1 Pz VI Missing?

13/7/44

Pz VI 10

In Transit

Pz VI 11

Bef Pz VI 2

In repair

Pz VI 16

15/7/44

Pz VI 19

In Transit

Pz VI 10

Bef Pz VI 3

Berge Pz V 5

In repair

Pz VI 10

LOSSES

Pz VI 3

16/7/44

Pz VI 19

Bef Pz VI 3

Berge Pz V 5

In repair

Pz VI 10

LOSSES

Pz VI 3

20/7/44

Pz VI 17

In Transit

Pz VI 10

Bef Pz VI 1

Berge Pz V 5

In repair

Pz VI 14

LOSSES

Pz VI 3

31/7/44

Pz VI 30

5/8/44

Pz VI 18

Bef Pz VI 2

26.SS & 27.SS PANZER DIVISIONS

August 1944

Both units were formed on 10th August 1944 – neither exceeded Brigade strength.

Certain parts of each formation fought in the later stages of the Normandy Campaign. Eventually both units were disbanded and incorporated into the 17.SS Panzer Grenadier Division.

26.SS & 27.SS Panzer Divisions
Original German Theoretical Organisation Chart
August 1944

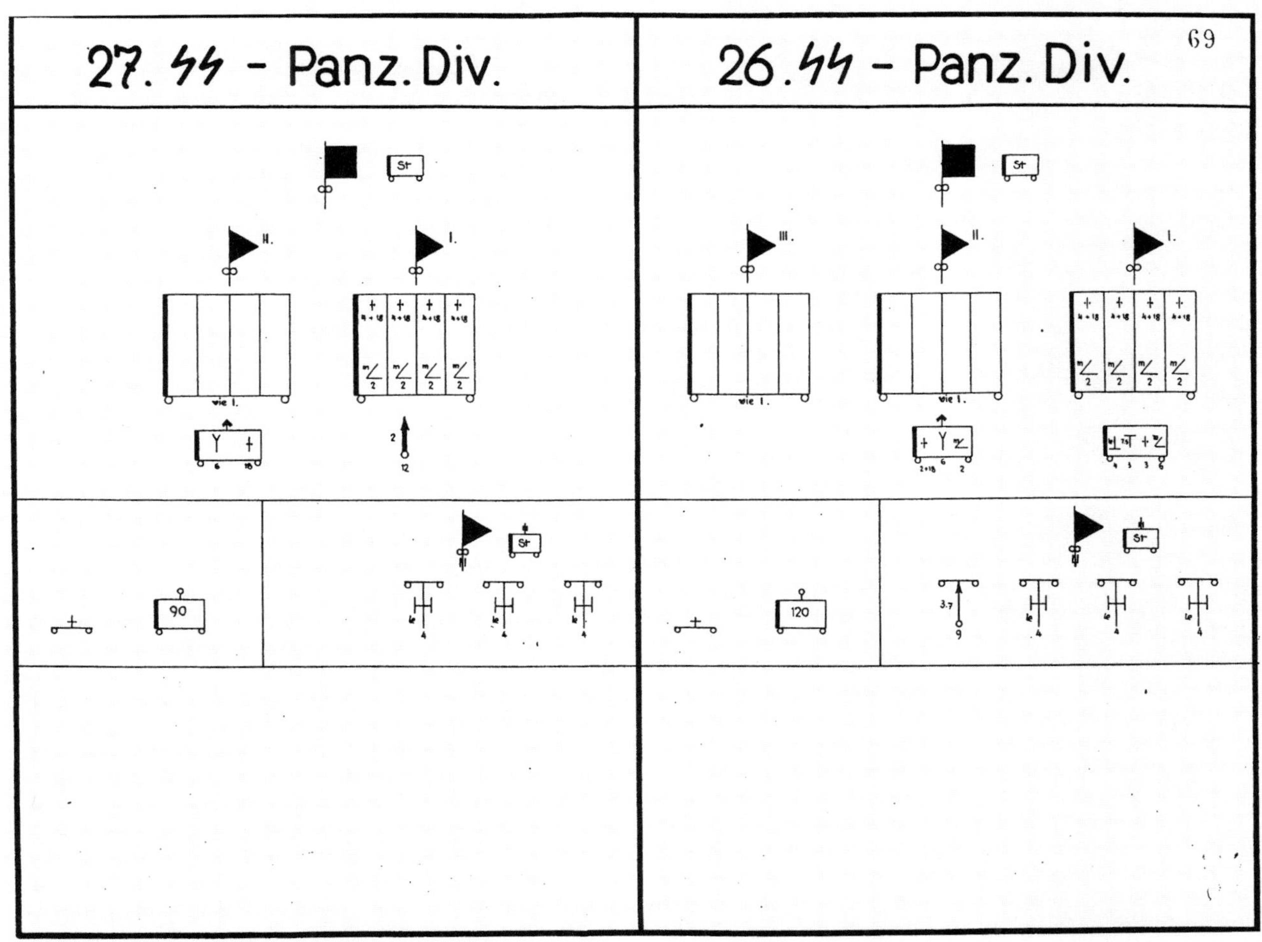

SOURCE MATERIAL

Bundesarchiv – Militärarchiv, Freiburg, Germany

RH 10
RH10/91
RH10/104
RH10/112
RH10/113
RH10/117
RH10/118
RH10/312
RH10/313
RH10/318
RH10/319
RH10/321
RH10/324

RH 20
RH20 - 7/135
RH20 - 7/136
RH20 - 7/295
RH20 - 7/379

RH 20
RH21 - 5/51K
RH21 - 6/1
RH21 - 6/2
RH21 - 6/3

RH 24
RH24 - 84/13
RH24 - 84/14

RS 3
RS 3 - 2/7
RS 3 - 2/42 (Parts 1 & 2)
RS 3 - 2/50
RS 3 - 2/51
RS 3 - 2/57

RS 3 - 9/3
RS 3 - 9/4
RS 3 - 9/5
RS 3 - 9/8

RS 3 - 10/4
RS 3 - 10/9
RS 3 - 10/13
RS 3 - 10/15
RS 3 - 1017
RS 3 - 10/20

MSGZ - 4829 - 4839